Vigilante!

Books by William E. Burrows

Vigilante!
Richthofen

William E. Burrows

Vigilante!

Harcourt Brace Jovanovich
New York and London

For permission to reprint copyrighted material, grateful acknowledgment
is made to the following: The Caxton Printers, Ltd.: From *Bald Knobbers,*
by Lucile Morris, copyright 1939 by Lucile Morris; The New York Times
Magazine: From "Tony Imperiale Stands Vigilant for Lawandorder," by
Paul Goldberger, © 1968 by The New York Times Company; The University
of North Carolina Press: From *The Carolina Backcountry on the Eve of the
Revolution,* by Charles Woodmason, edited by Richard J. Hooker, published
by The University of North Carolina Press, 1953, for the Institute of Early
American History and Culture.

Library of Congress Cataloging in Publication Data
Burrows, William E 1937–
Vigilante!
Bibliography: p.
Includes index.
1. Vigilance committees—History.   I.   Title.
E179.B96   973   76–2725
ISBN 0–15–193655–2

First edition

B C D E

To the memory of Frederick D. Elfers
Foreign Service of the United States
— First Among Equals —

Contents

Author's Note and Introduction

THIS IS the first part of the book to be read, but the last part to be written, and it is here that the writer is supposed to justify what follows. I will not do that, because what follows should justify itself. I do think, though, that I must justify what does not follow.

We live in one of a line of attached two-family homes in Forest Hills, a conservative, carefully manicured replica of Tudor England, in the borough of Queens, New York. Behind the attached houses there is an alley wide enough to accommodate the cars that fit into the garages under the houses, and also the garbage trucks that twice a week roll past the tidy back porches to pick up accumulated refuse. Our spot for depositing garbage is beside the back porch, but, because we live in the upper stories and have no access to that porch, we must lug our green-plastic garbage bags down the stairs, out the front of the house, and fifty or so yards to the corner, where we must turn right, walk the length of the apartment building at the end of the block, make another right, and then go another fifty or so yards to where the garbage cans are. The trip therefore becomes a long U.

Not long after we moved in, my wife and I decided to eliminate the last leg of the garbage trip by leaving our loaded bags behind the apartment building. In doing so, we saved ourselves the two-way journey down the alley while leaving the garbage right in the line of the garbage truck and still absolutely out of sight from the street.

One day about two weeks after we had shifted our drop point, a neighborhood woman literally caught my wife holding the bag and politely but firmly explained that everyone in the area left their garbage exactly where it was supposed to be left—behind their own houses, not behind other people's—and that we should do so, too. The admonition was taken politely and then ignored.

Early one morning about a week after that, I walked out of our front door and almost right into a very large bag full of someone else's garbage. The bag had been placed there very early that morning, and in a spot where it could not be missed. Nor could the warning be misunderstood.

I was at that time writing this book and was therefore up to my ears in burning crosses, skulls and bones, 3–7–77 warnings, and the like. I therefore knew that the full bag of garbage, just as surely as the full noose, was the warning mark of a vigilante. We laughed about it that evening, of course, but while we laughed we understood that, in classic vigilante fashion, we had been "regulated"—brought into line under the threat of someone in our neighborhood who was exercising vigilance. That person had not called the police, or even the sanitation department, but, instead, had taken the matter into his or her own hands. And it had worked perfectly. Being new to the neighborhood and not wanting any trouble, we began leaving our garbage in the correct place and never again found anyone else's in front of our house.

This book is, to my knowledge, the first reasonably comprehensive account of the American vigilante reaction. The reason it is the first, I have come to understand, is not because research material is lacking; to the contrary, it abounds. The problem is one of definition.

During both the research and the writing of the book, I ventured out rarely, but each time I did so I was fair game for people who wanted me to take a stand on whether this or that group fitted into the vigilante category and, if so, why. How, they asked, would I classify: lynch mobs, the Black Panthers, the Ku Klux Klan, the Minutemen, block associations, Boston parents against busing, assorted cowboys, the Jewish Defense League, anarchists, the Weather Underground, Joseph McCarthy, the House Un-American Activities Committee, Charles Bronson, taxi drivers with two-way police hookups, auxiliary police, Patricia Hearst, Robin Hood, tenant patrols, the Red Guard, Al Capone, Joan of Arc, the National Guardsmen who killed the students at Kent State, ghetto dwellers who mug and steal, and even those gangs of teen-age punks who beat up junkies and drug pushers and occasionally throw them off high roofs? No matter what I answered, someone always disagreed and ended up unsatisfied.

Vigilantism, to dredge up that well-worn line from Corinthians, is all things to all men, and anyone who attempts to force it into some nice, neat scholarly slot soon sees that the task is impossible. That, however, does not mean that vigilantism cannot be studied and understood; to argue otherwise would mean that we cannot study and understand war, simply because some define it as soldiers locked in armed conflict, while others see it as street gangs fighting on corners and still others as department stores undercutting each other on prices. Like war, love, or justice, vigilantism can be practiced without having an all-encompassing definition. And if it can be practiced it can—and must— be examined, especially now. The American vigilante seems to be staging a slow but steady comeback.

Hammacher Schlemmer, in New York, one of the nation's most fashionable gimmick emporiums, sells an expensive closed-circuit-television security system for home or office and calls it the "Electronic Vigilante."

The annual three-day Sweetwater, Texas, rattlesnake roundup, besides thinning the local diamondback population, is billed as a combination picnic, carnival, fund-raising event, and "vigilante party," at which snake meat is deep-fried in buttermilk batter and cracker meal and sold like hot dogs.

Manhattan residents angered by illegally parked out-of-state cars unscrew fifty-three of their license plates and deposit them in the lobby of a newspaper office with an explanatory note signed by the "East & West Side Vigilance Committee."

An American aircraft carrier launches a supersonic reconnaissance plane loaded with secret photo and ground-mapping equipment designed to gather intelligence by day or night and in any weather. The jet's military designation is RA-5; its manufacturer calls it the "Vigilante."

Three dry-cleaning chains and six other businesses in Houston, Texas, hire about fifty armed guards to protect their stores against robberies, which have grown to crisis proportions. A national news magazine calls the guards "vigilantes."

Authorities in Moscow use bulldozers, dump trucks, and water-spraying vehicles to break up an unsanctioned outdoor art show held in a vacant lot. Thugs roam through the ranks of the by-standers and, with the police watching but not moving, beat up three American correspondents. The *New York Times* reporter on the scene describes the bullies as "young vigilantes."

A California sports promoter organizes something called the World Hockey Association. He sells franchises in several cities, but at the outset reserves one of the paper teams for himself; before it is sold to a French-Canadian group and renamed the Quebec Nordiques, it is christened the San Francisco Vigilantes.

An English historian sends a story to an American newspaper in which she describes the right-wing "private armies" that have started in her country (again, on paper) in reaction to the power of left-wing unions, the general economic malaise, and the trouble in Northern Ireland. While dismissing the seriousness of these groups, she notes that they represent the first "real evidence of middle-class vigilantism."

Actor Charles Bronson makes a movie in which he plays a "bleeding-heart liberal" who, after his wife is killed and his married daughter turned into a mental vegetable by three sadists, uses a silver-plated revolver to exterminate every mugger he can find. The reviewers dismiss the picture as so much rabble-rousing junk, but audiences break box-office records to see it, after reading advertisements that portray Bronson as being a "Vigilante, city-style—judge, jury, and executioner."

The lawyer who defended Russell Means after the Indian occupation of Wounded Knee in 1971 writes an article in which he charges that the trial amounted to a case history of official lawlessness and so did the confrontation that led to it. Needed food and medicine were deliberately kept out of the occupied area, he charges, by "White ranchers and Indian Vigilantes."

In Mendoza, Argentina, a group of hooded citizens calling themselves the Pius XII Morals Squad uses chains, belts, and ropes to brutally beat nine prostitutes as the women walk their rounds. The Reuters correspondent describing the attacks calls those wielding the weapons vigilantes.

Former Teamsters Union president James Hoffa warned that if Alabama Governor George Wallace became president of the United States the first thing Wallace would do would be to destroy organized labor. "I know what happened to organized labor in Alabama—" Hoffa told a press club audience "—the dogs, the clubs, the vigilantes."

Bob Woodward, one of the *Washington Post* reporters who broke the Watergate story, asks his chief source, the fabled Deep

Throat, whether FBI Director L. Patrick Gray had known about telephone taps on newsmen and White House aides. "Affirmative," answers D.T., after swallowing a shot of Scotch. "There was an out-of-channels vigilante squad of wiretappers that did it." And so on.

Essentially, and as it has evolved in the United States during the past 200 years, vigilantism means an individual or, most often, a group acting in its own best interest (or in what it perceives to be its own best interest) in order to survive, and almost always outside the bounds of the established legal system. When you think about that, though, you realize fairly quickly that it includes just about every extralegal act from depositing garbage in front of someone's door to roughing up civil-rights workers to committing mass execution.

Further thought leads to the inescapable conclusion that everyone is a potential vigilante. Everyone is capable of going outside the system to protect his own best interest or survival if he thinks such action is necessary. What is the distinction between three ghetto youths who throw a drug pusher off a roof and thirty disgruntled ranchers who string up rustlers? Indeed, do vigilantes have to be violent and cause physical harm, or can they accomplish their aims through more subtle, and even pseudolegal, means? There are some, including John W. Caughey, author of *Their Majesties the Mob*, who hold that McCarthyism was nothing so much as a sophisticated vigilante operation. And if one were to tell Caughey that Senator Joseph McCarthy and his minions never actually executed anyone, Caughey would very likely answer by mentioning the Hollywood Blacklist and pointing out that there are other ways of killing people besides stopping their bodily functions. Where, then, do you draw the line?

I drew the line around violence, because violence or the threat of it lies at the very heart of the matter. Violence was and continues to be the ultimate recourse that has given vigilantes their social bite and made them a force to be reckoned with. Without violence in some form, actual or potential, vigilante action would mean next to nothing, because it would be incapable of intimidation and, therefore, of "regulation." Those who have been threatened by vigilance, who have wandered under its shadow, have always taken it seriously, because they have understood, sometimes through firsthand example, that it amounted to certain deadly punishment. In anything short of a multivolume study, then, only the more violent manifestations of vigilance can be met head on. But it is important to remember that vigilance is in reality a series of concentric and gradually blurring circles extending well beyond what is covered here. To those who would pick at the limits I have imposed, I can only say by way of apology that the practical alternative was no book at all, and the subject clearly deserves one. It is such a rich field to mine, in fact, that it deserves others.

This, then, is a selective and interpretive account of American vigilantism—an account that had its origin on the New Frontier, not the old, so it's not really about cowboys. Rather, it's the continuing story of a wide variety of citizens who have taken the law, or what they considered to be the law, into their own hands to punish those they thought were their enemies. That they have done, with the best of motives and with the worst, in the northern and eastern regions as well as in the southern and western, and with remarkable restraint as well as with incredible ferocity. What they have done is worth consideration, I think, because the evidence strongly suggests that the vigilante reaction remains in America, waiting to be fired, like so much brush in the heat of our seemingly endless August. Americans, after all, are a people who have always responded with more than enough rope.

I have divided my "rope" into four parts. The first, chapters one and two, attempts to define vigilance in a workable way and to set it in the context of the American character and experience: in other words, what it is and why it happened and continues to happen here.

The second part, chapters three through eight, is a reconstruction in action-narrative form of six carefully selected vigilante episodes. Each is a model illustrating a particular kind of vigilantism and is representative of from dozens to hundreds of others. The South Carolina episode was the prototype vigilante action and also contained the first real antivigilantes; their struggle was waged in the then new American frontier situation and against the backdrop of the coming revolution. Shelby County, Texas, was chosen as a blood-feud model, which, like many others (particularly in the Appalachians and in the Southwest), went out of control and degenerated into senseless slaughter; in the end, hardly anyone involved could remember why it had started. San Francisco could not possibly have been left out, since it was the biggest and most famous and became the political standard for most of those that followed; it marked the turning point from criminal to political vigilance. Montana represented the ugly outcome of a truly desperate crime situation and typified the frontier response to intolerable frustration at the hands of vicious predators. The Missouri Bald Knobbers were a prime example of religious or morally sanctimonious vigilance, the kind that began at Plymouth and recently manifested itself in front of my door. The New Orleans Mafia massacre provided the ethnic or purely racial side of the vigilante phenomenon; it also was the womb from which the current Mafia fetish emerged.

The third part, chapters nine and ten, draws together fact and fiction as they evolved into vigilante mythology and then moves into current events. It shows how, by selectively ignoring what is grotesque and dangerous about vigilance and concentrating, instead, on its heroic façade, Americans have fashioned a brittle but enduring recourse against their social and economic frustrations.

The final chapter offers some conclusions and a prediction. It is the noose at the end of my rope.

Acknowledgments

THIS BOOK is a selective and highly interpretive undertaking, with roots that run deep and in many directions. Those mentioned here, however inadequately, have contributed in varying ways to the book's development by giving me the benefit of their time, their expertise, and, in some instances, their strong encouragement. Much of the information on these pages is theirs, but they are, of course, in no way responsible for the selection of material or for the conclusions drawn from it.

Academic diggings in this interdisciplinary project were helped mightily through the efforts of: Professors Robert Crowder, Judith Rodin, and Phoebe Ellsworth, of the Yale University Department of Psychology; Archibald Hanna, Curator of the Western Americana Collection at Yale's Beinecke Rare Book and Manuscript Library; Jerry Kearns and Elizabeth Betz, of the Library of Congress; William Leary and "Chip" Stovel, of the National Archives; Professor Peter Fenner, of the Governors State University, Park Forest South, Illinois; Leon Weidman and the staff of the American History Division of the New York Public Library's research section; Mrs. Oliver Howard, of the State Historical Society of Missouri; and Professor Samuel Eliot Morison, of Harvard University, who took time from his own work in order to tell me what not to do.

Professor Richard Maxwell Brown, a gentleman whom I have, regrettably, not met, is in a class by himself where vigilantism is concerned. Wherever I went in search of vigilantes, I found that Richard Brown had been there first, separating sense from nonsense.

Acknowledgments

Work on "current events" was made possible, in large part, by Father Louis R. Gigante, the outspoken New York City councilman and fighting St. Athanasius Church priest; Dr. Michael Baden, Deputy Chief Medical Examiner for the City of New York; Assistant Chief of Police Anthony V. Bouza and John Battaglia, a sergeant in the Forty-first Precinct's anticrime squad; John F. Keenan, Administrative Assistant District Attorney in charge of trials and supervisor of the New York County Homicide Bureau; James P. Murphy of Manhattan's Odyssey House, a specialist on drug addiction and street lore; and everyone on the South Bronx's "Kelly Banana" who came out to talk about the realities of vigilance in the ghetto.

My deep gratitude also goes to Tony Lucas and Gay Talese, who, quite unawares, set research and writing standards more than a decade ago, at our common place of employment, that have served ever since as unfailing navigational points. Dick Severo, through his profound talent, honesty, and friendship, reinforces those standards with acute awareness. Bill Goodman supplied his usual liberal doses of encouragement, patience, and wisdom. How fortunate I am to have been touched by those four, and what pleasure it gives me to bring them my bone. The bone is for Professor Al Castagno, too, even though he is no longer here to see it.

Ernest Kroll, lately of Columbia University, is in a special category. This poet, journalist, historian, code breaker, collector, and unabashed student of just about everything has an exuberance and thirst for knowledge that proved to be highly infectious.

Researching and writing this book was, in many ways, easier than adequately expressing my gratitude to my family. Jo's full and cheerful support and her valuable judgment must therefore be rewarded in other ways. The same for Lara, who always remained on the other side of the door. Well, almost always. They also serve who draw monkeyclimbers with yellow crayons and drink their milk alone.

"Law or no law," exclaim the men of vigilance, "the cause is just because it is necessary."

—Hubert Howe Bancroft
Popular Tribunals

Vigilante!

1

The Vigilante Reaction

A COUPLE of hours before dawn on December 4, 1969, policemen armed with pistols, shotguns, and a submachine gun charged into a worn-out apartment house on Chicago's West Side. They went in blazing. After an estimated eighty rounds had been fired in ten minutes, two members of the Black Panther party were carried out dead, four others were wounded, and three were handcuffed and taken to jail. One of the dead men was Fred Hampton, the twenty-one-year-old chairman of the Illinois chapter of the party and a rising star on the national scene. The story of Fred Hampton's death was retold almost five years later by a Weatherman-turned-journalist named Bo Burlingham.[1]*
What made Burlingham's story different from all the others that went around after Hampton's death was his assertion that the FBI might have supplied the Chicago police with tactical information crucial to the successful assault on the Panther hide-out. The basis of the theory was an interview the author had had with Tom Charles Huston, a White House speech writer and

* Source notes are on pages 289–296.

3

specialist in left-wing extremism at the time of Hampton's death. Although most of the story pieced together the FBI's alleged involvement with the police, in many ways the most interesting part was Huston's justification for knocking out the Panthers and other radical groups in the first place.

What seems to have frightened Huston and his White House colleagues, according to Burlingham, was not the possibility of a revolution. "A handful of people can't frontally overthrow the government," he quotes Huston as saying. "But if they can engender enough fear, they can generate an atmosphere that will bring out of the woodwork every repressive demagogue in the country. Unless this stuff was stopped," Huston added, referring to radical violence, "the country was going to fall into the wrong hands. We were getting lots of pressure from below. According to our reports, local law enforcement people wanted a real crackdown against violent groups, and we expected some sort of vigilante action to develop. The real threat to internal security—in any society—is repression. But repression is an inevitable result of disorder. Forced to choose between order and freedom," the former Nixon aide concluded, "people will take order."

What Tom Charles Huston was saying, then, was that the Nixon administration thought it necessary to squash some citizens in order to prevent them and others like them from being squashed by still other citizens in a kind of counterreign of terror. It was using repression against the Panthers not because it was afraid of their revolutionary potential, but because their very existence could have triggered still greater repression by some shadowy force preferring order to freedom and riding under the banner of vigilantism. Huston was making a clear distinction between official and unofficial repression; between the kind supposedly practiced under law by the constitutionally elected government, on the one hand, and that practiced by armed citizens taking the law into their own hands, on the other. The dubious logic of liquidating a group in order to prevent its being liquidated by another group need not be dwelt on. But Huston was really talking about more than the murder of a few hundred black radicals. He was invoking the dreaded prospect of widespread vigilante reprisals as a result of allowing the Panthers to go on disrupting the system. If the government didn't wipe out the Panthers, Huston was warning, the people in the street were going to do it. Tom Charles Huston might merely have been pulling the specter of vigilantism out of his political hat as a handy excuse for spilling blood, but, if that was true, so was at least one well-known member of the opposition. His name was Tom Hayden.

After explaining in an interview, at about the same time as Burlingham's story appeared, that the struggle against the establishment had turned overwhelmingly political and much less violent, Hayden was pressed on whether or not he could conceive of any situation in which it would be necessary to pick up a gun. "There *are* certain circumstances where there's a need for armed security," said the former theoretician of Students for a Democratic Society. "But that's in self-defense against police and vigilante attacks, and that's different from picking up a gun as part of a revolution."[2]

Now, either both of these men—one a conservative and the other a radical—have conveniently summoned the ghosts of remorselessly tough cowboys and others with short patience and long ropes to justify a resort to violence, or else each one actually sees, or thinks he sees, something lurking out there in the deep shadows. Whatever it is, Anthony J. Imperiale and Rabbi Meir Kahane don't want it on their doorsteps, either. Imperiale, a barrel-chested former karate teacher who was elected to the New Jersey Senate on a law-and-order platform, organized the Newark North Ward Citizens' Committee in 1967 for defense against the blacks who had rioted there during the summer. He has studiously denied that vigilantism was in any way a part of North Ward theory or practice. Kahane, the founder of the paramilitary Jewish Defense League, has done the same.

"As for the absurd cry of 'vigilantes,' it is clear that a vigilante group is one which, despite the fact that there is adequate law enforcement, takes the law into its own hands and executes summary justice," explains Rabbi Kahane. "When we have seen, over weeks and months and years that, for whatever reason given, the police have proven themselves inadequate to enforce the basic duties of a state, it is criminal *not* to act."[3]

Whether or not Rabbi Kahane's definition of a vigilante is accurate, he at least makes it perfectly clear that he doesn't want to be called one. But, again, one what? What, in fact, are these four very different men thinking about when they conjure up vigilantism?

"Vigilante" comes from a Spanish word spelled exactly the

5

same way and meaning "watchman" or "guard." Its root, *vigil*, is of Latin origin and translates as "being awake or observant." But this explains almost nothing, because Americans have taken the word far beyond the state of passive observation and have recast it to describe part of their own life style—a life style that has been called many things, but never passive.

A vigilance committee, according to John Russell Bartlett's *Dictionary of Americanisms*, is "a portion of the citizens of a place who, assuming that the regular magistrates are unable or unwilling to execute the laws, undertake to watch over its safety, and punish criminals." And A *Dictionary of American English* defines a vigilance committee as being "a voluntary association of men professing to supplement the efforts of the police and the courts in maintaining order, punishing crime, etc." That "etc." turns out to be the most interesting part of the definition. (Everybody agrees, by the way, that a vigilante is someone who belongs to a vigilance committee.)

Vigilantism in its "classic" sense refers to "organized, extralegal movements which take the law into their own hands," says Richard Maxwell Brown, a professor of history at the College of William and Mary and a respected contributor to the literature on the subject. These movements, he goes on to explain, are distinguished from the more spontaneous lynch mobs in two ways: first, they have a regular (though illegal) organization, and, second, they exist for a definite (though possibly short) time, ranging from a matter of weeks to a year or more.[4]

The essence of his definition is, as far as it goes, irrefutable, and most students of American history who are interested in the subject would probably agree. The reason amateurs tend to get confused is that almost all of us have different ideas of what law we're talking about and differing concepts of specific periods of time. In addition, the term "movement" isn't entirely accurate when applied to vigilantes.

No vigilante episode was ever really part of a movement. It's not just a matter of semantics, either. To me, a movement is a truly sustained social or political action with a commonly agreed-upon motive. The antihorsethief and prohibition movements fall into that category; so does the student movement to end American participation in the war in Vietnam. Even the Ku Klux Klan, which is now well into its second century, could easily be dropped into the hate movement. But no localized group of vigilantes—and they were always local—was a true movement. To use "movement" greatly exaggerates the scope of the largest of them, even including the great San Francisco army of 6,000. While nineteenth-century Americans were in many instances acutely aware of vigilante actions elsewhere in the country, and in some cases consciously used the San Francisco and Montana explosions as models, there was almost no interorganizational liaison (California and Montana, again, were exceptions). There were no national co-ordinating staffs, no pamphlets, no newsletters, and no "how-to" handbooks or guides on the subject. There was not, in short, a master program. It was very much every community for itself.

A better term than movement is "reaction," which more accurately describes the sudden, relatively isolated, and combustible nature of the vigilante phenomenon: angry men banding together in reaction to real, imagined, or trumped-up wrongs, punishing their victims, and then quickly dissolving back into the relative anonymity and boredom of their families and businesses.

There are no rules on how long is long enough for a group to be considered vigilantes, nor has anyone really defined the exact nature of the laws vigilantes take into their hands. A lynch mob can exist for two days (which is a long time), but so can a full-fledged vigilance committee, like the one in New Orleans in 1891 (which is a short time). On the long end—years—time is a consideration; on the short end—days or weeks—time means little and tends to become irrelevant.

The "law" part of the definition is of considerably more than esoteric interest since, one way or another, law along with violence is at the heart of vigilantism. No vigilance committee would ever have existed in the first place without some law, however tenuous, that it felt it had to uphold. And the persistent paradox of vigilantism is that it must, by definition, break the law by enforcing it. That immutable fact of life has been known to almost every vigilante.

In late 1863 and early 1864, for example, Montana was part of the Idaho Territory. As such, it was subject to territorial statutes, which, like written laws elsewhere, prohibited robbery and murder. In the absence of effective law enforcement, however, a large vigilance committee was formed. Its members went out in the dead of winter and, with ruthless efficiency, rounded up every bandit and cutthroat they could lay their hands on and

7

hanged them. What got the good citizens out of their warm cabins and into the deep snow was the discovery that the leader of the gang of road agents that was plundering them was none other than their sheriff, Henry Plummer. Understandably, that news made them angry. The overwhelming evidence indicates that the Plummer gang was, indeed, a collection of bandits and killers and deserved everything it got. Yet those who used the ropes had to face the fact that they, too, were going outside the law; the same piece of paper that made it a crime for Plummer's men to kill made it a crime for the vigilantes to kill. The vigilantes justified what they did on grounds of sheer survival: no one, least of all their elected sheriff, was going to protect them, so they felt they had to do it themselves.

This conflict between one law and another, between written and natural, runs deep into vigilante rationale. It's a conflict always to be reconciled, and when vigilantes have surfaced it has been reconciled emotionally. Kill or be killed. Them or us. If the people who are being plundered and perhaps murdered cannot, or think they cannot, get adequate help from the constituted authorities, they face the dilemma either of chalking up their losses and probably getting hit again or of catching and punishing their oppressors. When unchecked, such "popular justice" becomes anarchy, and there has probably never been a vigilante who didn't understand that. The chronicles of vigilante actions are soaked with the stories of men who have agonized over this conflict, as well as the stories of others who never gave it a second thought.

The vigilante has traditionally rationalized his actions by convincing himself that he lives in a state of anarchy in the first place, since the authorities are unwilling or unable to protect him from predators, so he is really trying to preserve the essence of law and order until he is relieved of that burden by effective lawmen and judges. The question of whether vigilantism restores or erodes social order has been argued practically since the phenomenon began. Every vigilante has defended it, and so have many of their friends and admirers, including Owen Wister, the author of the first real cowboy novel. *The Virginian*, which appeared in 1902 and remained immensely popular for decades, provides the classic defense of vigilantism. It is even dedicated to roughriding Teddy Roosevelt, a friend of Wister's since their days at Harvard and himself a lifelong advocate of vigilantism. (Roosevelt, as a matter of fact, volunteered to join the Montana vigilante group of 1884, the deadliest of them all, when he was punching cattle in North Dakota and rhapsodizing in writing about the manly joys of life on what remained of the rugged frontier. He was turned down by the typically secretive vigilante leadership because even then young Roosevelt was known to have had a big mouth.)

Wister painted a picture of a tight-jawed, Cooperesque character who made "Smile when you say that" (actually, it was "When you call me that, smile") a household expression for the following half century, and who always did what had to be done, no matter how distasteful, in order to rid the range of rapacious rustlers and restore order in the only way believed possible. The Virginian was so straight that he helped hang Steve, an old and good friend, who was thought to be a rustler. Wister laid out the classic defense of vigilantism as a quasilegal, if not thoroughly legal, American right in an exchange between the Virginian's sweetheart and Judge Henry Dow, a wise and respected pillar of the community. Molly, an eastern schoolmarm who isn't familiar with the ways of the West, has just learned that her boyfriend helped string up the rustlers. Her sensibilities are severely shaken.

"Judge Henry," said Molly Wood, . . . "have you come to tell me that you think well of lynching?"

He met her. "Of burning Southern negroes in public, no. Of hanging Wyoming cattle-thieves in private, yes. You perceive there's a difference, don't you?"

"Not in principle," said the girl, dry and short.

"Oh—dear—me!" slowly exclaimed the Judge. "I am sorry that you cannot see that, because I think that I can. And I think that you must have just as much sense as I have." The Judge made himself very grave and very good-humored at the same time. The poor girl was strung to a high pitch, and spoke harshly in spite of herself.

"What is the difference in principle?" she demanded.

"Well," said the Judge, easy and thoughtful, "what do you mean by principle?"

"I didn't think you'd quibble," flashed Molly. "I'm not a lawyer myself."

"I don't mean to quibble," he assured her. "I know the trick of escaping from one question by asking another. If you can show me that I am wrong, I want you to do so. But," and here the Judge smiled, "I want you to play fair, too."

"And how am I not?"

"I want you to be just as willing to be put right by me as I am to be put right by you. And so when you use such a word as principle, you must help me to answer by saying what principle you mean. For in all sincerity I see no likeness in principle whatever between burning Southern negroes in public and hanging Wyoming horse-thieves in private. I consider the burning a proof that the South is semi-barbarous, and the hanging a proof that Wyoming is determined to become civilized. We do not torture our criminals when we lynch them. We do not invite spectators to enjoy their death agony. We put no such hideous disgrace upon the United States. We execute our criminals by the swiftest means, and in the quietest way. Do you think the principle is the same?"

Molly had listened to him with attention. "The way is different," she admitted.

"Only the way?"

"So it seems to me. Both defy law and order."

"Ah, but do they both? Now we're getting near the principle."

"Why, yes. Ordinary citizens take the law in their own hands."

"The principle at last!" exclaimed the Judge. "Now tell me some more things. Out of whose hands do they take the law?"

"The court's."

"What made the courts?"

"I don't understand."

"How did there come to be any courts?"

"The Constitution."

"How did there come to be any Constitution? Who made it?"

"The delegates, I suppose."

"Who made the delegates?"

"I suppose they were elected, or appointed, or something."

"And who elected them?"

"Of course the people elected them."

"Call them the ordinary citizens," said the Judge. "I like your term. They are where the law comes from, you see. For they chose the delegates who made the Constitution that provided for the courts. There's your machinery. These are the hands into which ordinary citizens have put the law. So you see, at best, when they lynch they only take back what they once gave. . . . The courts, or rather the juries, into whose hands we have put the law, are not dealing the law. They are withered hands, or rather they are imitation hands made for show, with no life in them, no grip. They cannot hold a cattle-thief. And so when your ordinary citizen sees this, and sees that he has placed justice in a dead hand, he must take justice back into his own hands where it was once at the beginning of all things. Call this primitive, if you will. But so far from being a *defiance* of the law, it is an *assertion* of it—the fundamental assertion of self-governing men, upon whom our whole social fabric is based. There is your principle, Miss Wood, as I see it. Now can you help me to see anything different?"

She could not.[5]

It wasn't until *The Ox-Bow Incident,* which was published thirty-eight years later, that a serious writer grappled with vigilantism and came out strongly against it. Here is the essence of Walter van Tilburg Clark's position.

"If we go out and hang two or three men," he finished, "without doing what the law says, forming a posse and bringing the men in for trial, then by the same law, we're not officers of justice, but due to be hanged ourselves."

"And who'll hang us?" Winder wanted to know.

"Maybe nobody," Davies admitted. "Then our crime's worse than a murderer's. His act puts him outside the law, but keeps the law intact. Ours would weaken the law."[6]

Clark's novel constituted a literary turning point in American thinking about vigilantism, but until it took hold Owen Wister's grim hero was the personification of the way the majority of Americans wanted to see their vigilantes and, therefore, themselves: burdened by the moral responsibility of bringing out the rope, but doing it just the same, because duty couldn't be shirked. Here is an exchange that takes place between the narrator of *The Virginian,* a confessed dude, and the hero, as they ride through the lovely cottonwoods where the hangings took place.

"You never did this before," I said.

"No. I never had it to do." He was riding beside me, looking down at his saddle horn.

"I do not think I should ever be able," I pursued.

Defiance sounded in his answer. "I would do it again this morning."

"Oh, I don't mean that. It's all right here. There's no other way."

"I would do it all over again the same this morning. Just the same."

"Why, so should I—if I could do it at all." I still thought he was justifying their justice to me.

He made no answer as he rode along, looking all the while at his saddle. But again he passed his hand over his forehead with the frown and shutting of the eyes.[7]

The act of stringing up his best friend, then, seems to have given our intrepid hero something of a migraine. Yet he'd hang Steve again if he thought he had to, because it was clearly his duty, personal feelings notwithstanding. It's also important to note that, for his part, Steve accepted his fate bravely and even cheerfully, as a man should. Steve had always known the likely consequences of pinching someone else's cattle, so when the time came to pay for his crime he accepted punishment with calm understanding and whimsey (to the extent of borrowing a newspaper, only hours before his lynching, to follow the progress of local elections whose outcome he knew he would never see). So Steve went out like a man, not like a miserable, whimpering cur, and that was a trait his executioner respected more than any other. Steve's accomplice, on the other hand, slobbered all the way to the gallows and was therefore beyond contempt. The Virginian tells his companion that Steve "stayed game" to the end. Here's what he says about poor sniveling Ed.

"It cert'nly was bad seeing Ed take it that way, I reckon. And you didn't see him when the time came for business. Well, here's what it is: a man may be such a confirmed miscreant that killing's the only cure for him; but still he's your own species, and you don't want to have him fall around and grab your laigs and show you his fear naked. It makes you feel ashamed."[8]

Again and again this twin theme runs through descriptions of nineteenth-century vigilante executions: summary hanging is a morally painful but necessary business, and the culprit who accepts his fate with understanding and good cheer is a worthy adversary. The wretch who cries and begs for his life, on the other hand, is almost not worth the rope required to stretch his neck. Almost.

The reasoning behind this pervasive propaganda is obvious enough: it eases the conscience and justifies vigilante violence and killing. Anyone who gleefully hunts, captures, and hangs someone else is no better than a butcher. Such a man would pull wings off flies, too, and is hardly the stuff from which heroes are molded. There's no glory in tangling with craven cowards, any more than there is in beating up children or arguing with mental defectives. True stature can come only with getting the best of a truly worthy opponent—an opponent who is fierce and who doesn't cry when he loses the game.

The mark of the vigilante organization, then, is the reluctant citizens' defense of the law of survival as they interpret it in a given situation. It is important to note, though, that the law of survival is nearly always wedded to written law in vigilante ideology. In other words, the men who form a vigilance committee do so, they tell one another, only because robbers and murderers are breaking the law—municipal, territorial, or state statutes, which were written to protect them but which they think aren't being enforced by the authorities. At the bottom of their thought process, however, is the fear that if they don't get so-and-so, so-and-so is going to get them. And, as the vigilante story unfolds, we will see that it is not necessarily a fear of being killed; it can be economic fear (this was usually the case), political fear, racial fear, or even the fear that immoral people are corrupting the community and must be stopped. Whatever the excuse, the vigilante always sets out to preserve, not to destroy. Irrespective of his breaking one law to uphold what he considers to be a higher one, the true vigilante has always been a conservative and something of a patriot; a believer in the ultimate worth of the Constitution, however abstract that document has appeared to him, and in "the American way" in the most altruistic sense of the term. He has seen himself as temporarily bending or circumventing the law of the land, but never as harming or destroying it. To the contrary, some of the ugliest vigilante episodes were launched because one group of citizens thought the Constitution made them more equal than another group. Vigilante action has always been class action—a violent manifestation of class warfare.

To sum up, the classic vigilance committee (1) is formally organized, with a hierarchy (hence is a "committee") and often a written manifesto or bylaws; (2) exists for as long as a year and disbands when its goals are judged to have been met; (3) bases its existence on the imperative of survival in the face of the inadequacy of regular law enforcement; (4) makes known that it is acting out its last-resort role with deep sorrow; (5) professes to work for the ultimate strengthening of the legal system, never for its destruction; (6) represents the establishment. It should be emphasized that these characteristics provide a fairly solid, but in no sense an invariable, framework within which to define vigilante groups. Think of it as a kind of kaleidoscope: all the spots usually converge, but occasionally some don't.

Certain groups are in some ways related to vigilantism, but are not strictly part of it. The Ku Klux Klan is the most obvious of these; others are the modern-day Minutemen, the Jewish Defense League, and even the Black Panthers and the Weather Underground. During and after Reconstruction, millions of white southerners were convinced that the emancipated blacks were going to tear the fabric of their society into even thinner shreds than had the Civil War, and the Klan became their first line of defense against an imposed system which they thought threatened their social, economic, and, in many cases, physical survival. The same is true, in the sense of political survival, of the Minutemen, the Sons of Liberty, and other far-right groups, which apparently feel that the international Communist conspiracy is well on its way to undermining their country from within as well as without. The Jewish Defense League has taken it upon itself to combat anti-Semitism with counterforce, violent and otherwise. All these groups, and others in any way allied with them, use some form of the survival argument to justify their existence. But survival is an ambiguous word. Carrying this argument to the level of the absurd, Friends of the Earth could be called a vigilante organization because its members are fighting for the ecological survival of the planet. Where vigilantism is concerned, survival involves a real or imagined immediate physical threat to life and property by criminals.

In that context, the Jewish Defense League comes closer to being a vigilante group, but still it is only a marginal one. The others' enemies are ethnic or racial minorities or political undesirables, and in no way do they constitute a serious and immediate threat to life or property. Furthermore, all of these groups, as well as their chosen enemies, seem destined to be around for a long time and are anything but short-term operations. Not only are they consciously breaking the law when they go after their opponents (most of whom are in no sense physically dangerous), but also they give no sign of ever wanting to stop. If they have to be classified, then, their durability and sociopolitical goals put them more in the movement category than among the true vigilantes.

This is also the case with respect to the Black Panthers and other revolutionary groups. Rightly or wrongly, the Panthers are convinced that they are targets for attempted or actual extermination, and so they have armed themselves and shot back in an effort to uphold the law of survival. The Panthers are especially frustrated because they feel, with some justification, that the same law-enforcement authorities who are supposed to be protecting them are the agents of their oppression. Yet the Panthers and other radical groups are not vigilantes. They are dedicated to overturning the system and therefore are obviously not concerned with preserving its laws and social structure. Vigilantes always see themselves as patriots.

Does this categorizing business really matter, particularly when there are so many gray areas? Only to the extent that unless some kind of manageable framework is established—even an elastic framework—the subject gets out of hand. If the Panthers are vigilantes, then a reasonably good case can be made for calling the Bolsheviks vigilantes, too, and where does it end?

The American vigilante phenomenon has gone through three distinct phases, though with considerable overlapping.° The first

° Vigilantism, while not uniquely American, has found its most fertile environment on American soil. The American variety is a strictly indigenous response to a uniquely American situation and was not transported from the Old World. Yet vigilantism has existed there in modern times, as well as in Asia, Africa, and South America. Further, foreign vigilantes come in all political stripes. A Falangist group in Spain calling itself *Guerrilleros del Cristo Rey* (Soldiers of Christ the King) preaches purity, fire, and inquisition; at least five other groups, some with foreign neo-Fascist connections, have committed terrorist actions against political enemies, and, it is suspected, with police sympathy. Death squads are legendary in Brazil, and in October 1975, the "Group for Action and Liberty" emerged in Argentina to counter left-wing assassinations. In Portugal, on the other hand, armed civilians wearing Communist party badges and passing out leaflets saying "People! Continue to be vigilant because somebody wants to put our freedom in danger!" were stopping and searching political suspects in March 1975. Committees of Defense of the Revolution were formed in Cuba nineteen months after the revolution to counter sabotage and now claim to have 80 per cent of the country's adults as members. But there are nonpolitical foreign vigilantes, too. Village headmen in Thailand's grassy countryside occasionally lead their tribesmen on hunts for buffalo thieves and, although it is illegal, severely punish any buffalo rustler they catch. And in September was classic vigilantism, which erupted initially in South Carolina's back country on the eve of the Revolution and concerned itself with punishing ordinary badmen—horse and cattle thieves, counterfeiters, and assorted gangs of desperadoes. Classic vigilantism had as its main target the killers and spoilers who infested the early frontier. The second, or neovigilante, phase started with the great San Francisco committee of 1856 and had as its target ethnic and religious minorities and political opponents, usually clustered in urban areas. Neovigilantism was essentially urban and had little or nothing to do with cactus, horses, and gunslingers. The current phase, pseudo vigilantism, a less deadly but potentially volatile mixture of the first two, can be said to have started in response to the soaring crime and the racial upheavals of the 1960s. Both criminals and blacks have been the objects of pseudovigilante activities, and in a number of instances blacks themselves have organized vigilantelike groups to fight drug addiction among their own people.

The American vigilante may have turned mean while growing up, but he started out as a helpful child, and one born of necessity. He was conceived as the only feasible defense against the perils of a constantly expanding frontier that usually left effective law enforcement far behind. Settlers who abandoned the relative security of the urban footholds back east, with their stabilizing schools, churches, municipal governments, courts, constables, and familiar neighborhoods, and pushed across the Appalachians into the great wilderness beyond were taking serious chances. They were laying their lives on the line, against Indians, desperadoes, and the elements, in order to grab timber, land, gold, and other resources. It was perfectly natural, given such a situation, that they would want to bring with them as much of the old stability as possible. In effect, those people wanted the best of two worlds: to carve up virgin Kentucky or Ohio woodlands and mine unclaimed California and Montana gold, but to do so under the benevolent eyes of the Philadelphia or Boston police force and with the blessing of the New York or Baltimore political establishment. But that was obviously impossible. The price they had to pay in return for a chance to get the frontier's resources

1975, eight pistol-toting Brazilian vigilantes arrested government officials who were trying to find the winner of a $2.6 million soccer lottery in a remote part of the country. The vigilantes later explained that they thought the officials were out to kidnap the lucky father of six.

often was acute social instability, which translated into almost constant danger. They all knew that the alternative to establishing some kind of stability was to be plundered by the predators —to have their communities ravaged and their hard-earned wealth taken away from them. That was intolerable. Do-it-yourself law enforcement seemed to be the only answer.

If the early pioneers took the law into their own hands begrudgingly—as was usually the case, since it was more profitable to plant crops or make chairs than it was to chase bandits—at least they were ideologically suited to it. The ideology of vigilantism, which began to take shape during the first few decades of the nineteenth century, had three basic components: popular sovereignty, the right of revolution, and the law of self-preservation. And those rested, like a tricorn, on a head of violence. As every nineteenth-century American schoolchild knew, violence worked. It had been spectacularly successful in yanking the colonies out from under the Crown in the first place. As a crucial tool for survival, in fact, it could be traced all the way back to Plymouth and Jamestown, when all those bloodthirsty savages, wild animals, and even an occasional renegade white had had to be subdued or liquidated for the apparent good of the majority.

The concept of popular sovereignty—democracy—was the single most important political element contributing to the vigilante reaction. Obviously, no monarch would have allowed a bunch of armed subjects to ride around the countryside hanging the people they hated. If that kind of thing had caught on, the rabble might eventually have raised their sights, and then where would he have been? So one of the key reasons for vigilantism's taking hold in America was the belief that the rule of the people superseded all other rule. And from that followed the premise that they had the power to act in their own best interest in the absence of effective constituted authority. That's what Judge Henry Dow was getting at when he told Molly Wood that if people make the law they can and should be able to unmake it.

The right of revolution justified the overturn by force of any authority considered by the people to be ineffective or harmful to the maintenance of real law and order. It provided the philosophical basis for insurrection, as in the hackneyed but true-to-life scene in which the angry mob storms the jail, subdues the sheriff and deputies, and lynches the prisoner. In doing that, vigilantes and lynch mobs were perfectly aware of the fact that they were kicking the props out from under whatever lawful authority existed. But the vigilante credo had it that when lawful authorities contributed to injustice, either willingly or out of help-lessness, they almost deserved what the redcoats had gotten in 1776.

Finally, vigilante ideology rested on the ultimate argument of survival as the first law of nature—kill or be killed. If no one else was going to protect a man's life and property, natural law dic-tated that he had to do it himself or suffer the consequences. It was as simple as that, or so vigilantes assured one another time and again.

Ideological justifications may have been strictly a matter of the mind, but the problems of everyday life on the frontier (which included, at one time, the area between the Hudson and the Mississippi) were hard realities. Chief among these was isolation, with its attendant transportation and communications problems and a very uneven law-enforcement and judicial system.

Until the Civil War, the average frontier community was far from a railroad and was usually linked to other communities by poor roads, which became corridors of dust under the sun and seas of mud under the rain. Even where there was a railroad, the peace officer in pursuit of an outlaw was bound to go exactly where the train went, while his quarry had the pick of any point on the compass. Fugitives would often head for the most difficult terrain in the area and, when there was more than one on the run, split up after arranging to meet at some distant place. A lone sheriff, or even one blessed with a deputy, was thus confounded by having to chase perhaps four outlaws, each heading in a different direction over the most obscure trails he could find. That kind of pursuit could take weeks, during which the town was left unguarded, and most likely the lawman would still re-turn empty-handed. In addition, posses were used far less often than the movie makers would have us believe. Who in his right mind would want to close a barbershop, livery, or dry-goods store, abandon a cattle herd, or perhaps miss a planting or har-vesting while he spent weeks following his paid official through the worst terrain in the area? Almost without exception, only the most spectacular crimes warranted pursuit by a posse unless the bad guys were known to be close by or enough bored citizens could be rounded up for the chase.

The considerable financial expenditure necessary to support

adequate law enforcement was another factor that made vigilance committees tempting. The amount of cash that might have to be shelled out for the pursuit, capture, jailing, trial, and conviction of a lawbreaker could easily have emptied the coffers of most frontier towns or counties. It was therefore no accident that the leadership of vigilante groups was invariably held by the local elite—the leading merchants, ranchers, and professional people— who bore the brunt of taxes and who therefore had an understandable desire to keep them as low as possible. The Las Vegas, New Mexico, vigilance committee broke into the town jail one night in the early 1880s, removed all the inmates, and ran them out of town. The "petty thieves, bunko men, and would-be bad men—were eating their heads off at the city's expense." Northern Indiana regulators marched in 1858 under a banner that said, "No expense to the County."[9]

The quality of lawmen and judges was another crucial factor, since it varied enormously across nineteenth-century America. To make matters even worse, criminals in newly settled areas lacking real community traditions and solidarity often produced witnesses who blatantly lied for them, and, when possible, they even packed juries with their friends or bribed and intimidated judges and juries. Occasionally, toughs standing trial openly threatened whole towns, which wasn't hard to do when a sizable number of residents were either sympathetic to the accused or actually counted themselves as their friends.

In recounting a Montana trial Thomas Dimsdale noted that "the roughs would swagger into the space allotted for the judge and jury, giving utterance to clearly understood threats, such as 'I'd like to see the G—d d——d jury that would dare to hang Charley Reeves or Bill Moore,' etc. etc." Dimsdale guessed that the threats "doubtless had fully as much weight with the jury as the evidence had." The jury, in fact, wound up accepting the accused men's explanation that the Indians they had massacred had murdered friends of theirs on the way to California fourteen years earlier. "But the truth," Dimsdale noted, "is they were afraid of their lives—and, it must be confessed, not without apparent reason."[10]

Frontier society—indeed, society everywhere in the United States—was far more rigidly stratified in the eighteenth and nineteenth centuries than it is today, and that also had a bearing on vigilantism. Perched on top of the social and economic ladder, the leading business and professional people, well-to-do farmers and ranchers, and other prominent citizens looked down with loathing on those clinging to the bottom rungs—at the bandits and killers, to be sure, but also at the shiftless, apparently lazy, and violence-prone poor. So, too, did the middle layer of craftsmen, teachers, tradespeople, and modest landholders. The pervasive belief of nineteenth-century America that the country was a boundless land of opportunity contained the corollary that those who failed to seize that opportunity were bums who would prey on the achievers. The achievers in such a rough-and-tumble society therefore had an obligation to remain vigilant and, where the law could not protect their property, to do it themselves. This was the framework within which vigilante groups worked. The transition from classic to neovigilantism was marked by a shift in emphasis: from seeing badmen of any stripe as threats to targeting racial and religious minorities as the troublemakers. Nativism had taken over.

Given the class basis for vigilantism, it was logical that vigilante organizations were invariably started and led by the elite and had solidly middle-class, upwardly aspiring memberships. A substantial number of nineteenth-century financial, political, and cultural notables embraced vigilantism, mostly as young men, and many of them never renounced it.

President Andrew Jackson had once advised Iowans to use vigilante action against a murderer. Theodore Roosevelt tried to get a piece of the action in Montana in 1884, and, aware that several innocent men were hanged, he wrote that the result of the executions was "in the main wholesome."[11] Senator Francis M. Cockrell, of Missouri, whose tenure started in 1875 and ended in 1905, was a vigilante advocate, as was William J. McConnell, one of Idaho's first two senators, its governor from 1893 to 1896, and the author of *Frontier Law: A Story of Vigilante Days,* published in 1924 and considered by its author to be a sufficiently good book on citizenship to warrant his dedicating it to the Boy Scouts. Dr. John E. Osborne, a leading Wyoming physician, who was governor from 1893 to 1895, not only participated in the vigilante execution of "Big Nose" George Parrott at Rawlins in 1881, but also, apparently unsatisfied that the corpse provided sufficient warning to other outlaws, Osborne skinned the body, cut away the top of the skull, and pulled out the brain. The skin was cured and made into a tobacco pouch, razor strops, a medical-instrument bag, and a pair of lady's shoes, which were displayed in the National Bank for years. Alexander Mouton, a wealthy sugar planter, who served as a United States senator and as governor of Louisiana, became the leader of a vigilance committee after he left office. Governor William Pitt Kellogg, another Louisianan, supported a vigilante action in Vermillion Parish that accounted for twelve victims. Texas produced James Buckner Barry, who was in two vigilante actions and went on to the state legislature. New Mexico boasted two former vigilantes as governors, Miguel Antonio Otero, a merchant's son, and George Curry, a Roughrider friend of Roosevelt's, who eventually became the provincial governor of the Philippines and one of his state's first congressmen. The master list includes two presidents, five United States senators, a congressman, eight governors, a minister to Uruguay and Paraguay, and, undoubtedly, scores of state legislators, city councilmen, mayors, and other local functionaries.

William Tell Coleman and Leland Stanford, both leaders of the San Francisco committee of 1856, exemplify the kind of businessman involved in vigilantism, and so does Granville Stuart, the Montana rancher who led the 1884 group and went on to Uruguay and Paraguay. Stanford was one of the guiding lights of the Southern Pacific and Central Pacific railroads, governor of California during the Civil War, and a United States senator from 1885 until his death in 1893. The year after he went to the Senate he founded the university that bears his son's name. These people were anything but members of a backward, hell-for-leather rabble.

The literati supporting or condoning vigilantism included Owen Wister; Hubert Howe Bancroft, who devoted two books of his multivolume history of the Far West to vigilantism; Thomas Dimsdale, the Oxford dropout who went on to become the editor-in-chief of the *Montana Post* and the territorial superintendent of public education; and Nathaniel Langford, who wrote *Vigilante Days* and became the "father" of Yellowstone National Park.

"As late as World War I," Professor Brown says, "the American elite looked with favor upon the vigilante tradition. In 1918 a group of distinguished writers formed an organization to promote the war effort. Significantly, they chose to call themselves 'the Vigilantes.'" Invoking America's vigilante heritage, their pamphlet explained that "there has been a disposition to associate the Vigilantes with those beloved rough-necks of the early

California days, who established order in frontier towns and camps by methods distasteful to tender souls. We find no fault with this. In fact, we are rather proud of being linked up with the stern and vigorous pioneers who effectually squelched the anarchists and I.W.W. of their day." The members of the Vigilantes included Booth Tarkington, Hamlin Garland, Irvin S. Cobb, Edgar Lee Masters, Ray Stannard Baker, and, again, Theodore Roosevelt. Its "underwriters," or associate members, included Vincent Astor, Simon Guggenheim, Coleman Du Pont, George F. Baker, Jacob H. Schiff, George W. Perkins, and Dwight Morrow.[12]

Whether or not they were regionally prominent or completely unknown outside their immediate communities, American establishmentarians between 1767 and 1902 managed to organize at least 326 identifiable vigilante organizations, and probably more than 150 others, which, because of secrecy or poor record keeping, are lost. Professor Brown has painstakingly pinpointed each of the 326 (116 of them eastern and 210 western). Together, they claimed 729 known victims, and undoubtedly, there were many more.[13]

Known variously as regulators, committees of public safety, slickers, stranglers, or, in parts of Texas, simply "mobs," vigilantes used intimidation, flogging, banishment, and execution to maintain the order they thought necessary for survival. Membership ranged from barely a dozen to more than 6,000. Texas led in the over-all number of organizations, with 52; San Francisco's was the largest; the Montana operation of 1884 was the deadliest, with 35 executions, followed by Lewiston, Idaho (31), Bannack and Virginia City, Montana (30), the Montana territorial groups of 1862–1864 (25), San Saba County, Texas (25), Madison and Hinds counties, Mississippi (21), Southern Illinois (20), Shackelford County, Texas (19), San Antonio, Texas (17), South Carolina (16), and Cheyenne City and Laramie County, Wyoming (16).[14]

On many occasions, vigilante groups got so far out of hand that they provoked the creation of antivigilante, or moderator, organizations, such as those in South Carolina and East Texas. As might be expected, even the most well-meaning vigilante leaders sometimes lost control to the more sadistic and violent types among their followers, and the excessive brutality that followed stimulated retaliation. Then, too, criminals occasionally joined vigilance committees to camouflage their illegal activities or to cover their trails when lawmen were in pursuit. Vigilante leaders who were less well-meaning sometimes formed groups not to punish criminals, as they claimed, but to pound their economic or political rivals into submission or extinction. Naturally, if the rivals were powerful enough to pose that kind of threat they were powerful enough to fight back, and they usually did so, at the head of moderator organizations. Sometimes vigilance groups were peaceful and confined themselves to beating drums, not heads. The Merchant's Vigilance Association of New York City, formed in 1845 to expose trade abuses and prevent fraud, evolved into the Better Business Bureau.

The vigilante reaction, then, is a complicated one and not suited to easy generalizations. It has brought order and destroyed it, consumed guilty and innocent alike, and been invoked by men with the most honorable of intentions and with the meanest. If there's one thing it has always been, however, it's a barometer of its time, a gauge of how Americans have coped with the social and economic challenges confronting them, from dealing with unabashed thieves and killers to the gentlest of immigrants. It's a barometer that has fluctuated wildly, unpredictably, and often lethally. And it's still there, just under the surface.

2

The Honorable
Judge Lynch

ALTHOUGH THE Puritans at Plymouth had disliked Thomas Morton for a variety of reasons practically since the day he first set foot in their colony, it was unquestionably the May Day party he threw for his friends and assorted Indians that really was the last straw for Governor William Bradford and his somber flock. Morton threw his badly timed party on May Day 1627. The citizens of Plymouth didn't like Morton's eighty-foot Maypole, which the Indians had helped erect, after it had been strung with flowers and ribbon. They didn't like the barrel of strong beer and the bottles of liquor that were freely passed around to whites and Indians alike. They didn't like the sight of citizens of the Crown dancing around a pole with a bunch of dangerous savages. Finally, they didn't like Morton's specially written May Day poem, which was pinned to the pole, or his song, which was sung by the revelers. The poem was scandalous and the song lascivious, according to Governor Bradford. The Governor probably found four lines particularly disgusting.

> Give to the Nymphe thats free from scorne
> No Irish stuff nor Scotch over worne.
> Lasses in beaver coats come away,
> Yee shall be welcome to us night and day.[1]

Morton was no Marot; even by Plymouth standards, he was at best a mediocre musical talent. But that was not what really made his neighbors so angry. When it is remembered that May Day is a pagan holiday, it becomes clear that he was taking something of a chance by openly celebrating it, almost within sight of the other colonists, and especially with Indians, who were getting drunk on his alcohol. The relationship between the precarious English colony of 200 and the tribes surrounding it had always been a touchy matter for Governor Bradford and his council, and the prospect of armed and loaded Indians outnumbering them by at least five to one was a positive nightmare.

Now Thomas Morton may have been a whimsical trouble-maker and something of a gadfly, but he was certainly no fool. He was a nature-loving free spirit, a bit of what used to be called a beatnik, who loved to roam through the quiet forests of his new land. He had a definite taste for hunting and other outdoor sports, as well as for the steady drinking and ribald humor characteristic of the reign of James I. But, in taking over a few abandoned cabins on the slope called Merry-Mount (now part of Quincy, Massachusetts) and throwing them open for the amusement of his white cronies and Indians of both sexes, Thomas Morton was thumbing his nose at an establishment of deadly serious Puritans. He did so not only because he thought that Bradford, Miles Standish, and the rest were starchy and emotionally moribund, but also because he had come to America to make money by trading with the Indians, and the best way to do that, he correctly judged, was to keep them happy. That had been the whole point of his crossing the Atlantic, buying a small piece of a trading post overlooking Boston Bay, and then taking it over when his partners emerged stunned from the New England winter and headed straight for the relative warmth of Virginia.

Morton kept the Indians happy by trading surplus muskets and potent rum for bear, otter, marten, deer, beaver, and black-wolf skins, all of which were plentiful in Massachusetts but worth a fortune back in England. For a while, business seems to have been good, largely because Morton kept braves and squaws alike happier than they had been in quite some time. As the Indians became adept at using the muskets, they were able to bring more skins to Morton, who was therefore able to buy more muskets with his profits and then pass them out to the Indians—more Indians—who soon brought in still more pelts, and so on.

But it wasn't to last. In the first place, the Puritans viewed all this as sacrilegious and unlawful—giving liquor to the Indians wasn't against the law, but giving them guns was. Second, Morton was cutting deep into their own trade, since it hadn't taken the Indians long to decide that they preferred his firearms and firewater to their hand axes, cheap trinkets, and blankets. Finally, and most important, those armed Indians were considered potentially dangerous, especially by the vulnerable plantation owners who lived outside the stockade. And, as if the Indian menace weren't bad enough, there was reason to assume that all the fun and profits at Merry-Mount were attracting unsavory white men, too.

"Here was a vast country without any pretence of a police," notes Charles Francis Adams, one of those who chronicled the episode. "It was the yearly resort of a most lawless class, caring only for immediate gain. Once let such a gathering place as Morton's become established, and it would indeed become a nest of unclean birds. Desperate characters, runaway servants, criminals who did not dare to go back to civilization, would flock to it and there find a refuge, until, as Bradford pointed out, the outnumbered settlers would 'stand in more fear of their lives and goods from this wicked and debauched crew than from the savages themselves.' "[2]

Accordingly, a year after Morton's party, several of the plantation owners around Plymouth met, agreed that he had to stop such activities, and sent letters describing what they saw as their common danger to the magistrates inside the stockade. The officials, in turn, sent a messenger out to Merry-Mount with a letter that Bradford described as friendly and neighborly, but which nonetheless put it to Morton that he had to end his evil practices immediately. The master of Merry-Mount was anything but an ambiguous man. In addition to berating the messenger, who returned to Plymouth severely shaken, Morton answered in writing by telling the magistrates that they were meddling in matters which didn't concern them, that they had no jurisdiction over Merry-Mount, and that he fully intended to continue trading with the Indians in whatever manner he pleased. A second letter from the magistrates soon arrived. This one informed Morton that he would do well to watch his tongue and reminded him that his trading enterprise not only endangered the community, but also defied the law. The second warning was answered about the way the first had been, except that Morton added several expletives, which have come down to us deleted, and ended by informing the magistrates that if anyone from Plymouth came out to molest him he would be ready for them—a warning that was undoubtedly taken seriously, since Morton probably owned more muskets than the Puritans did.

Although the legal basis for the magisterial order was in some doubt even among the magistrates, they felt that if Morton was not stopped all order in New England might be lost. He had successfully browbeaten them once, the magistrates reasoned, and would certainly try to do so again. They therefore called in Miles Standish, the settlement's chief scout and law enforcer, and sent him with eight deputies to bring in Morton. The Puritans' chief "hit man" found his quarry at Wessagusset, a few miles from the trading post, and made the arrest. It is suspected that someone in the area fingered Morton, because Standish knew exactly where to find him and never even went near Merry-Mount.

Instead of acting belligerent, Morton turned into the most seemingly virtuous and astonished of prisoners, inquiring with a great show of innocence as to the reason for his capture. Standish dutifully told Morton that he had broken the law and had ignored two appeals to stop doing so, but when the master of Merry-Mount insisted on being told the names of those who were charging him, Standish became silent. While Morton was declaring to his captors that he stood solidly on his rights as an Englishman, wouldn't answer the accusations of anonymous men, and should be set free immediately, Standish prepared to hold him under guard in a nearby cabin for the night and to move him to Plymouth the following morning. Nobody in Plymouth would have accused Miles Standish of being careless—he detailed six men to guard the prisoner and even ordered one of them to get into bed with Morton.

The so-far perfect execution of the magisterial order made Standish and his men so happy, according to Morton's account, that they decided to celebrate the apparent end of the threat with some of the residents of Wessagusset. Ordinarily, no one would have been more eager to join the party than the prisoner himself, but under the circumstances he thought it better to spend the evening waiting to see what would happen. He was eventually rewarded by seeing all his guards fall into their beds exhausted, and when he figured every one of them was out cold he left. Unfortunately, the outer of the two doors slammed loudly enough to wake some of those inside. What followed is best described by Morton himself, who did so delightfully.

"The word which was given with an alarme, was—o. he's gon!—he's gon!—what shall we doe, he's gon!—the rest (halfe a sleepe) start up in a maze, and, like rames, ran theire heads one at another full butt in the darke, Their grand leader, Captaine Shrimp, tooke on most furiously, and tore his clothes for anger to see the empty nest and their bird gone. The rest were eager to have torne theire haire from theire heads; but it was so short, that it would give them no hold."[3]

While Morton ran through a night filled with gathering storm clouds, trying to get back to the safety of Merry-Mount as quickly as possible, "Captaine Shrimp" wisely decided to wait until morning to take up pursuit. But Morton knew that Standish and the others would head straight for Merry-Mount at first light, and so he returned there determined to set up the strongest defense possible, not an easy task, since five of his seven colleagues were off looking for furs (a bit of intelligence probably known to Standish).

Sure enough, the posse from Plymouth showed up the next morning and walked brazenly up to the trading post's front door. While Standish and his men started to break down the door, Morton, musket in hand and followed closely by one of his quivering men (the other was too drunk to help), came out and made a show of resistance. Miles Standish contemptuously pushed away Morton's musket and rearrested him—an act that probably saved the trader's life, because his weapon had been filled with powder halfway to its muzzle and would likely have blown up in his face had he pulled the trigger. The defeat was made complete when Morton's only functioning follower ran nosefirst into the point of a sword held by one of Standish's men. He bled a little all the way back to Plymouth.

The council that tried Thomas Morton on charges of endangering public safety was divided on whether to execute him or send him back to England to answer charges there. Mention of sending him back to England so enraged Standish, according to Morton, that the Captain threatened to kill him with his own hands, rather than let him leave Plymouth in one piece. (Miles Standish thereby became the first in a long succession of American policemen who have argued that they took their lives in their hands to arrest and bring in dangerous criminals only to have the courts go easy on the culprits and nullify their work.) But cooler heads prevailed. Thomas Morton was returned to the mother country, in the company of a guard who carried letters dated June 9, 1628, that charged the prisoner with trafficking in firearms and maintaining a place filled with loose persons "living without all fear of God or common honesty; some of them abusing the Indian women most filthily, as it is notorious."[4]

Thomas Morton, buoyant soul that he was, hadn't seen the last of the New World, however. The former master of Merry-Mount was prepared to spend "a heape of gold" for his defense, but that proved unnecessary, because no formal charges were brought against him, either because the royal proclamation under which the Plymouth Colony functioned wasn't clearly law or because Morton managed to endear himself to the powerful men behind the New England Charter by convincing them that he had been purged on purely religious grounds and, anyway, was a better businessman than his persecutors.

Thomas Morton was back in New England a year and a half after he had left. But, after coming out on the short end of a major intrigue, he was once again dragged before the magistrates. This time, however, they were determined to make a lasting example of him, and their verdict was harsh and immutable. The "Sachem of Passonagessit," as he liked to call himself (the disgusted residents of Plymouth referred to him as "the Lord of Misrule"), was sentenced to be returned to England, to have his goods sold to pay the transportation cost and reimburse some Indians from whom he had allegedly stolen a canoe, and to have his home burned down, "because the habitation of the wicked should no more appear in Israel." He was promptly placed in stocks and ticketed to be sent back on the *Gift*, but her captain refused to carry him, so passage was arranged on the *Handmaid*. Even at the final hour the stubborn Morton refused to walk aboard. So he was hoisted onto the ship's deck with a tackle, and nearly starved at sea because no provision had been made for feeding him. In a final display of the renowned Puritan vindictiveness, Thomas Morton's ship sailed out of the bay and was within clear sight of Merry-Mount on the night his cabin was burned to the ground. It lighted the area where the Maypole had been with a pulsating orange glow visible all the way to Plymouth.

The Plymouth elders and Standish, their gunslinger, weren't vigilantes, in the strict sense of the word, because to the extent that there was law in their colony they were its properly constituted guardians. Yet certain aspects of the "Maypole of Merry-Mount" episode are of interest here because they formed the germ of a phenomenon that would grow into the vigilante reaction—namely, the use of force and ultimately of violence, without due process, to protect what was construed as the public welfare. While even Morton himself admitted that he had been a thorn in the Puritans' side, his actual "crimes" during that second visit seem to have been confined to taking a canoe from some Indians and firing at them, wounding one and tearing a hole in another's clothes.

"His was a case of civil persectuion only," wrote Charles Francis Adams about Morton's second appearance before the Plymouth authorities. "The man before them was a poor, lawless creature at best, and the Massachusetts magistrates had made up their minds in advance. They meant, in the preacher's holy phrase, to purge him from the land. He was not only what they termed a 'libertine,' but his presence at Mt. Wollaston was a standing menace to the company. The best use to which he could be devoted was that of an example to others. . . . That he was an undesirable character to have about an infant colony . . . does not admit of question, and it was the avowed policy of the company to permit none regarded in this light to remain. Similar methods of dealing with improper and undesirable characters have since not been uncommon among the mining communities of the interior and the Pacific slope; but it is somewhat singular that the rough camp-law there practiced should find its earliest precedent on the first page of the records of Massachusetts Bay."[5]

Not so singular, actually. Thomas Morton was punished by a people who frowned on any divergence of opinion within their own community as being unhealthy and dangerous (even though it had been divergence of opinion in their former land that had sent them there), who had no real convictions regarding democratic ideals on an individual basis, who despised the loose behavior of English society almost as much as they despised such behavior in their own tenuous domain, and who, above all, were constantly frightened for their lives and possessions. Governor Bradford, the magistrates, and most of the ordinary members of the Plymouth settlement were no less aware of British democratic principles than was their victim. But when they were in danger, or thought they were, the leaders of the colony didn't hesitate to put Morton in stocks, confiscate his belongings, destroy his home, and throw him out of their country, without bothering to hear his defense. Special circumstances, then, were understood to require special measures. If anything, Thomas Morton should have considered himself lucky to have escaped from the New World without having had his ears cropped, or worse. He should have considered himself lucky, but, being the kind of man he was, he probably didn't.

The "Maypole of Merry-Mount" incident is important to the vigilante story because it's one of the earliest examples, if not *the* earliest, of the most pervasive fact of life facing everyone who came to America during the following two centuries: they were involved, often on a life-and-death basis, in a new game having no universally accepted rules. They were people who constantly probed ahead of social stability in order to fill a lucrative but dangerous void. Common law was all well and good back home, where everyone—constables, barristers, solicitors, members of Parliament, judges, and even criminals—operated within an accepted social and legal framework. But that framework was next to meaningless when applied to the American frontier, because it wasn't acknowledged by all of the players. What could a Hudson Valley farmer do when he was ambushed by a band of Iroquois? Call a constable? Invoke the Sixth Commandment? Explain to the Indians that they'd be subject to an appearance before the King's Bench if they didn't leave him alone? Could the residents of a tiny settlement a hundred miles up the James River from the nearest Virginia Colony garrison remind the white predators who materialized out of the woods to steal livestock and tools, or even women and children, that crown law imposed severe penalties for thievery and abduction? That an unsavory record would forever damage their chances of getting good jobs? That their families would suffer excruciating embarrassment if their names appeared in the newspapers?

Seventeenth-, eighteenth-, and nineteenth-century America was wide open and up for grabs. The frontier, rolling implacably forward from the footholds scattered along the edges of the eastern seaboard, did so in a continuing state of flux, as divergent and often opposing groups maneuvered to establish their new identities and carve out a piece of the spoils. And each—English, French, German, Spanish, and Dutch; farmers, ranchers, trappers, bankers, and bandits; whites, blacks, reds, yellows, and tans—carried with it different rules for playing the game and different responses to the incursions of others. As with any chaotic situation in which a profit motive is involved, the lowest common denominator—violence—was the only principle understood and respected by all. Historian Richard Slotkin, in fact, has gone so far as to say that violence had a definite regenerating effect, that from the time of the Puritans Americans formed their new national identity by perpetrating violence against the land and against one another, gaining strength and purpose from it.[6] Whatever validity there may be to Slotkin's theory, at least one fact is inescapable: the friction generated by the diverse millions who poured into America and scrambled frantically for its resources produced an enormous amount of violence. The Republic itself was born to the crackle of musket fire and the application of torches, and that success was wasted on no one.

The last decade has produced a great deal of self-flagellation in America, much of it justified, some not. We have told ourselves, for example, that we are incorrigibly violence prone, and there has been a lot of headshaking about it. Well, we are violence prone, but, given the right combination of circumstances, everybody is violence prone. Civil violence is not peculiar to America. America is only about 350 years old, and the people who landed here came from other places and brought their violent proclivities with them. It was their unique interaction in the open American situation that brought violence to the surface; other kinds of interactions have produced equally awful results elsewhere. The modern histories of Germany and the Soviet Union, Northern Ireland and Hungary, Algeria and Nigeria, Chile and Argentina, and scores of other lands make the point. All those people had their reasons for committing violence. So did Americans. In order to make sense out of the violence in America, including the vigilante variety, it is necessary to see that violence as the response to peculiarly American circumstances. What happened at Merry-Mount in 1627 and 1628 illustrates the situation as it relates to vigilance and lynching. And lynching, by the way, is an American word, but in no way a strictly American phenomenon.

Trying to determine who committed the first lynching is like trying to determine who built the first fire. The German Vehmic courts, for example, existed as far back as the thirteenth century. Such elaborately organized secret bodies came into existence to end lawlessness throughout much of Germany, but particularly in Westphalia, where they started a reign of terror to combat feudal anarchy and particularly plundering or heretical noblemen. Nobles could be either members of the tribunals or victims, but the courts' nickname—"free courts"—reflected the fact that all freeborn men were eligible for membership (and also that the courts claimed exceptional jurisdiction because of the exceptional circumstances of the times). Death was the only punishment inflicted by the Vehmic courts, and executions were carried out on the spot. A culprit was given six weeks and three days to answer the summons nailed to his door, and if he failed to show up for his trial three more notices were sent. The scoffer who continued to stay away after this procedure had been followed was subject to execution by the first court member who met him. When the accused did show up, he was tried before the full membership, in either open or secret session, and with the presentation of evidence and testimony by witnesses. Standing before the court leaders (who generally sat at tables on which a sword and a rope had been placed), the accused was given a chance to defend himself. If he wasn't himself a member of the court, he had to produce favorable witnesses from among the members of the tribunal (twenty-one meant guaranteed acquittal). If he was a member, he could clear himself just by swearing innocence. The power of the Vehmic courts gradually eroded as sovereign law took hold in Germany, but they weren't finally abolished until the time of Jérôme Bonaparte, the King of Westphalia—specifically, in 1811.

Lynch law was used against the burgomaster of Stujhely, Hungary, in November 1902, after he set fire to his own house and caused the deaths of his wife, his parents, and his three children. The man had become angered by some trivial matter and had immolated them in revenge, an act that so enraged others in the town that they strung him up before the civil authorities could get him to jail. In prerevolutionary Russia, it was relatively common for horse thieves to be clubbed to death by villagers, each striking the victim so as to leave no more than a bruise. Then there was the practice of tying a thief's ankles to the tail of an especially active colt and riding it at full gallop until the man was literally kicked to pieces. Other horse thieves were tied to benches or logs while village women pricked the soles of their feet and other sensitive areas with pins and needles until the victims died in agony. "Halifax law," as it used to be known in Britain, allowed the summary trial and execution of criminals without giving them the benefit of anything like a defense. It seems to have started in the forest of Hardwick, near the parish of Halifax, where the burghers tried and condemned to death anyone charged with stealing goods valued at 13½ pence or more. The accused was usually beheaded on market day, for the familiar reason—to make him an example to others who might be tempted to take what didn't belong to them.[7] The symbolic value of public punishment, including executions, runs throughout the history of lynching and vigilante operations.

Lynching, in America, wasn't always synonymous with killing. Most early lynchings, in fact, consisted of beatings, floggings, or confinement in stocks or irons. Public flogging was a popular ritual in much of seventeenth- and eighteenth-century America and was considered a more than adequate punishment for most transgressors.

Aside from the Salem witch trials, one of the earliest known instances of capital punishment in America was in late December of 1763 at Paxtang (now Harrisburg), Pennsylvania, after Conestoga Indians went on a scalping rampage. Appeals for help by the settlers to the Quaker authorities had been ignored, so the men in Lancaster and Cumberland counties formed ranger companies for their "protection." When word came that a Conestoga thought to have been involved in the murder of whites was spotted in a nearby Indian settlement, Matthew Smith, one of the area's staunchest citizens, called together a group of Paxtang rangers and led them to the Conestogas. As they bore down on the Indians' cabins, one of the rangers thought he recognized a brave who had murdered his mother. He shot and killed the Indian. That signaled a charge into the cabins. When the shooting stopped, six more Conestogas were dead, and fourteen others had fled to what they assumed was the safety of the Lancaster County jail. It didn't take the rangers long to discover that their quarry was being protected by Quaker lawmen, however, so fifty of them marched on the jail and broke in. The remaining Indians, including women and children, were massacred.

Three elements of this story are worth noting. First, the avengers reacted violently only after they found they couldn't get satisfaction from the authorities; second, they were led by a prominent member of the community, who undoubtedly stood more to lose to the Indians than many of the others; third, the rangers eventually stormed a jail, indicating that, however weak they thought the local law enforcement to be, it did in fact exist.

The Revolution provided a backdrop for all sorts of summary punishments and reprisals, from Maine to Georgia, as Tories and Whigs—loyalists and revolutionaries—clashed while the social and political order went through convulsions. Many loyalists made no bones about where their sympathies lay, and that infuriated their highly insecure Whig counterparts. Revolutions are, after all, very passionate undertakings.

That being the case, committees of correspondence, inspection, and safety started to spring up in many Connecticut, Massachusetts, and New Hampshire towns between 1774 and 1777. The committees, which were elected at town meetings, not only helped control disaffection and subversion, but also provided a bit of grass-roots legitimacy during the transition period before 1776, when such bodies as the Massachusetts provincial Congress were still in considerable doubt as to their authority and permanence.[8]

But, however lofty the patriots' motives and supposedly beneficial their actions, their power rested on force and, when needed, violence or the threat of it, in civil matters as well as military. The case of Edward Perry, a lumberman from Maine (then part of Massachusetts), who had a contract to sell masts to the Royal Navy's yard at Halifax, Nova Scotia, illustrates the workings of the committees. The committees of Georgetown and Woolwich seized a large number of Perry's masts in April 1775 and demanded that he post a bond of £2,000 as a guarantee that he wouldn't ship them to the British. The money was paid by Perry's friends, but he was nevertheless put in confinement, finally being deported all the way to Sturbridge, and threats of violence were made against his employees.[9]

The tarring and feathering of Tory sympathizers, which was done by mobs, not committees, was much quicker and undoubtedly far more satisfying. On September 7, 1768, a customhouse waiter in Salem, who had been accused of informing the Crown's customs collectors that certain items had been taken aboard a vessel to avoid payment of duty, was publicly "plummed." "Between the Hours of Ten and Eleven A.M. he was taken from one of the Wharves, and conducted to the common, where his Head, Body and Limbs were covered with warm Tar, and then a large Quantity of Feathers were applied to all Parts," reported the *Salem Gazette*. "The poor Waiter was then exalted to a Seat on the Front of a Cart, and in this Manner led into the Main Street, where a Paper, with the word *Informer* thereon, in large Letters, was affixed to his Breast, and another Paper, with the same Word, to his Back. This Scene drew together, within a few Minutes, several Hundred People, who proceeded, with Huzzas and loud Acclamations, through the Town."[10]

"Last Thursday Afternoon a young Woman from the Country was decoyed into one of the Barracks in Town," reported the *Boston Gazette* of November 6, 1769, "and most shamefully abused by some of the Soldiers there:—the Person that enticed her thither with promises of disposing of all her marketing there (who also belonged to the Country) was afterwards taken by the Populace and several times duck'd in the Water at one of the Docks in Town; but luckily for him he made his escape from them sooner than was intended;—however, we hear, that after he had crossed the Ferry to Charlestown, on his return home, the People there being informed of the base part he had been acting, took him and placed him in a Cart, and after tarring and feathering him (the present popular Punishment for modern delinquents) they carted him about that Town for two or three Hours, as a Spectacle of Contempt and a Warning to others from practicing such vile Artifices for the Delusion and Ruin of the virtuous and innocent: He was then dismissed, and permitted to proceed to the Town where he belonged, for them to act with as they should see fit."[11]

By the time of the Revolution, then, the pattern of lynching was well established in America and was thought to be an especially useful tool for keeping actual or potential troublemakers in line. Victims were almost always put on public display and occasionally adorned with signs explaining their crimes, in three words or less. The use of signs had started in Europe, not in America, but it was here that they achieved widespread popularity, on the theory, of course, that such graphics would discourage anyone else from considering the same kind of crime. Nineteenth-century vigilantes repeatedly hanged their victims in public places in towns or along heavily traveled routes, and signed their work, in an equivalent of today's highway billboards warning against speeding and drunken driving. Young Malcolm Campbell, who was to become well known as a Wyoming sheriff, had no sooner arrived in Cheyenne, in 1868, when there were four vigilante hangings, all of them public displays. "Undoubtedly, these incidents went far in shaping my future life and in guiding my feet properly in those trails of danger where I was later to apprehend some of the most dangerous outlaws of the plains," he was to recall.[12] We'll never know, though, how many others ignored the advertising.

Indians, gangsters, and political enemies weren't the only subjects of lynchings in young America, nor were lynching parties confined to frontier areas or those in turmoil. Lynching was also popular as a weapon against citizens who didn't behave themselves like good Christians, even if they carried on behind their own doors. Ugly drunkenness, blatantly crooked business practices, and wife beating or child abuse often prompted community "regulation." Again, the punishment was meant not only to chastise the wrongdoer, but also to serve as a warning to the rest of the community. The following episodes, which illustrate that kind of activity, probably formed precedents for what was to become the late-nineteenth- and early-twentieth-century White Cap movement, which spread across wide areas of the United States and punished all manner of minor miscreants, sometimes with considerable violence.

"We hear from *Elizabeth-Town*," said the *New York Gazette* of December 18, 1752, in a story about happenings in New Jersey, "that an odd Sect of People have lately appeared there, who go under the Denomination of *Regulars:* there are near a Dozen of them, who dress themselves in Women's Cloaths, and painting their Faces, go in the Evening to the Houses of such as are reported to have beat their Wives: where one of them entering in

---

first, seizes the Delinquent, whilst the rest follow, strip him, turn up his Posteriors and flog him with Rods most severely, crying out all the Time, *Wo to the Men that beat their Wives:*—It seems that several Persons in that Borough (and 'tis said some very deservedly) have undergone the Discipline, to the no small Terror of others, who are in any Way conscious of deserving the same Punishment. 'Twere to be wish'd," added the writer, evidently a man with some sense of humor, "that in order for the more equal Distribution of Justice, there wou'd arise another Sect, under the Title of *Regulartrixes* who should dress themselves in Mens Cloathes, and flagilate the Posteriors of the Scolds, Termagants, &c., &c."[13]

A year later, "Prudence Goodwife" related in a letter how her husband had beaten and otherwise maltreated her, and went on to describe his retribution. The letter contains the earliest known use of the word "regulators," meaning to regulate, or bring into moral balance, the state of the community. "My Case being happily nois'd abroad," the woman explained, in what appears to be something like a 1753 version of a Dear Abby letter, "induced several generous young Men to discipline him. These young Persons do stile, or are stiled, Regulators: and so they are with Propriety: for they have regulated my dear husband, and the rest of the Bad Ones hereabouts, that they are afraid of using such Barbarity; and I must with Pleasure acknowledge, that since my Husband has felt what whipping was, he has entirely left off whipping me, and promises faithfully he will never begin again. Tho' there are some that are afraid of whipping their Wives, for fear of dancing the same Jigg; yet I understand, they are not afraid of making Application, in order to have those dear Regulators indicted; and if they should it might discourage them for the future, to appear to the Assistance of the Innocent and Helpless; and then poor Wives who have the unhappiness to be lockt in Wedlock with bad Husbands, take care of your tender Hides; for you may depend upon being bang'd without Mercy."[14]

The man from whose name "lynching" was coined had far more serious motives than punishing wife beaters and used a more lethal instrument than a stick. Although several candidates, including James Lynch Fitz Stephen, the mayor of Galway, Ireland, in 1493, have been credited as the source of the word, the winner, appropriately, is an American named William Lynch, of

Pittsylvania, Virginia.* Colonel (or Captain) Lynch seems to have been first identified in print by Edgar Allan Poe, who had this to say about him in an editorial in the *Southern Literary Messenger* of May 1836:

"Frequent inquiry has been made within the last year as to the origin of Lynch's law. This subject now possesses historical interest. It will be perceived from the annexed paper, that the law, so called, originated in 1780, in Pittsylvania, Virginia. Colonel William Lynch, of that county, was its author; and we are informed by a resident, who was a member of a body formed for the purpose of carrying it into effect, that the efforts of the association were wholly successful. A trained band of villains, whose operations extended from North to South, whose well concerted schemes had bidden defiance to the ordinary laws of the land, and whose success encouraged them to persevere in depredations upon an unoffending community, was dispersed and laid prostrate under the infliction of Lynch's law. Of how many terrible, and deeply to be lamented consequences—of how great an amount of permanent evil—has the partial and temporary good been productive!"[15]

Poe went on to support his claim that Colonel Lynch was *the* Lynch by printing the manifesto allegedly written by William Lynch or a confederate and used by the group. I do the same here, not to prove the case for William Lynch but for a far more important reason: it is a prototype of the kind of vigilante manifesto that will be found elsewhere, used always in an attempt to set the moral justification for vigilante action. It might also be noted here that as far back as 1836 Poe was questioning the use of summary justice and calling it a mixed blessing.

Whereas, many of the inhabitants of the county of Pittsylvania, as well as elsewhere, have sustained great and intolerable losses by a set of lawless men who have banded themselves together to deprive honest men of their just rights and property, by stealing their horses, counterfeiting, and passing paper currency, and committing many other species of villainy, too tedious to mention, and that those vile mis-

* James Elbert Cutler identified him in 1905 as a Colonel Robert Lynch, another Virginian of the same period, and Richard Maxwell Brown apparently agrees. Still others think his name was Charles. I think the case for William is better, and there is a possibility that they are one and the same.

creants do still persist in their diabolical practices, and have hitherto escaped the civil power with impunity, it being almost useless and unnecessary to have recourse to our laws to suppress and punish those freebooters, they having it in their power to extricate themselves when brought to justice by suborning witnesses who do swear them clear—we, the subscribers, being determined to put a stop to the iniquitous practices of those unlawful and abandoned wretches, do enter into the following association, to wit: that next to our consciences, soul and body, we hold our rights and property, sacred and inviolable. We solemnly protest before God and the world, that (for the future) upon hearing or having sufficient reason to believe, that any villainy or species of villainy having been committed within our neighborhood, we will forthwith embody ourselves, and repair immediately to the person or persons suspected, or those under suspicious characters, harboring, aiding, or assisting those villains, and if they will not desist from their evil practices, we will inflict such corporal punishment on him or them, as to us shall seem adequate to the crime committed or the damage sustained; that we will protect and defend each and every one of us, the subscribers, as well jointly as severally, from the insults and assaults offered by any other person in their behalf; and further, we do bind ourselves jointly and severally, our joint and several heirs etc. to pay or cause to be paid, all damages that shall or may accrue in consequence of this our laudable undertaking, and will pay an equal proportion according to our several abilities; and we, after having a sufficient number of subscribers to this association, will convene ourselves to some convenient place, and will make choice of our body five of the best and most discreet men belonging to our body, to direct and govern the whole, and we will strictly adhere to their determinations in all cases whatsoever relative to the above undertaking; and if any of our body summoned to attend the execution of this our plan, and fail to do so without a reasonable excuse, they shall forfeit and pay the sum of one hundred pounds current money of Virginia, to be appropriated towards defraying the contingent expenses of this our undertaking. In witness whereof we have set our hands, this 22d day of September 1780.[16]

Besides providing a fine example of organization leaders' traditional penchant for run-on sentences, in emulation of lawyers, Lynch's law is notable in other respects: it was based on loss of property, not of life; it complained of inadequate law enforcement and judicial process, not a lack of them; it put a premium on secrecy, because it was blatantly illegal, but it did so on a piece of paper every member had to sign, because that lent it an aura of legality; it was predicated on the individual's right to take the law into his own hands, but it explicitly provided that he had to follow the orders of a few leaders and could be penalized for not doing so. The original Lynch mob, then, was no mob at all. It was a true vigilante group. And, like others that paralleled or followed it, it had to justify a series of very basic contradictions. The justification, as always, was expedience in the interest of survival.

It was expedience, for example, that apparently convinced Colonel Lynch to inflict capital, rather than corporal, punishment on his group's victims. The manifesto made it clear that corporal punishment was to be used, but it doesn't seem to have had the desired effect on the rogues infesting Virginia, so the rod was occasionally spared in favor of the rope. Lynch, obviously aware of the stigma attached by some to "the regulation," explained to a surveyor named Andrew Ellicott that, although his men had hanged some criminals, he—Lynch—had never actually voted for the death penalty. Furthermore, he said, part of the responsibility for executing outlaws had to be shared by their own horses. Why? Because a condemned man would be seated on his horse, with the noose around his neck and the other end of the rope tied to a tree limb. Man and horse would be left that way. Eventually the horse would wander off, because of either hunger or boredom, and when it had gone far enough its rider would be left hanging by his neck in mid-air.

"The Lynch-men associated for the purpose of punishing crimes in a summary way without the tedious and technical forms of our courts of justice," said Ellicott, in recounting his conversations with Lynch. "Upon complaint being made to any member of the association of a crime being committed within the vicinity of their jurisdiction the person complained of was immediately pursued and taken if possible. If apprehended he was carried before some members of the association and examined:— if his answers were not satisfactory he was whipped till they were so. Those extorted answers generally involved others in the supposed crime who in their turn were punished in like manner. These punishments were sometimes severe and not infrequently inflicted upon the innocent thro spite or in consequence of answers extorted under the smarting of the whip to interrogatories put by the members of the association.

"It seems almost incredible that such proceedings should be

had in a civilized country governed by known laws it may nevertheless be relied on. I should not have asserted it as a fact had it not been related to me by Mr. Lynch himself and his neighbor Mr. Lay, one of the original association together with several other Lynch-men as they are called."[17]

Lynch's admission to Ellicott that occasionally an innocent man had been punished along with those definitely guilty would be echoed by other vigilantes during the following century, and with about as much remorse. The theory, which clearly ran contrary to every legal principle on which the country had been founded, simply had it that a few good apples were bound to turn up in every barrel of bad ones but, most regrettably, no foolproof sorting out could be made when community survival was at stake.

In adopting this ends-justify-means approach, lynchers may have been acting contrary to legal precepts, but they did so very much in accordance with the political and social spirit of the times. Hadn't the glorious end of breaking away from a tyrannical monarchy justified the raising of a ragtag army that had shot at and killed many British soldiers who not only had done no personal harm to Americans but also had never wanted wretched garrison duty in this Godforsaken wilderness at all? No matter. The Crown had been repressive, and since they couldn't shoot at King George his minions had to do. Wasn't it possible that an occasional harmless Indian got caught and killed with the dangerous ones? It wasn't only possible, it was probable, and many people knew it. Yet how could the inhabitants of a precariously situated settlement, with limited supplies and manpower, afford the luxury of sorting out the motives and dispositions of every Indian they saw? The only sure way of reducing the security problem, and therefore of surviving, was to reduce the Indians— all Indians. Well into the twentieth century, the maxim of shooting first and asking questions later has been an integral part of American lore. The frontier, from Vicksburg to Vietnam, after all, is strewn with the bones of too many innocents who asked too many questions. The chain of events running from the first attack on an Indian camp through Pittsylvania and the actions that will unfold here logically culminated at My Lai in 1968. The pattern is always the same.

If details of the Lynch-men's "regulation" were ever recorded, they have been lost. We don't know how many people they whipped or hanged, nor do we know the extent of the crime wave that brought them into existence. Lynch himself went on to represent Pittsylvania County in the Virginia House of Delegates in 1787–88—a political achievement shared by many future vigilante leaders. He was granted land in Pendleton District, South Carolina, in June 1798, and he died there, in relative obscurity, on July 15, 1820. His obituary in the *Pendleton Messenger* said:

Died.]　On the 15th ult. Capt. William Lynch; aged 78. He was an old revolutionary soldier, a friend to the widow, and orphan, and a good farmer: he died in possession of christianity and the good will of all honest people who knew him.[18]

It is ironic that the man who gave us the word "lynching" was buried in the soil of South Carolina, the scene of America's first full-scale vigilante war.

3

South Carolina: "We are *Free-Men* ... Not Born *Slaves*"

THE PATIENT and respectable men of the South Carolina back country decided, in the early summer of 1767, that they had been pushed to their limit by governmental indifference, corrupt and inadequate law enforcement, and what amounted to a full-scale crime wave that was devouring their crops, livestock, money, wives, daughters, and other possessions. They decided, that summer, that their world needed regulating, and, having come to that conclusion, they reacted with vengeance. They became the first true American vigilantes. The time, after all, was ripe; self-determination was in the air in 1767.

By that year, His Majesty's Province of South Carolina was divided into two roughly parallel parts: the coastal low country, which stretched some fifty miles inland, and the back country, which began where the low country ended and wandered unevenly westward, across swamps, fertile farmlands, and pinewoods, until it nudged the Piedmont. The Piedmont was Cherokee country and was therefore left alone by everybody with sense. For all the inhabitants of the two colonized sections had in common, though, they might as well have lived on different continents.

The low country was where Charles Town was located, and, since Charles Town was the seat of the provincial government, the center of commerce, and the repository of such culture as existed in South Carolina on the eve of the Revolution, the low country was the dominant partner in a shaky provincial alliance. Low countrymen of substance carried on a thriving but specialized trade with the back country, especially in flour, deerskins, and cattle. Trade, in fact, was one of only three elements that kept open whatever lines of communication existed between the two sections. The other two elements were decidedly negative— the possibility of a slave revolt or an Indian uprising. People in the low country were always worrying about a slave revolt, since they had most of the slaves, and they knew that if a revolt ever happened they'd need every able-bodied white man they could find. Then, too, if the Cherokees decided to come out of the Piedmont and move eastward looking for scalps, the back country would turn into a buffer and be the first line of defense. Every white musket would be needed if the Cherokees came.

Still, back countrymen were looked down on as being mainly yokels and second-class citizens, a fact that was reflected in their treatment by the provincial authorities in Charles Town. The government, which was headed by a governor, a lieutenant governor, and a governor's Council, all appointed by the king, was highly centralized, as was the so-called popularly elected Assembly. The Assembly was popularly elected by the low country, not the back country, and that grated on back countrymen. The four counties in which all South Carolinians lived were politically meaningless and had neither power nor officials to represent the citizens locally. Instead, local government was carried on for the most part by parish churchwardens and vestrymen of the Church of England and by justices of the peace and constables. The churchmen cared for the poor as best they could and supervised Assembly elections; the justices, who also were under the Crown, had limited jurisdiction in civil cases and no jurisdiction in criminal cases, and exercised their maximum power on the rare occasions when they were able to call out the militia to help some constable who was over his head in police work. All healthy whites (and, in time of real trouble only, healthy blacks) had to serve a stint in the militia.

During the years when almost all South Carolinians had lived in the low country, the system had worked fairly well. Charles Town was close enough in those days so that the power of its government was always felt. It was never very hard to drag some criminal into the capital and let the law take its course. Likewise, the political bonds between parishes around Charles Town and the Governor were kept reasonably taut because they were reasonably short.

But the opening of the back country had brought problems. For one thing, while transportation routes existed and often were heavily used, they were difficult. Rivers and streams linking the back country to the coast were hard to navigate and wandered, so rough trails and roads that pointed to Charles Town were the main routes on which people got back and forth. The distance between the capital and some far-out settlement might have been as much as 250 miles, requiring a man to stay in the saddle for about a week or on the seat of a wagon for two or three times that long. Making use of Charles Town's legal apparatus was therefore not something to be done whimsically, and neither was covering vast back-country areas in order to keep the peace.

Second, the back country was badly underrepresented in the Assembly, because the real seat of power, in London, refused to open new parishes as the frontier moved west and north. The back country had only one parish—Saint Mark—in 1767, and two of the forty-eight members of the Charles Town Assembly. Not only did that lack of parishes, which were equivalent to our electoral districts, limit political representation; it also limited the number of clergymen sent to bring God to the rich and food to the poor. As a consequence, while many back countrymen met the fifty-acre land requirement for voting during that early summer of 1767, there almost wasn't anyone to vote for. And even that would probably have been tolerable for a while if it hadn't been for the devastating effects of the Cherokee War of 1760–1761. The war had fundamentally dislocated and brutalized almost everyone in the back country. The combination of these factors set the stage for regulation.

Settlement of the back country had begun in the 1730s, and, under an official expansionist settlement plan designed to counterbalance the low country's growing and potentially dangerous slave population, new towns were started throughout that decade. Germans, Swiss, and Irishmen, French Huguenots, Welsh Baptists from Pennsylvania, British-bred Virginians, and even a scattering of real low-country South Carolinians had begun to move into the area during the 1740s and '50s. Places like Orangeburg, Saxe Gotha, New Windsor, New Bordeaux, Long Canes, and Fredericksburg Township had sprung into being as some of the wagons came to a halt, while others had continued moving cautiously westward, probing at 3,000 Cherokee warriors and their families who lived in about sixty camps in the foothills of the Appalachians and along the Blue Ridge. They probed and traded, and many did well, but it wasn't to last.

Largely because of French intrigues, relations between the British and the Cherokees began to sour in the late '50s. In 1758, a large group of Cherokees deserted General John Forbes, before he attacked Fort Duquesne in western Pennsylvania, and on their way back home got into a battle with some Virginians and lost several men. Attempts by both red and white leaders to calm the situation failed, and isolated fighting soon erupted in Rowan County, North Carolina, leaving thirteen whites dead. Other settlers were picked off elsewhere, and by January 1760 a general attack was launched against the South Carolina frontier, hitting hardest at the Scottish-Irish community of Long Canes.

Although the town itself was warned about the impending attack by traders who had been ambushed several days earlier and also by an Indian girl, the people in a wagon train plodding through the bog at nearby Long Cane Creek weren't so lucky. At ten o'clock on the morning of February 1, 1760, after the residents of Long Canes had fled for the safety of Augusta, Georgia, a large party of mounted Cherokees hit the wagons from all sides. Maneuvering in the sludge was impossible, and when the attack was over close to forty of the caravan's 250 men, women, and children had been killed or captured. Two days later, twenty-three women and children who had left Long Canes under the protection of a single armed man were jumped near Stevens Creek. The militiamen who came upon the "cruelly mangled Bodies" the next day described the scene as a massacre. Wounded children were found days later wandering in the deep woods; at least nine, their scalps cut off and suffering from other tomahawk wounds, were brought into Augusta. Twenty-seven other whites were killed, at about the same time, in another engagement, on Rayburns Creek, as the Cherokees launched a

47

successful series of hit-and-run skirmishes in the north, burning and otherwise destroying property all along the Bush River and trying to pick off targets of opportunity.[1] Back-country families streamed to the protection of forts, while the homes and plantations they abandoned were looted and burned.

The settlement of Ninety Six was hit on March 3, in an attack that began just after sunrise and continued under steady fire until reinforcements chased off the raiding party some thirty-six hours later. Several Cherokees died in that siege and two whites were wounded. A letter from James Francis, one of the defenders, to Governor Henry Lyttleton points up the escalating brutality that was beginning to infest the back country. Francis described his joy at seeing the Indians drop under gunfire, and added, "We have now the Pleasure Sir, to fatten our Dogs with their Carcasses, and to Display their Scalps, neatly ornamented on the Top of our Bastions." On March 12, while the defenders of Rabb's Fort watched in horror, one of their scouts was killed and scalped. The horror suddenly turned to rage, so they left the protection of the stockade, killed and counterscalped two Cherokees, and drove the rest away. The remains of the Indians were fed to dogs. Forty Cherokees were chased into a deserted house near the Catawba River about a week later. The Indians managed to hold out until the place was set on fire, and as they came running through the doorway they were cut down by heavy gunfire. Since the Assembly in Charles Town had only recently raised the bounty on Indian scalps from £25 to £35, the triumphant colonists sent nineteen of them back to the capital. One of the dead Indians, in turn, had "Six green white Scalps" on him.[2]

Peace came in December 1761, and none too soon, since the Cherokees were crippled and without supplies and the settlers were about as badly devastated and exhausted. Vast areas of the back country came out of the war depopulated. About half of the 3,000 colonists who remained in the Piedmont's upper valleys were confined to miserably crowded settlers' forts. Many had been hit with smallpox during 1759 and 1760; in March of 1760, two-thirds of those at Fort Ninety Six had the disease and fourteen died of it. Finally, relief supplies sent to the settlers in the forts were often stolen by the fort commanders, which did nothing to bolster the people's confidence in the system.

Even before the shooting stopped, desertions were taking place in the field. Loyal recruits from North Carolina fought a battle with South Carolina provincials on the Wateree River in the spring of 1761; the provincials had deserted from their regiment. The rangers, who had always been a disciplinary problem, began seriously to resist further service in May and actually began turning on those they were supposed to protect. "These Rangers, instead of annoying the Enemy, fell to plundering of, and living at free quarter on the poor Scatter'd Inhabitants," noted one disgruntled observer. "The forts into which they retir'd were fill'd with Whores and Prostitutes and there maintain'd at the Public Expence." The rangers stole clothing and other articles from stores and liquor from individuals, wasted ammunition and supplies, and otherwise "liv'd in an open, scandalous debauch'd Manner with their Doxies, instead of going on Duty." Many a victim of the Indians began to complain that he suffered more at the hands of his supposed protectors than he did at the hands of the Cherokees.[3]

The back country, then, was a disaster area when the Cherokee War ended. Starvation had narrowly been averted only because of emergency measures taken by the government in Charles Town. But the people came out of their forts nearly broken, spiritually as well as socially and economically. They had been hunted and attacked by brave and tenacious Indians, plundered by many of their own paid leaders and protectors, and forced to witness the cowardice and corruption of others. Their homes and shops were in many cases nothing more than piles of charred rubble. Tracts of wheat, corn, tobacco, oats, and other crops had been trampled or burned out. Their cattle, sheep, and horses had been stolen or slaughtered for either food or revenge. Some in the back country had been wracked by disease; most left the war virtually penniless and without the means to quickly begin again.

The social and economic havoc left in the wake of the war, plus an unresponsive government that gave no sign of trying to cope with the back country's feeble political institutions, laid on top of an already unstable society in which people were still groping for their permanent identities, set the stage for the next nasty problem—the rise of a large and vicious criminal class, often operating in gangs, which was dedicated to preying on the war's survivors and taking from them whatever they had left or had begun to rebuild.

The back-country society that emerged from the Cherokee War was set in three basic strata. At the very top were the large landholders, gentlemen of substance, who, in the absence of cohesive social and political rules and effective law enforcement, became the wise men and arbiters of their communities. They dispensed advice, settled minor disputes, and, in general, ran things on an unofficial level. Small landholders, planters, merchants, and professionals formed the bottom layer of this class. It was the respectable class. Next came the lower people, a varied bunch of "crackers," who lived on the edges of their communities: poor planters, loafers, gamblers, hunters, military deserters, mulattoes, squatters, debtors, runaway slaves, and others whom the respectable folk considered to be either a menace or a nuisance. These people lacked the energy or the ability, or both, either to rise to leadership in the communities or to become full-fledged criminals. At the extreme, says Richard Brown, they were content to "chip at the edges of respectable society by squatting, poaching, or sneak thievery."[4]

The bottom level belonged to the outlaws, and, if those men had nothing else, they had energy, initiative, and, in many cases, remarkable organizational ability. Many not only formed tight-knit groups that were linked to other groups outside their provinces, but also, by the time all hell broke loose in the summer of 1766, had actually set up whole criminal towns throughout the back country.

Since color was not the problem it was later to become, whites, mulattoes, blacks, and assorted others often lived together in the larger criminal enclaves. Most had their own women and children and even took care of elderly relatives. Bastard children born into the towns had no other allegiance, and in the summer of '66 were developing into a second generation of bandits and killers. When there weren't enough women to get the chores done and to satisfy the men's sexual appetites, the outlaws just went out and abducted more to replenish their stock. The new girls usually were taken from the homes of respectable families, possibly because that added a touch of class to the towns, but more likely because it was a way of striking at the hearts of their parents and communities. Once brought back to an outlaw town, a recruit was put through a ritual of being raped, beaten, and then roughly schooled in what was expected of her. There's evidence that some of the belles adapted rather well to their new lives. Thirty-five of them were rescued at one point, but, according to a contemporary quoted by Brown, they had "grown too abandon'd ever to be reclaimed."[5]

A more pervasive problem—and one that was to be repeated many times as the frontier moved westward—was the relationship the outlaws enjoyed with some of the more respectable segments of society. Out of either fear or greed, many merchants and minor officials became the bandits' allies and spies, sometimes on salary, and always in the capacity of either preventing the issuance of warrants, warning of attack, leading pursuers off the track, or acting as fences for stolen goods. Shopkeepers who didn't want to be robbed were obliged to trade ammunition and other supplies for articles brought to them by the outlaws. Teamsters were naturals for helping to move stolen goods to other areas, and there was little reason for saloon owners to betray the men who brought in huge sums of money for their beer and liquor. Five years after the Cherokee War, the outlaws were organized into bands, had established nearly impregnable strongholds with all the comforts of home, had developed contacts and allies throughout society's middle strata, and had declared war on the respectables.

In a petition to the Charles Town Assembly the following year, Charles Woodmason, an Anglican minister, prolific writer, apologist for the Regulators, and something of a back-country character, was to beg for help and describe the situation in the gloomiest and most dramatic terms.

Our large Stocks of Cattel are either stollen and destroy'd—Our Cow Pens are broke up—and All our valuable Horses are carried off—Houses have been burn'd by these Rogues, and the families stripp'd and turn'd naked into the Woods—Stores have been broken open and rifled by them (wherefrom several Traders are absolutely ruin'd) Private Houses have been plunder'd; and the Inhabitants wantonly tortured in the Indian Manner for to be made confess where they secreted their Effects from Plunder. Married Women have been Ravished—Virgins deflowered, and other unheard of Cruelties committed by these barbarous Ruffians—Who, by being let loose among Us (and conniv'd at) by the Acting Magistrates, have hereby reduc'd Numbers of Individuals to Poverty—and for these three Years last past have laid (in a Manner) this Part of the Province under Contribution.

No Trading Persons (or others) or with Money or Goods, No Responsible Persons and Traders dare keep Cash, or any Valuable

Articles by them—Nor can Women stir abroad, but with a Guard, or in Terror—The Chastity of many beauteous Maidens have been threat[e]ned by these Rogues. Merchants Stores are oblig'd for to be kept constantly guarded (which enhances the Price of Goods) And thus We live not as under a British Government (ev'ry Man sitting in Peace and Security under his own Vine, and his own Fig Tree), But as if [we] were in *Hungary* or *Germany*, and in a State of War— continually exposed to the Incursions of *Hussars* and *Pandours;* obliged to be constantly on the Watch, and on our Guard against these Intruders, and having it not in our Power to call what we possess our own, *not even for an Hour;* as being liable Daily and Hourly to be stripp'd of our Property.[6]

John "Ready Money" Scott, a merchant and justice of the peace, was among the first to be hit when the crime wave started to crest—possibly because his nickname made him irresistible. Apparently having decided that his money was, indeed, ready, four bandits came to get it on the night of July 29, 1766. The four, George Burns, Thomas Gray, Jeremiah Fulsom, and Nathaniel Foster, crossed the Savannah River from the Georgia side and went directly to Scott's house. While Foster guarded the yard, Gray knocked on the door, was admitted, and pretended to be friendly. Suddenly Burns and Fulsom pushed into the house, each with a blackened face, and went for Scott and his wife. While Gray feigned fright, screamed "Murder," and ran outside, Burns jumped Mrs. Scott and threw snuff in her eyes. The lady was temporarily blinded and was probably sneezing heavily. Meanwhile, her husband was trying to make for the door, but was intercepted by Fulsom, who smashed him over the head with a lightwood stick (lightwood isn't really light at all), then dragged him back and tied and blindfolded him. Fulsom next got a glowing hot iron and used it to get the magistrate to tell him where he kept all that ready money. With the cash safely in their pockets, both bandits left the house, rendezvoused with the others, rowed back across the Savannah, and divided the take. It was as easy as that.

Throughout the rest of that summer and well into 1767, large gangs of thieves and killers roamed the back country almost at will, stealing anything they could get their hands on and stopping many who got in their way. On November 22, John Huggins, of the northern Waxhaw area, asked four suspicious-looking men what they were doing prowling around his house. Two of them ran away, but one of those who remained hit Huggins with a musket and, in the scuffle that followed, shot him in the neck and left him to die.

On the day after Christmas 1766, provincial Chief Justice Charles Shinner ordered the militia around the Camden area to follow him in pursuit of the notorious Thomas Moon and the Black brothers. Moon and the Blacks were the leaders of a gang that had been terrorizing communities in that part of the back country for more than a year. The militiamen refused to join in the pursuit. Shinner himself abandoned plans to return immediately to Charles Town when he heard that Govey Black, one of the brothers, planned to ambush him with eleven gang members. A battle did actually take place near the Broad River on May 6, after which ten horses, thirteen saddles, and some weapons were recovered, but the bandits escaped and went right back to raiding farms and plantations in the area. The following month, the outlaws ran into an expedition led by the cocky and optimistic Governor William Tryon of North Carolina. Tryon came out of the encounter with fewer horses than he had when he started.

On June 16, the massive gang led by Moon, the Blacks, and the Tyrrels appeared at the plantation of one Robert Buzzard, at Cannon's Creek. Buzzard, an extraordinarily brave man, asked to see their passes. "There's our pass," answered one of the bandits, pulling out a pistol and shooting Buzzard in the chest and shoulder. The outlaws galloped away, apparently in a momentary panic, but they returned a few days later to steal all of Buzzard's possessions, including his horses and furniture.[7] The tempo began to pick up. An old storekeeper named Dennis Hayes was visited by seven or eight members of the gang on the evening of June 28. Dressed as Indians, they broke into his home at about nine o'clock and tied his hands behind his back. Next, they stole £3,000 worth of goods and raped both Mrs. Hayes and the couple's ten-year-old daughter. Charles Kitchen, of Broad River, was next. He was robbed, burned, and had an eye gouged out. A few days later, one of Kitchen's neighbors, Gabriel Brown, was beaten, severely burned, and left for dead after he was robbed. And a week after that a Charles Town resident who happened to be near Godfrey Dreher's mill, at Saxe Gotha, was jumped, badly beaten, and robbed. There was talk among the solid citizens of the back country of taking the law into their own hands and counterattacking, as that summer of 1767 wore desperately on, but they would need more pushing before it happened.

The people of Camden and Fredericksburg Township were next. John Pane's blacksmith shop was broken into on the night of July 11; in addition to making off with several pieces of gear, the thieves led away a locally celebrated stallion. Hugh Brennan got word that they were on their way to his place, so he hid everything of value and was therefore able to greet the dawn with his goods intact. Before that night was over, however, a man named Davis was pounced on six miles away, near his home on the Lynches Creek Road. He was tied and tortured with hot irons until he told his captors where he kept his money. Davis probably didn't talk fast enough, though, because after they took his money they left him tied and in agony to watch while they set fire to his house and rode away. On July 26, five outlaws struck at James Miller's home, at Turkey Creek, and stole cash, deerskins, and all his clothes. Back-country folk were now talking darkly about killing the predators, but still they did not consolidate. They only talked about the fools in Charles Town and about killing the predators.

The day after wiping out Davis, the same five attacked the homestead of Michael Watson, a prominent member of the Clouds Creek community. They carried off everything worth taking and, for good measure, set fire to the house and nearby corn and wheat fields. Then they headed for Watson's father's place. The elder Watson managed to elude them, so the disgruntled bandits took, instead, Conrad Adler's pocket watch and money and even the silver buckles from Mrs. Adler's shoes. Meanwhile, the elder Watson, his sons Michael and William, and two other men decided to go after the outlaws. After a thirty-mile chase, they caught up with them at the home of Robert Ford, who was rumored to be in cahoots with various bandits in the area but not one himself. Two of the gang leaders were captured near Ford's place and immediately led the Watsons and the others to it; the other three outlaws were inside.

"Peace or war?" shouted someone in the house to the five men standing out in the open in front of it.

"Peace," answered William Watson.

The initial gunfire from the house killed three of the five men, including the elder Watson and one of his sons. The other Watson, although subsequently wounded, not only shot back, but also somehow managed to get close enough to the killers to rip open two of them with his knife. The outlaws rode off, helping their wounded. The surviving Watson, of course, added his story to those of the other back-country victims. His story was the one that did it.

There was not much of a formal organization during those first months of August and September. Starting in the heat of August and continuing into early autumn, elements of respectable society simply began to fragment into a number of "Mobbs," which began prowling in search of the outlaws. They abandoned their farms and plantations, shops and mills, and came together in mounted and heavily armed groups. The back-country irregulars didn't have to do much serious hunting to locate their quarry; they had a pretty good idea where most of the outlaw towns were, and they hit them as hard as they could. They shot up the towns all during that August and September, tying suspects to trees and flogging them, putting the torch to houses, reclaiming stolen goods, and recapturing abducted women. Word of the reprisals got back to Charles Town and to the new governor in short order.

Governor Charles Greville Montagu was a fop and a mental lightweight who had been in the colonies for less than two years and who never gave much indication that he really understood them. He had begun his term of office by executing acts of clemency for five bandits who had been condemned to death by the Court of General Sessions the previous March. As soon as he heard about the back-country irregulars, Governor Montagu condemned them. And he did more than that. On October 6 he issued a proclamation ordering those committing "riots and disturbances" to stop immediately. Now Montagu may not have been the most intelligent and perceptive of colonial administrators, but he wasn't a complete fool, either. British political authority in the colonies rested ultimately not in Commons or in the Colonial Office, or even in functionaries like himself, but in the military—in the armed redcoat on garrison duty. The British soldier, with his musket and bayonet, was the main rock of stability in a sea already beginning to swell with political and economic restiveness. But the British army had only so many men with muskets and bayonets. It did not take a genius, then, to conclude that every organized group of armed Americans to some extent reduced the relative strength of the British army. Allow a hundred Americans to roam the countryside today, and it could well be a thousand tomorrow, and then what? What if they actually decided to challenge the army? That rather ugly possibility—that the Regulators might one day turn their attention from rogues to redcoats—was undoubtedly the reason behind Governor Montagu's proclamation. The Regulators ignored the edict, but the outlaws didn't; they were so encouraged by it that they began striking back. The outlaws started setting fire to the homes of known Regulators.

And it was then, in early October 1767, that the now enraged back countrymen reacted by formally establishing their Regulation. They "chose a thousand Men, to execute the Laws against all Villains and Harbourers of Villains," and "assum'd the Title of Regulators."[8]

Since they were all well aware of the illegality of their organization, particularly in view of Montagu's proclamation, the Regulators took oaths and signed secret papers swearing to support one another under all circumstances. Regulator groups sprang up simultaneously in the Peedee district, Dutch Fork, the Congarees, Camden, Ninety Six, and elsewhere, as fast as men could ride with the word. They were led by the most respected of the respectables: Gideon Gibson, the fiery planter from Marrs Bluff; Moses Kirkland, the owner of two mills and a ferry; James Mayson, the magistrate, militia major, and determined crime fighter from Ninety Six; Robert Cunningham, another militia officer, from Sandy River; Thomas Woodward, Barnaby Pope, Edward McGraw, Benjamin Hart, William Wofford, John "Ready Money" Scott (whose presence is understandable), and others.

The Regulators had been going on continual search-and-destroy operations in the swamps and pinewoods for about a month when, on November 5, the increasingly exasperated Governor Montagu sent word to the Assembly that he wanted legislation passed that would suppress them once and for all. The assemblymen were, of course, South Carolinians. They therefore told the Governor they would enact nothing until they had more information about what was going on in the back country. They didn't have long to wait.

Hart, Scott, Kirkland, and Woodward rode into Charles Town on November 7 and presented the Assembly with a list of long-standing grievances, which had been drawn up by their friend and sympathizer Charles Woodmason, the Anglican itinerant and back-country gadfly. The beginning of the document, which Woodmason claimed had been signed by 4,000 Regulators and other back countrymen, has already been quoted in part. The heart of the petition asked, often in moving language, for the establishment of a circuit or country court system, solid laws for punishing criminals and idlers, and an expanded parish system to ensure more equitable representation in the Assembly. It also mentioned the construction of court and jail houses and other long-needed means of relief. Woodmason, who had gotten his poetry into the *Gentleman's Magazine* of London, was probably the most formidable penman in South Carolina at the time. He used his pen deftly on that petition.

We are *Free-Men*—British Subjects—Not Born *Slaves*—We contribute our Proportion in all Public Taxations, and discharge our Duty to the Public, equally with our Fellow Provincials Ye[t] We do not participate with them in the Rights and Benefits which they Enjoy, tho' equally Entituled to them.

Property is of no Value, except it be secure: How Ours is secured, appears from the foremention'd Circumstances, and from our now being obliged to defend our Families, by *our own Strength: As Legal Methods* are beyond our Reach—or not as yet *extended* to Us.

We may be deem'd too bold in saying *"That the present Constitution of this Province is very defective, and becomes a Burden, rather than being beneficial to the Back-Inhabitants"*—For Instance—To have but *One* Place of Judicature in this Large and Growing Colony—and that seated *not Central*, but *In a Nook* by the SeaSide—The Back Inhabitants to travel Two, three hundred Miles to carry down Criminals.[9]

The words were moving. The observations were incisive. The message was poignant. But Charles Woodmason wasn't one to let a good thing alone. The twelfth through the fourteenth requests concentrated on the problems of the Anglican church in the back country, matters that were of no concern to the Regulators and probably bored the assemblymen. Worse, Woodmason jabbed at the assemblymen and insulted the lawyers among them. In the sixteenth request, for example, he called for the lowering of ministerial and legal fees.

That a proper Table of Fees be fram'd for all Ministers Ecclesiastical and Civil, to govern themselves by; And that the Length and enormous Expence of Law Suits be Moderated. *This Province being harder rode at present by Lawyers, than Spain or Italy by Priests* [my italics].[10]

And that wasn't all. In May 1766, the South Carolina Assembly had shown its gratitude to William Pitt for his opposition to the Stamp Act by appropriating £1,000 with which to erect a statue of the British statesman in Charles Town. Woodmason, who had supported the Stamp Act and who had fallen into disfavor with the Assembly because of it, reserved mention of the statue for his parting shot.

Lastly We earnestly Pray That the Legislature would import a Quantity of Bibles, Common Prayers, and Devotional Tracts, to be distributed by the Ministers among the Poor, which will be of far greater Utility to the Province, than erecting the Statue of Mr. Pitt.[11]

Although Woodmason didn't sign the petition, there's no doubt that the members of the Assembly recognized the hand behind it. Accordingly, they tabled it the day they got it, which probably confused the four Regulators who had delivered it. The subtleties of their friend's barbs no doubt went over their heads. Someone seems to have explained the situation to them, however, because three days later the embarrassed back countrymen told the Assembly that the insulting sections of the petition had been put in accidentally. The Assembly was apparently more than willing to buy that story, because the same day—November 11, 1767—it began drawing up a circuit-court act, which was to be signed by the Governor the following April and forwarded to London for approval. The Circuit Court Act of 1768, which laid the basis for a better one the following year, was destined to become one of the most important pieces of legislation in the early history of South Carolina.

Meanwhile, the Assembly decided to take its own steps to relieve the situation in the back country. Governor Montagu's November 5 message to the Assembly ordering it to suppress the Regulators had also stipulated that the body should act on the "unhappy situation of the Settlers." That was a command the Assembly was in the mood to honor, so two weeks later it created two ranger companies, with a total of fifty-four men, who were authorized to hunt down the outlaws. Kirkland and another Regulator were made captains and leaders of the units, and Thomas Woodward was appointed a lieutenant. That meant that the Regulators were legitimatized in spirit, if not in fact, by the government. That development, too, got around. When the ranger units passed through parts of North Carolina tracking gang members from their own province, people along the way simply called them Regulators.

During the next three months, or for as long as their mandate lasted, the Regulator-rangers pursued their quarry throughout North Carolina and as far as Augusta and Loudoun counties in Virginia. The South Carolinians were good trackers and determined hunters, and there was no shaking them. One outlaw band was trapped near what is now Mount Airy, North Carolina, and sixteen of its members, including one of the Black brothers, were hanged where they were caught. The pursuers recaptured stolen horses and slaves in Virginia and made it back to South Carolina without having had one of their own killed.

Dozens of outlaws were either shot up or strung up, but many others were brought into Charles Town for trial in the Court of General Sessions. Edward Wells was hanged for robbing Dennis Hayes; George Burns and Thomas Gray were also hanged, for robbing and torturing John "Ready Money" Scott; others were severely whipped or burned on the hand for their parts in the crime wave. There was no question but that by March 1768 the Regulator-ranger operation was an unqualified success—so much so, in fact, that Governor Tryon of North Carolina was to complain the following October that the horse thieves chased out of South Carolina were roosting in his own province.

But, with organized crime effectively smashed, the Regulators began showing their dark side—a side that was to be repeated scores of times during the following century and a half. They didn't know when to stop. Those respectable people, still worked up and swollen with pride over their accomplishments, began looking around for more action. The organization, after all, was in being; it would have been a shame to waste it. The Regulators therefore decided to begin correcting the lower people's faulty morality and work ethic.

Careless hunters who skinned animals but didn't bother to bury the carcasses, gamblers, anyone who was foulmouthed, vagrants, and idlers were put on the punishment list. Vagrants and idlers were especially irritating because the back country suffered from a chronic labor shortage. Slaves were expensive. It hurt a man to see orchards go unpicked, wheat and corn unharvested, cows unmilked, fences and roofs unrepaired, and paths uncleared while all sorts of lazy scoundrels took handouts from the church and pilfered whatever was within easy reach. Virginia, North Carolina, Georgia, and other provinces had vagrancy laws to cope with the problem. The Virginia and North Carolina statutes provided that vagrants could be whipped as they passed from one district to another until they reached their homes. If they were unable to get work once they got home, a county court could indenture them for as long as a year, and if no one would take a chance on hiring them, because of their reputations, thirty-nine lashes were administered before they were turned loose. The South Carolina legislature hadn't had the common sense to write such a fine law, so it was clearly up to the Regulators to correct the oversight. This they did, in June 1768, by adopting a code calling for vagrants to be rounded up and forced to work so many acres in so much time, six days a week. The alternative was flogging. The plan was enacted by a "Congress" of Regulators that met at the Congarees and drew enthusiastic landholders from as far as the Peedee River and probably Ninety Six, all of whom hurried back home to implement the scheme as soon as possible.

Then the Regulators moved into domestic relations and vice control. Shady ladies were dunked, whipped, and "expos'd" (literally as well as figuratively) in public. Mrs. Bennet Dozier complained to Samuel Boykin, a young planter and dedicated Regulator, that her husband was neglecting her and their children. She is quoted as begging Boykin to regulate her spouse. This he and two friends did. They went to the Dozier home, dragged Bennet Dozier outside, tied him to a tree, and laid on thirty-nine lashes. Typically, the account of the incident says that Mr. Dozier had a complete change of character after his whipping, began working his head off, and bore "no malice against Boykin" for the punishment.[12]

That theme, too, runs through the chronicles of vigilantism. Almost everyone who was stripped, flogged, tarred and feathered, held under water, beaten up, or given other kinds of corporal punishment seems not only to have repented immediately, but also to have practically gushed gratitude to his or her regulators for the trouble they had taken. It's hard to find an account in which someone who had been punished went right back to being a sluggard or a cheat and condemned those who had dragged him out of his house and smacked him around. To read these accounts, almost always written by sympathizers on the scene, you'd think that being regulated was almost a privilege—the Protestant ethic in its full, thorn-adorned flower.

Having killed or run off the outlaws, gotten bums off their backsides and into the fields, intimidated harlots and gamblers, and established healthier and more devoted families in their communities, the Regulators next came up with a perfectly natural question: if they could do all that, why did they need the government in Charles Town? Governor Montagu's nightmare was coming true.

As it became increasingly clear to the back-country notables that their 'territory could best be regulated by themselves, they began erecting barriers to keep the ignorant and misguided authorities from the low country out of their domain. The lone exception was the Crown-appointed provost marshal, who was permitted to serve writs of debt, but only writs of debt. In June 1768, John Wood, one of the provost marshal's deputies, was jumped because he was carrying other kinds of writs into the back country, including one for the arrest of Kirkland, McGraw, and another Regulator leader, named Hunter. Five men armed with muskets, pistols, and cutlasses tied Wood to his horse, struck and insulted him, and held him prisoner for five days in Barnaby Pope's house. They were preparing to try him when he managed to escape. Another process server was turned back, at about the same time, after a battle between Regulators and militiamen at Marrs Bluff that left one militiaman seriously wounded and several others carrying lash marks. Even Roger Pinckney, the Provost Marshal, was thrown out of Marrs Bluff when it became apparent to his militia guard that they had to choose between protecting him and siding with the Regulators. Their sympathies clearly lay with the back countrymen. Meanwhile, lawsuits from back-country residents who had been punished by the Regulators were pouring into Charles Town. The Regulators, it seemed, were turning into the outlaws, and it was becoming increasingly clear to Charles Town that something was going to have to be done about it.

Lieutenant Governor William Bull, a native South Carolinian who had taken temporary charge of the government while Montagu was in Philadelphia, understood the Regulators as well as he understood the need for Charles Town's sovereignty. He had sympathized with the back countrymen during the crime wave and had always been aware that many of their grievances were justified. Yet the law was the law. Accordingly, Bull issued two proclamations during the first week of August 1768: the first called for the suppression of the Regulators; the second promised them pardon for their crimes, provided they committed no more. The able and intelligent administrator was walking a tightrope. He knew that the now massive Regulator organization could be put down only by raising a large force of armed men in the low country. First, and most obviously, that would be divisive where the province as a whole was concerned. Second, Bull and many other low countrymen were haunted by the specter of a slave uprising, so sending all those armed white men off their plantations and into the interior would be a risky business. Bull would not take that chance. Better to use the carrot and the stick.

As it happened, the summer and fall of 1768 were relatively quiet in the back country, as the Regulators started turning their attention to provincial politics. Having secured their part of the province, and undoubtedly understanding that the low countrymen and even some of their neighbors were getting edgy, they decided to try to increase their representation in the Assembly. Charles Town newspapers carried stories that summer saying that the Regulators were holding election meetings throughout the back country and that thousands of them were planning to march on the capital. The march never materialized, but, by storming one low-country parish and turning out heavily elsewhere, they managed to get six of their candidates elected and sent to Charles Town. Low-country newspaper editors and other commentators noted, apparently with raised brows, that the Regulator constituents behaved admirably at the polls, acted with "decency and propriety," and patiently explained to anyone who would listen that they were only trying to exercise their rights and undo years of abuse and indifference. On November 16, 1768, the back-country delegation took its place beside its low-country counterpart for the Assembly's monumental opening session. Four days later, the Commons House of the Assembly of South Carolina was dissolved.

The cause of this minor catastrophe came not out of South Carolina, but from still another of the increasingly stubborn tests of will between London and Boston. Charles Townshend, the witty but often loose-tongued gentleman who had succeeded

George Grenville as chancellor of the exchequer in 1766, was determined to continue Grenville's policy of raising as much money as possible from the colonies. In the absence of Pitt, the ailing Prime Minister, Townshend had taken office with virtually a free hand to propose to Parliament whatever tax legislation he saw fit. Accordingly, he had proposed import duties on paint, lead, glass, paper, and tea, and, to make sure that the taxes were collected, he had also proposed the establishment of a Massachusetts Board of Customs Commissioners, who would earn their salaries from the duties they managed to collect; they would collect the revenue and be paid a percentage of the total by England, thus neatly laundering their share. Parliament had passed the Townshend Acts in 1767. The Massachusetts Assembly had reacted, in February 1768, by sending a letter to the other colonial assemblies urging them to oppose all British taxes. The Secretary of State for Colonial Affairs, Lord Hillsborough, had then angrily retaliated by ordering his colonial governors to prevent the assemblies in their provinces from supporting the Massachusetts plan. When word of that got out, one assembly after another fell into line behind the one in Boston. Montagu warned the South Carolinians not to support the Massachusetts proposal, so, naturally, they did support it, as one of the first acts of their new session. He then told the Assemblymen to go home and, in so doing, effectively ended the promising experiment of bringing the Regulators into the mainstream of South Carolina politics.

Irrespective of their fine conduct at the polls and behind the desks at the Charles Town Assembly, the Regulators effectively exercised a near-complete tyranny over the back country during the winter of 1768–69. Punishment of immoral lower people began to degenerate into the settling of old grudges and feuds with even respectable men, including magistrates and other officials. One by one, many of the established planters and other early settlers were singled out for warnings and then for visits by mounted Regulators, in many cases because of disputes dating back many years. But now the Regulators weren't picking on defenseless squatters, vagrants, whores, gamblers, and wife beaters; they were taking on men of their own social rank, connections, and resources. And those men, in turn, straddled a now-angry middle class, which had applauded the Regulation up to a year before but which, by the beginning of 1769, had had enough of arbitrary floggings and beatings and what amounted to a reign of terror. The system was ready to right itself; it was about to be moderated.

Retribution at the hands of the Regulators had increased all during that winter. Early in the new year, one John Harvey was punished on Nobles Creek while neutral witnesses looked on. Fifty to sixty Regulators took Harvey to a secluded place, stripped him to his undershirt, and tied him to a sapling with a wagon chain. Two hours later they began whipping him—ten blows each with rods and switches—until he had about 500 bleeding slashes across his back. During the flogging, one of the Regulators beat a drum and another played a fiddle, giving the scene a deliberately festive air. A bystander was asked if he wanted to help whip Harvey. He answered by asking why Harvey was being so brutally punished. "Because he was roguish and troublesome." Could the Regulators prove that? The Regulator answered by saying that he couldn't take the trouble to prove it. Another Regulator was later overheard to explain that Harvey, who was by then drenched in his own blood, had been found to have a horse that didn't belong to him.[13]

At about the same time, John Musgrove, a prosperous planter in the Saluda River area, received his second visit from the Regulators as part of a vendetta that included his brother, Edward. Both Musgroves were educated Englishmen who had been early and successful back-country settlers. Nonetheless, Edward, who was a militia officer, deputy surveyor, and justice of the peace, was brought before a grand jury; the complaint, filed by Moses Kirkland, accused him of being "a very bad person" and of encouraging and conniving with thieves and robbers. John had been physically assaulted by Regulators once, and that second time was forced to run from his home and hide. Jonathan Gilbert, a justice of the peace and a friend of the Musgroves, rode to Charles Town and related the episode to Montagu, Bull, and other members of the Council. Besides telling them about the Musgroves' ordeal, Gilbert handed over affidavits from the Saluda and Ninety Six areas attesting to the harshness of the Regulators. He then went on to name eleven of them, all leaders, who were chiefly responsible for the misery in the district. All those named were immediately deprived of their commissions as justices of the peace or militia officers. That was fine as far as it went, but, as the Musgroves, Gilbert, and others knew, it meant relatively little. The Regulators needed to be leaned on, and leaned on hard. And, since the low countrymen weren't going to use force, it clearly had to be applied by the back countrymen themselves. They would have to hire muscle.

Joseph Coffell, an "illiterate, stupid, noisy blockhead" from around Orangeburg, was perfect. He responded to the call by immediately making himself a "colonel" and rounding up a collection of ne'er-do-well friends who welcomed any chance to get back at the Regulators. Coffell's band of thugs and other miscellaneous rabble gave the Moderators instant credibility. A judge in Charles Town handed John Musgrove a bench warrant for the arrest of several Regulator leaders, including one Rudolph Buzzard. Musgrove handed it to "Colonel" Coffell. Coffell hired himself about a hundred troops and in a few days, warrant in hand, captured Buzzard. When some Regulators tried to rescue their cohort, five of them also were captured and the rest backed off. Coffell and his mercenaries saw the warrant as symbolizing official sanction, and they therefore acted with unconcealed zeal.

The government was at that moment beginning to wonder which of the two factions—Regulators or Moderators—was worse. Richard Richardson, of Saint Mark Parish, and William Thompson, of Orangeburg, both of whom were dedicated colonials, respected veterans of the Cherokee War, and destined to become celebrated patriots in the coming War of Independence, told the Council on March 16, and again six days later, that "Colonel" Coffell was having women and children thrown in jail and that his men were ransacking practically every house they came upon. Other reports were getting into the newspapers, most accusing the Moderators of stealing and arresting without warrants. Exasperated, Montagu and his Council decided, on March 22, to withdraw support from the Moderators, following which word was sent to the back country explaining that the group was operating illegally.

The Regulators, by that time smarting from Moderator successes, found no cause for relief. They knew that Montagu's latest proclamation would mean as little to the Moderators as it would have had it been directed at them. They therefore decided that the only way to settle the matter was to have one big shootout. Winner take all.

And so it was that on Saturday, March 25, 1769, an estimated

700 Regulators from the Wateree, Broad, and Saluda areas stood on John Musgrove's plantation facing about an equal number of Moderators, all of them armed to the teeth. After a few preliminary shots were exchanged, both groups tensed for what they assumed was going to be a withering fusillade in which many would be killed or wounded defending the cause of either Regulation or Moderation. It promised to be one of the epic battles of American history. It promised to be, but it wasn't. It didn't happen.

Just as everyone was about to let go, three riders were seen approaching. As they got closer, the leaders of both factions saw that they were Colonels Richardson and Thompson and one Daniel McGirt, another notable. The three rode to a point between the opposing muskets and therefore immediately requested that fire be withheld. They then explained that they were carrying orders from Charles Town commanding the Moderators to disperse. "Colonel" Coffell probably snickered. At any rate, no one dispersed, so Montagu's emissaries began talking. They talked in the loftiest terms about why bloodshed had to be averted and why everyone therefore had to clear the area. They cajoled and probably even pleaded, and eventually they got the leaders of both sides to come to agreement, right there in John Musgrove's field.

The Regulators agreed to drop their name, which aroused angry passions throughout the back country. They also agreed to permit the regular system of justice, which was soon to be reformed, to operate without interference. For their part, the Moderators (with Musgrove, not Coffell, in command) decided to obey the dispersal order. Although a few scattered Regulator meetings and floggings occurred later, the truce of March 25, 1769, marked the effective end of America's first real vigilantes.

Several of the leading Regulators wound up in the Charles Town Assembly, where they and their low-country peers enacted the Circuit Court Act of 1769, which revamped the judicial system and dealt specifically with several of the original Regulator grievances. Seven judicial districts were established, four to serve the back country exclusively. Sheriffs were provided for each district and replaced the provost marshal, who had never gotten around much, anyway. The sheriffs were to be appointed for two-year terms and selected from lists made by the court of common pleas in each district. Jurors were to be selected from the tax rolls, and special lists were to be kept of those living within five miles of the courthouses, to ease travel problems. Fixed tables of judicial fees were to be set up, on which claimants could see the maximum amount of money they would have to spend on court fees. In essence, all this gave the back country control over its own criminal justice system and at the same time helped to bring it into the mainstream of South Carolina politics.

The back country had, indeed, been regulated. Appropriately, in 1776 South Carolina would choose as its flag one with a wide-eyed rattlesnake, the coiled and vigilant serpent that bites only when attacked . . . or trod upon.

4

Texas: "You've stolen my life and you'll wade through blood for it"

ON THE morning of July 14, 1841, Charles W. Jackson appeared at the Harrison County, Texas, courthouse to go on trial for the murder of one Joseph Goodbread the year before. It was an open-and-shut case. Jackson had shot Goodbread with a rifle at almost point-blank range in the center of Shelbyville, a town in neighboring Shelby County. He had shot Goodbread right in the stomach while the man was talking to a friend, and at the sound of the report others had come running down the dusty street to see what had happened. Charles Jackson had stood there looking down at Goodbread to make sure he was dead as a crowd gathered around. An open-and-shut case, to be sure.

Yet as he headed for Judge John M. Hansford's desk in the Harrison County Courthouse that hot morning in 1841 Jackson showed no fear at all. In fact, he smiled arrogantly and seemed completely confident that he was going to leave the building a free man. Judge Hansford, who sat up front and therefore had an unobstructed view of the courtroom, began to understand the reason for Jackson's optimism as the defendant got closer. Charles W. Jackson wasn't really walking toward Judge Hansford; he was stalking toward him, with a rifle in his hand and the sheriff at his side. And behind them, one a murderer and the other a lawman, came 150 other armed men. They filed slowly into the room until they stood all around its walls, in the back corners, and even overflowed into the aisle and back rows. Some held their rifles with the butts resting on the floor, others cradled them in their arms, and still others held them butt-in-the-armpit with their fingers on the triggers. The men who had followed Charles W. Jackson into that courtroom were Regulators, and he was their leader.

John Hansford was a typical frontier judge. He therefore believed that the law could be mitigated under special circumstances. He embraced that philosophy because, like most other judges, he didn't want to get killed. He had been educated in medicine somewhere back east, had served his military hitch on a warship, and had gotten discharged after getting into some kind of trouble. So he had decided to migrate to Texas and take up law. Since his arrival, John Hansford had gotten involved with some of the men who peddled counterfeit land grants, had been awarded a judgeship in the district court, and indulged his fondness for whiskey at every opportunity (he had once vomited on the docket). Now he watched, trying to conceal his nervousness, as Charles W. Jackson bore down on him and about 300 spectators, at least half of them allied with Jackson and carrying guns, looked on.

Hansford forced himself to make a show of asking the sheriff why Jackson was being allowed to carry a rifle into court and then told the lawman that he was going to be heavily fined for letting him do so. But before the sheriff could answer Charles W. Jackson walked up to Judge Hansford's desk and laid his rifle across it. He then pushed a chair up to the desk, took off his jacket and shoes, and leaped onto the chair. From that position, Jackson looked defiantly down at Hansford and demanded that the trial begin. That did it. The Judge mumbled something, rearranged his papers, and adjourned the court until nine the next morning. As soon as John Hansford was able to get out of the building, he hurried to a friend's house, since there was no saloon in town at that time.

Charles W. Jackson had come from Kentucky. Even before he

gunned down Joseph Goodbread, he had been credited with killing one merchant and wounding another in Alexandria, Louisiana, narrowly escaping arrest several times, and having a large bounty on his head. He had a quick temper, enjoyed brawling and other kinds of violence, and swaggered in a way that tended to encourage people to start trouble with him. But there's no understanding the East Texas Regulator-Moderator War of 1840–1844 without keeping one small but significant fact in mind: Jackson was one of the good guys.

The bad guys were really mean. In 1840 they infested Shelby and Harrison counties, as well as other areas stretching north to the Oklahoma Indian territory and due south to the Gulf of Mexico. Shelby County was the worst pocket, since it fronted the Sabine River, which formed the boundary between the Lone Star republic and Louisiana. Until 1819, the river had been the military boundary between Texas and the territory claimed by Spain on the Louisiana side, and had therefore been a convenient frontier that allowed bandits to hit communities on either side and then flee to the other. The breaking up of the Murrell conspiracy had made matters worse. That scheme had called for what was then the entire southwestern part of the United States to be taken over by hoodlums, outlaws, and freed slaves, in effect creating a gigantic criminal nation. The mastermind of that plan actually had the men and guns with which to try the take-over, but was arrested and sent to prison in 1834, before the invasion could be launched. Many of Murrell's men had then fled to the Texas border region, after being thrown out of their own communities by their outraged neighbors.

Once in East Texas, these confidence men, bandits, petty thieves, killers, rustlers, land speculators, gamblers, extortionists, counterfeiters, and others formed an organization loosely patterned after Murrell's model. They took loyalty oaths, swore to help one another at every opportunity, developed recognition signs, and in effect declared war on the respectable people. The situation was especially insidious because, in many instances, the criminals seemed to be the most respectable people around. Cattlemen, planters, bankers, merchants, judges, lawmen, high-ranking militiamen, and even clergymen considered bilking the public to be their legitimate privilege. The less sophisticated rabble just took what they wanted: strongboxes, hogs, guns, plows, clothing, wagons, horses, fruit—anything.

Given those circumstances, the honest people were confronted with at least three problems that could not be solved simply by shooting at those who were trying to rob them. First, the honest man couldn't always tell who his enemies were, since many of them seemed to be the staunchest citizens in the community. Not only might an apparently friendly neighbor be a thief, but he also might relay dangerous remarks to someone higher up in the crime chain, thereby marking the bigmouth for an ambush. Second, justice was a farce. In the unlikely event that a conscientious sheriff brought in a criminal to appear before an honest judge (and the odds against that combination were enormous), juries could be bribed, intimidated, or packed, witnesses could be kidnaped, beaten, or murdered, and even the courthouse could be vandalized or destroyed. Whole towns were known to have backed down in the face of outlaw bands threatening to take them apart. Finally, the honest man knew that, where the outlaws were concerned, no holds were barred. Resistance didn't necessarily mean that he was going to be attacked directly. He was just as likely to have his home burned down, his herd run off and crops fired, or a member of his family bushwhacked or abducted. "Human life simply was not as valuable on the frontier as property," notes one Texas historian.[1] Like today, however, it was one's own property that was the most valuable.

Land graft was the biggest racket in Shelby County, the acknowledged heartland of the East Texas criminal class. Although it had started as early as 1829, it didn't achieve major proportions until 1838, when the newly established Texas Land Office began granting so-called headrights to people who had been in the area since the 1836 rebellion against Mexico. The land grants, each good for a tract of property, were negotiable; they could be sold or transferred. They were therefore counterfeited, in such quantities that one observer, Dr. Levi Ashcroft, who had come to the Shelby County area from North Carolina, wrote that the certificates "were frequently pawned in grog shops for a dozen drinks."[2] Which brings us back to Charles W. Jackson.

Jackson had settled in Shelbyville in the late 1830s, after barely winning a fight with a character named "Maulheel" Johnson and several of his cronies and then deciding that he would be better off leaving Louisiana for the wider spaces of Texas. One of the first things the mercurial Kentuckian did was run for the Texas Congress, and, probably because he was a newcomer, he got trounced. Instead of blaming his defeat on the fact that the older settlers hadn't known him well enough to vote for him, Jackson decided that he had been sabotaged by the gang of land-grant swindlers, which was thought to be led by one Sam Todd. The electoral defeat soured Jackson and convinced him that he had a score to settle with Todd and his mob. It's very likely that Charles Jackson would have joined Todd's gang had he been invited to do so, but his newness to the area and his attempt to get elected to public office precluded that possibility, so, instead, he became righteously indignant. When a new batch of bogus land titles started circulating, right after his defeat at the polls, he sat down and furiously began to write letters to politicians and government officials in Houston, Austin, and, for some reason, New Orleans, condemning the Todd organization and the county officers he thought were involved with it. As he passed through some woods one day soon afterward, somebody quite naturally took a shot at him.

Then a letter came. It was brief and to the point: if he didn't stop meddling in other people's business, he was going to get killed. The letter was signed by Joseph Goodbread, who was related to Sam Todd and was therefore one of the area's influentials. Jackson went into a rage. Waving the paper over his head, he asked a neighbor named Daggett what he should do about it. Daggett, who was an understandably cautious fellow, told Jackson to judge for himself. But Mrs. Jackson, a remarkably cynical woman, whose soul seems to have been gnarled by her husband, frontier life, or both, sighed and answered, "You've had to kill rascals all of your life and you might as well kill a few more before they'll let you alone."[3] Charles W. Jackson swore to Daggett and his wife that he was going to kill Goodbread.

Even then, Jackson might have cooled if it hadn't been for the interference of Alfred George, a man who was about to become sheriff, and who had an old score to settle with Goodbread. George had a short time before traded a slave to Goodbread in exchange for ten headright certificates, each having a face value of 5,605 acres. The black man was completely functional, but the certificates weren't, so Alfred George got very angry. He got so angry, in fact, that he stole the slave from Goodbread and hid him. Goodbread reacted by telling people in the community that George was a thief. Since George was a candidate for sheriff and, furthermore, was the one who had been cheated in the first place, he became still angrier. Knowing that there was bad blood between Goodbread and Jackson, George decided to get Goodbread once and for all by telling Jackson that Goodbread was going around telling people that he was going to shoot Jackson like a dog the next time he saw him. To Jackson, who had already had a threatening letter from Goodbread, it was perfectly logical. And the only thing to do about it, he reasoned, was to get Goodbread before Goodbread got him. That's why Charles Jackson had come into the center of Shelbyville, rifle in hand, the year before.

Goodbread had been sitting on a hitching rail chatting with a friend when Jackson walked up, eyes sparkling. He had spread his legs and swung the rifle down from his shoulder with his right hand while the left went into his pocket and pulled out the piece of paper.

"Goodbread," he had said, "here's your letter. I'm going to answer it."

Joseph Goodbread had sat very still. At first he had seemed to be trying to understand what was happening. Then he had apparently remembered what he had written. "Jackson," he had answered mildly, "I'm unarmed."

"So much the better. Get up on your feet."

"Charley, I was mad when I wrote that letter. I was too hasty."

"Stand up."

"I didn't mean to do any more than scare you a little, Charley," Joseph Goodbread had said. They had been his last words.

"Stand up." The muzzle of Jackson's rifle had pointed at Goodbread's stomach, and as he had pushed himself off the rail it had gone off.[4]

Alfred George, who had in the meantime been elected sheriff, in spite of his reputation (or perhaps because of it), stuck by his dupe. He took the Kentuckian to a justice of the peace, and, after posting a $200 bond and promising to appear at the next regular court session, Jackson was released. But he was indicted a short time later and, probably to his surprise, noticed that rather energetic preparations were being made for his trial. He therefore complained to his benefactor, the sheriff of Shelby County, that something was going to have to be done, and done quickly. George had promised to help Jackson even before Goodbread had been gunned down, and he now kept his word. He told the county officials that the Shelbyville jail wasn't secure enough to hold Jackson and asked for permission to move the prisoner to Harrison County. The officials obliged, handed their sheriff an order for a change of venue, and allowed him to ride out of town with Jackson. As soon as the pair was well away from the courthouse George turned Jackson loose. The argument about the jail's not being secure enough to hold Jackson hadn't really been farfetched, because at that time—the summer of 1840—Charles W. Jackson was already the leader of a band of Regulators.

His motives for setting up the Regulators were probably mixed. Obviously, it would be very hard to punish him for past crimes if he commanded a group of armed men—in effect, a private army. But it's also likely that Jackson had by that time become fed up with all the crime in the district, particularly since he had never been allowed to muscle in on it. A man who thought enough of his potential as a civic leader to run for the Texas Congress would certainly have decided that he was the perfect candidate to organize a regulator group and smash the criminals. And he had excellent credentials for the job: he was energetic and unscrupulous, had definite leadership qualities, and liked to shoot people. With those qualities going for him, plus the backing of armed and upright citizens, he might yet have gone to Congress. Or so he undoubtedly figured.

By the winter of 1839–40, when regulation came to Shelby County, it was an American tradition. It had been used in Jackson's home state of Kentucky as early as the 1790s and again in 1816–1817 and 1820–1822. Elsewhere in the South, regulation had erupted in the 1830s twice in Georgia, three times in Arkansas, twice in Virginia, and six times in Alabama. It had come to Tennessee as early as 1798, again in 1818, and still again in the 1830s. Regulators in Madison and Hinds counties, Mississippi, had strung up twenty-one alleged outlaws in 1835. But the South had no monopoly on amateur executions. Regulators had ridden over much of Illinois as early as 1816–1817, again in the early '20s, and once more in 1831. Even as Jackson's organization was getting started, the people in the northern Illinois counties of De Kalb, Lee, McHenry, Ogle, Boone, and Winnebago, reeling under the pressure of rapacious gangs of bandits, were gearing up to start their own celebrated, and by all odds thoroughly justified, regulation.[5] Regulation had come to Indiana in 1818 and 1819 and throughout the next two decades. It had struck in Iowa in the 1830s, in Ohio between 1825 and 1833 and once more during 1837–1839, and in Saint Louis as early as 1815. By 1839–1840, then, frontier regulation was as American as shooting Indians, and was thought to be every bit as necessary.

When the Regulators began riding in Shelby County, their purpose was to break the hold of the criminals there. If Charles W. Jackson's motives were less than pure, he at least had been joined by some of the most reputable citizens in the district—by good men who had filtered in from Kentucky, Tennessee, Arkansas, and Louisiana and had grown up thoroughly accustomed to regulation. As residents of East Texas went, most of those men were late arrivals and were therefore known to the older families as "newcomers." When they started, their purpose was reasonably honorable, but they were soon to find that, since the criminals they faced were usually members of the older families, their war quickly turned into one between newcomers and old-timers. It would then degenerate into a blood feud and, as the Regulators' popular consensus drained away, into senseless slaughter. But in the beginning the Regulators' targets were outlaws, and, as in other parts of the country, horse thieves were high on their list.

On the night of January 31, 1840, three men sneaked onto the ranch of Peter Stockman, one of the newcomers. Under cover of a driving rain that turned to ice as it fell, they carefully rounded up thirty-two of Stockman's best horses, linked up with other thieves once they had gotten off the rancher's property, and together herded the animals north, across the Red River and into Arkansas. When Stockman went out the next morning and saw that his best horses had been stolen, he sent two men after them. Fifteen of the animals were located and brought back, but there's no evidence that the pursuers tangled with the thieves. Yet when other newcomers heard about the incident, and heard Charles Jackson telling them that the outlaws around there needed regulating, they knew who he was talking about. Three old-time families were known to be the leaders of the Shelby County criminals in 1840. Their names were McFaddin, Strickland, and Humphreys.

The McFaddins and the Stricklands lived near each other in the northern part of the county. Sam McFaddin was the patriarch of the clan and had three sons: William "Buckskin Bill," Bailey, and Rufus. The Strickland family revolved around four very tough young men: Amos, Henry, Dave, and "Tiger Jim."

Squire Humphreys and Wade Hampton West, who was married to Squire's sister, Susan, represented the third major crime family. They and a few others seem to have had a hand in practically every type of crime in the county, from relatively sophisticated land swindles to plain hog stealing. And they tended to stick together. Murrell, after all, had left an all-for-one, one-for-all legacy. But, more fundamentally, those people had been transplanted from the backwashes of the Ozarks, the Appalachians, and other regions where kinship was an inviolable code—usually the only code that held the segments of a community together and kept large numbers of people from murdering each other. The fear of reprisal by kinfolk was taken seriously where the McFaddins, Stricklands, and others came from, and it was therefore taken seriously in Shelby County, too. Jackson and his Regulators nevertheless decided to move on the three families.

Soon after Stockman was hit and the Regulators formed, Charles Jackson and some of his followers grabbed young Squire Humphreys and Wade Hampton West. Humphreys was escorted to a tannery, tied face down on a large tanning log, and severely whipped across his back. He was told to talk—to admit having taken part in the Stockman raid and to name his accomplices. But he said nothing except to repeat several times that he hadn't stolen anyone's horses. Then a former plantation overseer suggested that Squire Humphreys be turned over and tied with his back to the log. That done, the man began lashing Humphreys just under his chin. Those watching the flogging marked the progress of the sudden red marks as they moved toward the middle of his chest.

"When I get to his belly," said the overseer, who had perfected his technique on slaves, "he'll belch the truth."

That was enough for Squire Humphreys. "Let me up. I'm guilty and I'll let the truth come," he said. "I'd rather be hung than whipped to death."

After being untied, he related details of the Stockman job while one of the Regulators took notes. Then he recounted his life, concentrating on the fact that he had been born into crime and had never really known anything else. Almost the first thing he remembered, he told the Regulators, was holding stolen horses in a thicket so they could graze. Humphreys's obvious intention was to gain sympathy. But as they listened Jackson and the others seem to have realized more than ever that they were dealing not just with men who committed crimes for convenience, but with crime as a family institution. Wade West's father, who happened to be there, said at one point that he took full responsibility for what his son had done. He told Jackson and his men that his boy had always been obedient and had only been following orders when he helped to steal Stockman's horses. The elder West asked Jackson to punish him but to let his boy alone. After some discussion, Humphreys and West were released, but were warned that if they weren't out of Texas within five days they'd be shot. That was Charles W. Jackson's first and last act of leniency.

A year and a half passed, during which Jackson killed Goodbread, intimidated Judge Hansford, and watched uneasily as crime continued. It was a time in which the Regulators seem to have been consolidating and holding their rides to occasional forays against "nigger-stealers." Texas, of course, was a slave state, as were neighboring Arkansas and Louisiana. Consequently, it was fairly common for Texans to cross the Sabine, grab a couple of "thousand-dollar niggers" from a Louisiana plantation, and bring them home for resale. The game worked the same way with Texas slaves, who were taken in the other direction. The Regulators rounded up several slave stealers in the autumn of 1841 and, contrary to usual vigilante procedure, turned them over to the authorities—not out of respect for the law, but out of respect for money, since there was a $200 bounty for each one.

Having accumulated some money and seen his Regulators reach a high point in prestige and power, Charles W. Jackson finally decided to declare war on the McFaddins, Stricklands, Humphreyses, and others. He noted ruefully that Squire Humphreys and Wade West hadn't left Texas, as ordered, and, since he had become an important man in the district, that must have embarrassed him. So he picked fourteen men to ride north with him into the outlaw families' stronghold around the McFaddin Creek area.

One of the fourteen, an athletic twenty-six-year-old Mississippian named Watt Moorman, was destined to play a far greater role in the war against the McFaddins and Stricklands than anybody imagined at the beginning of the ride. Moorman's having been chosen to accompany Jackson was in itself something of a commentary on the changing composition of the Regulators, nearly two years after they had formed. Moorman's father was a farmer, but, instead of taking advantage of the old man's relatively sound resources and position in the community, Moorman had quit school at fifteen and just banged around for a while. Eventually, he got a job in a store in Columbus, Mississippi, and, once in the big city, realized that good times could be had but that they cost money. One day he forged a check and left Columbus with his stake, and the next stop had been the wide-open and apparently up-for-grabs district of Shelby County. No one who knew Watt Moorman there had ever known him to work. He shared what he had with his friends and expected them to share what came their way with him. Mostly, he was known to have a persuasive tongue, a good shooting eye, and a volatile disposition, and always carried two pistols and a Bowie knife. Moorman, then, was in Texas looking for action.

The Regulators' first stop was at "Tiger Jim" Strickland's. It had by then turned cold, and as the men moved under the bare branches of oaks and hackberries their mood grew foul. Mrs. Strickland told them that her husband wasn't home. A guard was posted to prevent her warning others in the area, and the remaining fourteen pushed on to the McFaddin place, where "Buckskin Bill" and brother Bailey lived with their families. Neither of them was home, either. In apparent exasperation, Charles Jackson decided to burn down the house, and the pleas of the McFaddin women that winter had come and their children would suffer did nothing to change his mind. As the McFaddin homestead started to go up, one of the women, a child in her arms, tried to run inside while screaming that she preferred to die in the inferno, rather than freeze to death outside. She was held back, of course, which was the only humane thing to do.

Insisting that they were forced to "fall back upon their natural rights and seek satisfaction by their own hands,"[6] the McFaddins, the Stricklands, and their allies immediately named themselves Moderators and began ranging through the vast canebrakes, hickory groves, and pine forests searching for their enemies, and particularly for Charles W. Jackson, the house burner and terrorizer of women and children. Thirty men, led by a determined but careful friend named Edward Merchant, were assigned to get Jackson. A young surveyor named McClure, who had nothing to do with the feud, was gunned down during the search. He had somehow gotten in the way. Almost anyone, in fact, could have gotten in the way. The safest thing to do, given that situation, was to pick a side. That way, you'd at least have some guns behind you and not be caught helplessly in the middle. Sidney Lauer, a popular Shelbyville shopkeeper, was another neutral who got killed because he was in the wrong place at the wrong time. In fact, Lauer was in the worst conceivable place: he was riding with Charles Jackson the day the Moderators got the Regulator leader.

Jackson, who was naturally reckless anyway, became more so after he destroyed the McFaddin home and started the war. Instead of lying low and using bodyguards, Jackson moved at will, almost daring his enemies to attack. So when Merchant found out that Jackson had crossed the Sabine for business in Logansport, Louisiana, he saw his chance to get him once and for all. And, incredibly, the route to Logansport and back went right through the McFaddin Creek area. Lauer knew all that, but he decided to accompany Jackson anyway. They were passing through the hostile territory on their way back to Shelbyville when they were bushwhacked. Caught in a hail of buckshot coming from the side of the road, both men were swept off their horses; Lauer died instantly, and Jackson, the next day.

After a few days without a leader, the Regulators held a meeting and gave the job to Watt Moorman, who apparently was already showing the charismatic side of his personality. The Mississippian's first act after being drafted was to make himself "Colonel Commandant of the Shelby Guards," in the classic military style of vigilante leaders. His second act was to draw up a "hit list."

Figuring out who had been responsible for killing Jackson and Lauer wasn't especially difficult, since as soon as Moorman was made leader of the Regulators "Tiger Jim" Strickland, "Buckskin Bill" McFaddin and his brothers, Squire Humphreys, a notorious horse thief named Boatwright, and another friend, named Bledsoe, moved out of the area with their families. We can infer from that that Watt Moorman had a ferocious reputation even before he became the "Colonel Commandant of the Shelby Guards."

Nearly everyone in the county had by that time either joined one of the factions or was a sympathizer. Fearing that he'd get killed, Sheriff George disappeared and was replaced by John W. Middleton, an extremely prudent man. In theory, Middleton should have served notice to both sides that they were violating the law, put together a posse consisting of everyone who wanted to be neutral, and arrested as many of the Regulator and Moderator leaders as could be found. But John Middleton understood perfectly that trying to do such a thing would have amounted to blowing off his own head. There weren't many neutrals left in Shelby County by then, and certainly none who wanted to help arrest the leaders on both of the feuding sides. Middleton therefore decided to go after those who had fled and picked the Moorman group for his posse, thereby investing the Regulators with a touch of legality and respectability. With that, the pursuit of the fugitives began.

The Moderators' leaders decided to spread out. "Tiger Jim" Strickland headed for a friend's place on the outskirts of Crockett, a hard 100-mile ride to the southwest. The McFaddins, Humphreys, Boatwright, and Bledsoe went even farther; they kept going until they reached Montgomery, about forty miles north of Houston.

"Tiger Jim" Strickland was flushed from a camp he had made near his friend's house, managed to get away, and then, for some reason, tried to creep back up on the posse. Before the day was over, he was riding away furiously with a ball in his shoulder. The Regulator posse located the McFaddins and Humphreys in a house near Montgomery after nightfall a few days later. The Moderators were forced out of the place by threats to burn it down and agreed to return to Shelby County for trial. While negotiations were still going on, though, "Buckskin Bill" made a dash for freedom, but was hit in the heel by a long shot from Moorman's gun. The limping man had no sooner been brought back to the house when Bledsoe, who had been off somewhere else, stumbled right into the posse. He was shot to pieces.

One of the main characteristics of many true vigilante groups is worth mentioning at this point—that of the long pursuit. Classic vigilantes and their admirers were forever justifying what they did on the ground that they wanted to clear badmen out of their territory. They said, in essence, that they wanted only to make their communities safe by ridding them of outlaw elements. Yet in a number of instances vigilantes showed their underlying vindictiveness by following those on their death lists over hundreds of miles and, having caught them, bringing them back for execution. It was not simply a matter, then, of vigilantes wanting to sanitize their areas. The long pursuit clearly indicates that they wanted revenge—an eye for an eye—against their enemies. And there was another reason. A relentless chase was meant to show outlaws that merely hopping borders would be no guarantee of safety. Vigilantes wanted it known that they were not hamstrung by territorial sovereignty the way lawmen sometimes were; that they would get their man no matter where he went.

At noon on Saturday, October 9, 1841, the captured Moderator leaders were tried in Shelbyville, not by a court of law, but by an estimated 300 Regulator sympathizers gathered at a frontier town meeting. "Buckskin Bill" McFaddin and Squire Humphreys were condemned to death, but Rufus McFaddin, the youngest brother in the family, was spared because of his age.

The executions took place on a specially erected gallows beside the main road east of Shelbyville. It was a heavily traveled route and was undoubtedly chosen for purposes of maximum public exposure, another familiar vigilante trait. Both of the Moderators told their executioners that they regretted the death of Lauer, the merchant, but not that of Charles Jackson. Squire Humphreys is reported to have assured the gathering that he knew he deserved to die because he had broken his word about leaving the district in order to help kill Jackson and Moorman. Here is still another hallmark of classic vigilantism. Friends and sympathizers of those who did the hanging evidently felt cleansed by convincing themselves and others that those who had confronted the noose either had gladly accepted it or else at least had understood why their liquidation was necessary and just. In reading the literature, it's striking to count the number of times victims are described as having told their executioners that they bore no grudges against them. If even half of those reports are true, the frontier was infested with an astounding number of imbeciles.

"Buckskin Bill's" parting remarks are more credible. He cursed the Regulators and called them worse thieves than he was. "You've stolen my life and you'll wade through blood for it. You fellows that are grinning now," he said prophetically, "will bleed and die to pay for this murder."

"Do you think we'll die as you're dying to pay for murdering Lauer, McClure and Jackson?" shouted someone in the crowd.

"Oh, damn you, you ain't worth killing; here, help me up on

this horse." He apparently needed help because of the wound in his heel. A minute later, "Buckskin Bill" McFaddin's horse was led out from under him.[7]

The Stricklands and Boatwright were still at large. They hid for months in the Louisiana canebrakes, waiting for a chance to even the score. During that time, however, Henry Strickland was badly cut up in a knife fight and moved on. He was eventually killed in another fight. "Tiger Jim" Strickland stayed safely out of sight, but not long after the hangings Boatwright was spotted picking cotton on a plantation. A group of Shelby Guards crossed the Sabine, grabbed him, and brought him back to his county.

The way Dr. Levi Ashcroft, the former North Carolinian, told the story, even the Regulators were afraid to murder Boatwright in cold blood. On the other hand, nobody seems to have wanted to take the trouble of arranging another public execution, possibly because complaints were at that moment being sent by some of Shelby County's alarmed Moderators and neutrals to President Sam Houston. Instead, a lawyer named Charles L. Mann got hold of Boatwright and, in the seemingly friendliest way possible, convinced him that his chances of making a run for it and escaping were excellent. Boatwright thanked the lawyer, turned, and ran. Mann then shot him in the back. Newspapers on either side of the Sabine reported that the Regulators then "cut him to pieces and hung the fragments of his body on the surrounding trees." Such stories seem to have made their way back east and provoked some unfavorable comments. The *Redlander*, which was published in nearby San Augustine, defended Texas honor by calling Boatwright a notorious "horse thief, counterfeiter and highway robber," and added for good measure that he had been suspected of having murdered his wife.[8] Who could argue about chopping up a man like that?

The Regulators were in the saddle in every sense of the word during the winter of 1841–42. "Colonel" Moorman, who was by then affecting tight-cut military dress and moving with a bodyguard, began sending warning notes to selected undesirables.

Shelby County, January 4th, 1842

Mr. West:

Sir: Not finding you at home, this means of notifying you to leave our country by the 14th inst., has necessarily been adopted. If, sir, after the prescribed time, you are found within the limits of our county, you will be dealt with according to Lynch: this certainly cannot be comfortable; nevertheless you must and shall go, as the undersigned and others will convince you on a failure to comply with the requisitions.

By order of the Shelby Guards
C. W. Moorman,
Col. Commandant
B. F. Hooper,
W. Cook,
Chas. B. Daggett[9]

Moorman evidently had more luck with his letters than the county neutrals had with the ones they sent to Austin asking for help in stopping the feud. Sam Houston issued a proclamation on January 31, 1842, calling on the local authorities to "prosecute all offenders" and authorizing them to call for military help if they thought they needed it. They needed it, all right, but it wasn't available. Almost in the same breath, Houston said that his treasury was clean, that credit was not available, and that he therefore had no troops to send. Later, after more blood had been spilled, he would have to resort to the militia in desperation.

Meanwhile, "Tiger Jim" and some friends crossed the Sabine for a crack at Sheriff John Middleton, a man they must have hated almost as much as they did Watt Moorman. They put four balls into Middleton from ambush on the morning of March 26. He walked, not staggered, all the way home and five days later was back in the saddle looking for his would-be assassins. Middleton never found them, but he seems to have gotten their message and was soon replaced by a man named Llewellyn.

What was to turn out to be the bitter end started early in 1843 over, of all things, the theft of a few hogs. Henry Runnels, a Regulator, accused one Samuel N. Hall of pilfering in his pig pen. In keeping with Shelby County tradition, Hall not only vigorously denied taking Runnels's hogs, but also went home to get his gun. Runnels, of course, went home to get his gun, too. When he arrived at his house, he told a friend named Stanfield, who happened to be living with him, that he was going to settle the stolen-hog business by shooting Hall. Perhaps because he felt obligated for the lodgings, however, Stanfield went out and shot Hall. He was then arrested, put in jail, and somehow escaped. And before he could be recaptured he was caught by some of Samuel N. Hall's kin and hanged.

There was no such thing, though, as simply blaming Hall's murder on Stanfield, finding satisfaction in having executed the murderer, and letting it go at that. Never. Stanfield had been a friend of Runnels. Runnels was a Regulator. The Regulators were led by Watt Moorman. Watt Moorman therefore had to be killed, too. The next thing Moorman heard—and it seems to have been accurate—was that the Hall clan, together with relatives named Deal and Hicks, had brought in professional gunslingers and promised them $1,000 for killing Moorman, $700 for John Myrick, his deputy, and $500 for Runnels (who had tainted their dear departed's reputation by calling him a hog thief and had then gotten him killed). Being an inherently cautious lot, the professionals decided to start at the bottom of the list and work their way up.

Two gunmen appeared at Runnels's house one day and, pretending that they were on the trail of horse thieves, asked him for directions. Since the place to which they said they wanted to go was in the general direction of Shreveport, which was where Runnels had to take a load of cotton the next day, he invited them to spend the night. They did spend the night, but by the time Runnels got under way the following morning, they were gone. That evening Runnels set up camp and was about to start his supper when the two gunmen reappeared. He was inviting them to share his food and blankets when they killed him.

The new murder enraged the Regulators, who immediately took off after the killers. One, named Williams, was caught on the Louisiana side of the Sabine; the other escaped. Under sharp questioning, Williams admitted that he had murdered Henry Runnels. But he did more than that. He also fingered one John M. Bradley and some of Bradley's friends as having been involved in planning the hit. The Regulators were astounded, and very pleasantly so. John M. Bradley was the author of anti-Regulator letters appearing in the *Redlander*.

Bradley, as it turned out, was an example of the outwardly respectable Shelby County citizen who trafficked in crime. He owned a saloon halfway between Shelbyville and San Augustine that was said to be a hotbed of bandits and counterfeiters. He was a good family man, with a solid reputation (his brother-in-law was the governor of Arkansas), but one known in some quarters to be connected with swindlers; his good friend, in fact, was William Todd, the brother of Sam Todd, the land grafter. Finally, John M. Bradley was an openly declared Moderator, and that was enough. Watt Moorman let it be known that he and his men were after Bradley and his associates, including Amos Hall, Samuel's grieving brother and the most likely candidate for having called in the gunslingers.

Bradley, William Todd, and Hall reacted to word that the Regulators were looking for them by getting their guns and waiting for the attack in Bradley's house. They waited for some time, and when no Regulators appeared they took the opportunity to send word to their fellow Moderators that they wanted help. But no Moderators appeared, either; some expressed sympathy at Bradley's and the others' plight, but nonetheless flatly refused to get involved in another fight with Moorman and the rest. Finally, Bradley saw that he had no recourse but to go to the law, so he visited Sheriff Llewellyn and swore out warrants against several Regulators, including Watt Moorman. The warrants charged them with the murder of Williams in Louisiana; they were issued by a Judge Lister and served by Llewellyn himself.

Moorman told Llewellyn that he wanted three days in which to decide whether or not he cared to be arrested. The Sheriff agreed to that and left. Moorman's next move was to collect fifty of his men, see to it that they were well armed, and put them on alert in Shelbyville. Llewellyn, noting the appearance of armed Regulators in his town, found an equal number of Moderators and, by the authority vested in him as sheriff, turned them into a posse. It was the Moderators who now enjoyed quasilegal status, for a change. In addition to the hundred or so belligerents who were suddenly eyeballing one another in Shelbyville, almost everyone in the county was once more gravitating toward one side or the other and waiting to see what happened, as the tension increased. It was in large part their choosing sides, of course, that most increased the tension. But they couldn't be expected to understand that.

Then came word that Watt Moorman was going to give himself up—with one proviso. The condition stipulated that Moorman and his lieutenants would appear not before Judge Lister, who leaned toward the Moderators, but before Judge John Ingram, who was pro-Regulator. Moorman got his way. So, a few minutes after Judge Ingram began scanning the warrants, he announced that they were illegal because Williams had been killed in Louisiana. The case was dismissed before it actually became a case.

Sheriff Llewellyn had in the meantime joined his Moderator posse, which was camped two miles outside Shelbyville, and was therefore present when a rider showed up carrying counterwarrants for the arrest of Bradley, Todd, and Amos Hall as accessories to the Runnels murder. The warrants had been issued by Judge Ingram and were accompanied by this note:

A. Llewellyn, You have been so damned energetic in attempting to enforce the laws of the county, I herewith forward you writs against your particular friends, Bradley, Todd and Hall. We will now see if you are as persevering in the discharge of your duty as you have recently been, but we will see that you do your duty. If you do not, by God I'll make you.

C. W. Moorman[10]

The thing to do, naturally, was to take Bradley, Todd, and Hall before the Moderator judge. Lister scanned the papers and then announced that they were illegal. Runnels had been killed in Louisiana, he said, and that was obviously out of Shelby County's jurisdiction. Case dismissed.

That development made the Regulators so angry that they decided to kill James Hall, one of Samuel's and Amos's brothers. They got him by hiding behind a fence and shooting him as he plowed a field. Still another brother, John, was with James when he was killed and saw the murderers. But John was a mental defective and was therefore taken apart by the defense lawyer when the trial took place, more than a year later. Meanwhile, James Hall's murder shocked even some Regulators and sent the Moderators into heated discussions about liquidating every last Regulator, once and for all. A Moderator meeting was held six miles away, at Belle Springs, where John F. Cravens, a thirty-five-year-old deputy sheriff, was elected "Colonel" of the "Regiment." "Colonel" Cravens moved his regiment into Shelbyville the next morning and occupied it, not a particularly difficult thing to do, since the Shelby Guards were somewhere else at the time.

The composition of the Moderators had fundamentally changed since the Merchant-Jackson days of 1840. Many of the new members were recent settlers who didn't much care about the old feuds and who were reasonably receptive to a truce. Yet it's interesting that they joined anyway. Nearly everyone who came into the area at that time seems to have gravitated toward one faction or the other, apparently because it was the thing to do. Cravens and his assistants began setting membership standards and actually turned away some applicants (one of them being John M. Bradley, who had moved to the safer precincts of San Augustine but who nevertheless wanted Moderator protection). Still, enough of the old, bad elements hung on so that the Regulators could go on seeing themselves as the law-and-order faction. But, good and bad, peaceful and warlike, hundreds of men in Shelby County were regulating or moderating on a full-time basis by the summer of 1844, meaning that a lot of farming, ranching, and other business wasn't getting done. In effect, the area was supporting two small standing armies, and that was becoming intolerable.

When a team of neutrals arranged a dialogue between Moorman and Cravens, both leaders seemed to accept the idea, probably because of pressure from the moderate elements in their groups. On July 24, 1844, Moorman wrote his provisions for an agreement and sent them to Cravens. He pledged his men "not to Molest or in any manner disturb, any good and unoffending citizen." The catch, which Cravens noted, was that the definition of who was and who was not a good and unoffending citizen was to be left to Watt Moorman. With deep reservations, John Cravens signed the document. Watt Moorman then decided that John M. Bradley was not a good and unoffending citizen and would therefore have to be killed.

A spy named John Farrar was sent to San Augustine to reconnoiter. He returned to Shelbyville with the news that a big Baptist revival was going to be held in San Augustine's Masonic Hall the following Saturday night. Entertainment being what it was in East Texas in 1844, there was an excellent chance that everybody who could squeeze into the hymn and prayer meeting would do so, including Bradley. Moorman and five heavily armed henchmen rode into San Augustine on the big night, and as soon as they heard the revival begin they started moving on the Masonic Hall through the town's back streets. As the preacher exhorted the audience and the hymns were sung, Moorman waited silently at the entrance, trying to stay out of the light. Sure enough, there was Bradley, singing along with the rest of them.

When the meeting ended, John M. Bradley made his way slowly out of the packed room with the rest of the crowd. Everyone funneled through the front door, walking slowly and close on one another, before spilling onto the street. Just outside that door, Watt Moorman stepped up to his target and fired at point-blank range, hitting him in the stomach. The crowd's first reaction was stunned silence as John M. Bradley dropped to his knees. A moment later, though, women were screaming, and some people were shouting that they'd been hit, too. The residents of San Augustine began scattering in all directions. Bradley died a few hours later.

Murdering Bradley was the first step in a campaign of annihilation and purging. Moorman and other Regulator leaders met at one of their homes on July 28 and drew up a proclamation naming twenty-five Moderators who were to be ordered to leave the county within fifteen days or suffer the consequences. Sheriff Llewellyn's name headed the list, followed by Cravens, five members of the Haley clan, two Todds, two Stricklands, and others, including Isaac Hall, John Anderson, and Laurel Lang. Anderson was by all accounts (except Moorman's) a solid and well-respected citizen; William Todd was related to bad elements; Lang was a hog thief and a killer. All were tossed into the pot, and, over the objections of some Regulators, the list was approved. Moorman's younger lieutenants, all of them new to the area, endorsed it enthusiastically. Making trouble would allow them to prove themselves.

They got their chance when they were sent to notify everyone on the blacklist that he was marked for death unless he packed and left Shelby County. Their first stop was their last. Mrs. Thomas Haley saw the group trying to sneak up behind her home and quickly told her husband, who dropped two balls into his rifle and pulled its trigger from inside the barn. One of the balls killed a Regulator horse, and the other broke the arm of one of the proclamation servers. They decided that nailing the documents on the courthouse door would be just as effective. Moorman's eager but inexperienced youngsters had had an elementary lesson in the difference between theory and practice.

By the end of that day—July 29, 1844—both sides were preparing for a fight to the finish. Moorman sent the men he had under arms out of town to find a good "fort," and then he rode to the northern part of the county in search of recruits. The excuse

Moorman used for leaving town was that he was going fishing, a tale that even John Hall, the local half-wit, wouldn't have believed. Cravens was also busy. Having by then decided that the only way to end the feud once and for all was by killing everyone on the Regulators' "Provisional Committee," he pulled together fifty Moderators and sent fifteen of them out of town to find the enemy. The Regulators had taken over the farm of a sympathizer named Beauchamp, three miles west of town, and had quickly thickened a zigzag split-rail fence with several layers of fresh lumber.

When "Colonel" Cravens arrived with his regiment of Moderators, he decided to attack the farm from front and rear, splitting his force, which probably numbered about 200, in half. Both attacks were instant and obvious failures, since the Moderators had to charge across open terrain while the Regulators fired from behind their thick barricades. Cravens reluctantly decided to pull his forces back to a wooded area just out of effective rifle range and wait. Some of his men relieved their frustration by getting off an occasional shot in the general direction of the enemy fortification. Hours passed, and it was getting very warm.

One of the young Regulators, overcome by boredom, climbed on the fence and began flapping his arms and crowing like a rooster. He kept on trying to taunt the Moderators until a ball hit him on the side of the head, circled around the inside of his hatband, cutting a ring into his flesh, and disappeared. The boy fell off the fence, dazed but not seriously hurt. Then a Regulator knocked a Moderator out of a tree from a distance of about 150 yards, a shot so improbable in those days that he immediately nicknamed his rifle "Tremendous." It was getting warmer.

Three times the Moderators gathered for assaults on the Beauchamp farm, and three times they changed their minds. They finally retreated to a creek two miles away, where they watered themselves and their horses and pitched camp. After dark, the Regulators slipped out and went to Hilliard's Spring, fifteen miles north, where they were joined by thirty to forty other Shelby County men and more than a hundred sympathizers from Harrison County, who were led by still another "colonel," named Boulware. Everyone then began chopping trees for the construction of a custom-made defensive complex. It is highly doubtful that many of the men who worked in the darkness to build that fort remembered, or at least were thinking about, the original purpose of their organization. Their leader, who was by that time carrying a hunting horn with which to signal his forces, evidently had his heart set on possessing a real fort of his very own. That's what they had to think about.

The next morning, August 8, the Moderators picked up the Regulators' trail. They moved into Strickland's Church, an old log building two miles from Moorman's rising bastion, and settled in. New Moderators straggled into the church throughout the rest of the day, putting Cravens's strength at something over 200. Those involved in all this so exaggerated the numbers of men on either side that it's impossible to come up with accurate figures.

The Regulators attacked Strickland's Church on the afternoon of the ninth. A "Colonel" Davidson, one of an unusually large number of colonels around that day, was killed with two of his men by Moderator fire as they crouched under an embankment behind the church. Other Regulators were picked off by their own allies, since many of the Shelby and Harrison county men didn't know one another. Some Moderators had been positioned outside the building they were defending, and, with both sides crawling around without uniforms, mistakes were inevitable. Seeing that his troops were getting the worst of the battle, however, Moorman sent out a blast on his little hunting horn, and the Regulators slowly withdrew, under heavy fire. A Moderator figured that the Regulators had fifteen killed or wounded, with only six on his side hurt, none seriously; a Regulator calculated that the Moderators had lost sixteen dead and twenty-five wounded, with only two killed and one hurt on his side. Watt Moorman convinced himself that he had led the Shelby Guards to a stunning victory. Moderator scouts nevertheless found Moorman's fort deserted the next morning. The Regulators had been ordered to disperse and reassemble just south of Shelbyville, where it was easier to get food and ammunition. Moorman's dream of having a fort had to be abandoned.

Most of the Regulators and the Moderators were by then dispirited and exhausted, and the prospect of moving south and doing it all over again was simply too much for many of them. "The life of a feudist was no picnic," observed C. L. Sonnichsen, the western historian. "They had to hide in the woods like animals and eat cornbread and beef—if they ate at all. Water was scarce. The weather was hot. There were ticks and flies and other annoyances. And larger evils loomed in the background, for many had been unable to plant crops and more had been too busy to tend what they had planted. There was actual hunger in some families."[11] Many on both sides therefore took the opportunity to call it quits. They just picked up their rifles and went home, nursing bitter grudges. Those who remained camped near each other south of Shelbyville and, like two punch-drunk boxers, probed listlessly for some kind of opening.

The fighting around Hilliard's Spring and Strickland's Church had meanwhile prompted a new barrage of angry letters to President Houston, some describing the bloody turmoil in vivid terms and almost all asking that he take a personal hand in stopping it once and for all. This, Sam Houston was now ready to do. Instead of riding dramatically into Shelbyville, however, he stopped at San Augustine and from there issued an order for both sides to lay down their weapons and go home. He also called out the San Augustine, Sabine, Nacogdoches, and Rusk County militias, totaling 600 men, and instructed them to move on Shelbyville. Finally, Houston told the Marshal of the Republic, one "Sandy" Horton, to bring in ten leaders from each side.

When Watt Moorman heard that 600 militiamen, under the command of a real general, were marching toward him, he called together the remaining Regulators and told them that they'd have to disband temporarily and that it was every man for himself. All scattered. Some went back to their homes, and others left the county altogether. Moorman and a few others made their way to the fort at Hilliard's Spring, assuming that the militia would leave after both sides had disbanded and that they could wait out developments there. But the Moderators didn't disband. They surrendered. Ten of their leaders and nine Regulator lieutenants gave themselves up to Horton and, on instructions from Houston, were released on bail. Moorman was in turn tracked, captured, freed on bail, rearrested for John Bradley's murder, put in chains, and finally released again after posting additional bond.

Houston then had all twenty Regulator and Moderator leaders brought to him. They were subjected to a long and severe tongue-lashing, which dealt mainly with the stupidly disruptive effects their little feud was having on the struggling young republic. He then returned to the capital.

A treaty of peace was soon written and signed by two Regulator and two Moderator leaders and several other participants, none of whom included "Colonel" Cravens or "Commandant" Moorman. It said simply:

We the undersigned citizens of the Republic of Texas, in view of the disastrous consequences, anarchy and misrule attendant upon the late attempts in the county of Shelby and elsewhere, to turn the law from its legitimate channels, and to the end that law and order may prevail, peace and quietude restored, do hereby solemnly pledge ourselves to assist the civil authorities in carrying out, enforcing and maintaining the law of the country and to that end:

1st. Be it resolved, that we do hereby favor discarding the odious designation of Regulators and Moderators, and will henceforth be hailed and recognized by no other name than that of Texans.

2nd. Resolved, that we will forever forget and forgive and will frown upon and discountenance any and every attempt to revive the unfortunate divisions which have for so long distracted the country; that we will give the hand of fellowship to every worthy citizen, no matter under which party banner he may have rallied.

3rd. Resolved, that a voice has come to us from our firesides, from our wives and little ones, that its pleading for peace shall not pass unheeded, and we do therefore pledge our sacred honor to the strict observance and faithful performance of the foregoing resolutions.[12]

The treaty was quickly circulated, and everyone who read or heard about it agreed that it was a wonderful document—an inspiring document, which promised a glorious new beginning for the weary residents of Shelby County.

Alfred Truitt, one of the Moderator leaders who had signed it, might have been thinking about how wonderful it was a few days later, when, about to mount his horse, he saw Regulator Charles Luton coming his way. Luton was carrying a shotgun. Truitt pulled himself up and over the saddle and landed on the side of the horse away from Luton as a load of buckshot whistled over his head. The Moderator fired back from under the animal's belly, severely wounding the Regulator. Truitt was acquitted; Luton fled bail and apparently never returned.

At about the same time, a Moderator named Duncan started a fight with a Regulator named Harris. Duncan was shot dead, and Harris, who gave himself up in his own good time, also was freed of responsibility in the killing. Soon afterward, a county court session was electrified when somebody mentioned gunpowder and forty men jumped for their guns. A mass shoot-out was prevented by a margin of seconds.

Despite such occasional flare-ups, however, the feud quieted during the rest of 1844, as the residents of Shelby County began picking up the pieces of their shattered lives and tending to the more pressing problems that had been neglected during the fighting. Strangers passing through their fields, branches cracking outside at night, and other unfamiliar noises kindled emotions in the people of Shelby County that would take a long time to die. In early May 1847, sixty guests attending a wedding reception at the home of a man named Wilkinson were fed a stiff dose of arsenic, leaving at least twenty-three of them dead. One newspaper reported that Wilkinson had been a Moderator and wanted to kill as many former Regulators as possible. It was most unlikely, but showed that almost three years later the subject was still very much on the minds of the people in Shelby County. During the war with Mexico, the Shelby County contingent consisted of two companies, one Regulator, the other Moderator. They fought at each other's side warily, but the common trial by fire seems to have ultimately gone far toward healing the spiritual wounds. Still, it was to be five more decades before the people of Shelby County, Texas, could discuss the great Regulator-Moderator war without a trace of rancor.

Watt Moorman had tried to join both Shelby County companies when the war with Mexico started, but neither would have him. He was acquitted for the murder of John M. Bradley and finally settled in Louisiana, where, according to some accounts, he engaged in crime. Moorman's last undertaking, appropriately, had to do with a feud. He got into a vicious disagreement with a Dr. Burns of Logansport, who became convinced that Moorman was out to waylay and kill him. So one day, as Watt Moorman approached Burns's house, the doctor, hiding beside an open window, got off one lethal shot, which dropped the former "Colonel Commandant of the Shelby Guards" right there on the street. Moorman was not carrying the little hunting horn when he died.

5

California: "Gentlemen, as I understand it, we are here to hang somebody!"

THE TWO thick planks, each sixteen inches wide and hinged, looked like tongues as they slid silently out of the windows on the second floor of the building on Sacramento Street, close by San Francisco's busy wharves. It was forty-five minutes past noon on a clear spring day, and a large crowd had collected in front of the sandbag walls that protected the building's entrance. Some had been waiting since midnight, and now they grew expectant as the wooden tongues stuck out at them, pointing over their heads toward Washington Street, where the city hall and police station were located. In a few minutes, the planks would become the last objects Charles Cora, an Italian gambler, and James P. Casey, an Irish politician, stood on before each man plunged into eternity at the end of a rope.

The building from which the planks protruded was more than a building. It was a citadel. It had been used by an appraising firm, among others, but, since there wasn't as much to appraise in 1856 as there had been in '49, Truett and Truett had vacated. Then, only a week before the day Cora and Casey were executed, the rooms had been taken over by the Grand Tribunal—the renowned San Francisco Committee of Vigilance. Officially, number 41, which was on the south side of Sacramento, was known as the committee's headquarters, or simply as its rooms. Its popular name, however, was Fort Gunnybags, so called because of the sandbags that were piled eight feet high and formed a three-sided barrier extending from the front of the building well into the street. The sandbags turned the area in front of the building into a kind of stockade; gaps had even been left in them from which rifle or cannon fire could be directed at anyone threatening the premises. No one ever did, though.

Those who walked or were dragged into Fort Gunnybags had to pass a sentry box, from which a guard demanded the current password, which was sometimes changed twice a day because of a fear of spies. Once inside, the vigilante or his prisoner found himself in a large drill room, whose walls were strung with weapons of all kinds, flags, artillery harness, and bulletin boards holding general orders and notices for the committee's various companies. There was a commissary stand immediately to the left of the entrance, from which coffee was given to those standing guard duty. Above the stand hung the committee's celebrated insigne: a circle with a watchful eye at its center, the name of the organization ringing the eye, and around the circumference the words "*Fiat Justitia Ruat Coelum*. No Creed, No Party, No Sectional Issues." That drill room led into another drill room and armory, which also contained offices, and, in the courtyard behind them, sheds for horses and some cannons for heavy defense.

The second floor held two police offices (the committee's force, not the city's), seven cells, two Executive Committee rooms, an initiation room, the grand marshal's chamber, the enrolling clerk's room, a cubicle for the sergeant-at-arms, more weapons stores, and four flights of stairs, including one used only by the Executive Committee. The third, and top, level held an armorer's shop and a hospital, containing a large supply of medicine and bandages and several cots. The flat roof supported a heavy bell used for alerting the membership, two more cannons, trained along Sacramento Street in either direction, more sentries shouldering muskets, and a large American flag.

As impressive as was Fort Gunnybags, it was only a reflection of the men who planned and manned it. The leaders of San Francisco's Committee of Vigilance, after all, weren't a bunch of yokels with trail dust in their hair and saddle sores on their behinds. They were civilized men, established or aspiring gentlemen of the city. Most were urbane and reasonably well educated merchants, bankers, stock traders, land speculators, shipowners, lawyers, doctors, judges, morticians, and politicians. So they tended to wear silk cravats rather than cotton bandannas, accrue means rather than collect pay, live in dignified homes rather than under saddle blankets, and execute their enemies rather than kill them. All had gotten where they were by civilized means, and, as every one of them knew, organization was the hallmark of civilization. They had therefore organized their committee in the most efficient way known to civilized man. They had organized it like an army.

At the top of the chain of command was a forty-one-member Executive Committee, headed by a thirty-two-year-old importer named William T. Coleman. Coleman had been a member of the Committee of Thirteen, the secret leadership body of San Francisco's first real vigilante group, that of 1851. The Committee of Thirteen had never actually disbanded, but had only lain dormant until Coleman was persuaded, five years later, to revive it. He had then been elected president of the Executive Committee, which also included a vice-president and prosecuting attorney, a judge associate, a treasurer and deputy treasurer, a secretary, a grand marshal and deputy grand marshal, and a chief of police and his deputy. All were identified by secret numbers, not by name—a precaution that seems a little silly, considering that anyone with patience enough to stand outside Fort Gunnybags could have recorded the comings and goings of any number of municipal notables. Those notables and others in the Committee of Vigilance, by the way, corresponded with friends and relatives elsewhere on their own vigilante stationery, which depicted their fort in shades of gray and their seal in dark blue.

The rank and file, which stood at 2,000 by the end of the first day of the committee's existence and peaked at about 6,000 a few weeks later, represented an organizational tour de force. They were divided into four infantry and artillery regiments, cavalry battalions, pistol companies, a "Citizen Guard," and a medical staff. Regiments were composed of 100-man companies, on which military rank fell like snow. Clerks, shirtmakers, masons, dairymen, riggers, deliverymen, loaders, messengers, salesmen, teamsters, and carpenters overnight became commanders, colonels, lieutenant colonels, majors, captains, first lieutenants, second lieutenants, sergeant majors, quartermaster sergeants, orderly sergeants, second orderly sergeants, third orderly sergeants, fourth orderly sergeants, and privates. These men, many of whom were new aliens who spoke little or no English, were drilled day and night with a pageantry, if not a precision, that would have done credit to a military academy. Each company met in its own corner of Fort Gunnybags and kept its own muster, arsenal, drums, fifes, flags, and other accouterments of the military machine. They drilled and practiced incessantly, those sergeants and privates, but there's little evidence that any of them knew exactly what they were drilling and practicing for. Such, at any rate, was the strength of the San Francisco Committee of Vigilance, which gathered eight days after its second coming to hang one Italian gambler and one Irish politician.

Like a box within a box, the San Francisco Committee of Vigilance was awakened, after five years of fitful slumber, for reasons within reasons.

The ostensible reason for the Vigilantes' new presence was to punish Charles Cora and James P. Casey, two men who were seen by the Executive Committee as personifying the crime they insisted was poisoning their city.

Charles Cora was not the ruffled-shirt-and-diamond-stickpin species of gambler. He was a small, well-proportioned man, who dressed conservatively, spoke softly, and seems to have always shown manners. Gambling in those days was a reasonably honorable profession when it was done honestly, and apparently Cora was honest, because he wasn't very successful at it. But he was lucky in at least one respect: he lived with and was loved by his common-law wife, Belle. And Belle Cora was the proprietor of one of San Francisco's quality brothels, so she was very well off. She also was intelligent, fiery, and completely devoted to her man.

What her man had done to get himself in trouble was shoot and kill William H. Richardson. Richardson was a United States marshal. One night in mid-November of the previous year Richardson had stepped out of the Blue Wing, a saloon favored by lawmen, judges, white-collar criminals, and journalists, to get some fresh air. The Marshal was short, thickset, and generally nasty and, according to one newspaperman who knew him, tended to wear a facial expression strikingly similar to a bull-dog's.[1] He also carried a pair of derringers, was widely known to be a dangerous enemy, and hit the whiskey bottle with dedication. Anyway, as Richardson stood in front of the Blue Wing that November night in 1855, Charles Cora passed him on his way into the place and made some remark that he thought was humorous but that angered Marshal Richardson. So Richardson followed Cora into the Blue Wing and asked a friend who the smart aleck was. He was told, but, since he was drunk, he kept referring to the man he thought had insulted him as "Carter." The friend, who knew Cora, let it go at that and assumed Richardson would sleep off his anger. But the friend was wrong.

Richardson was still brooding over the "insult" two days later and, after another heavy drinking bout, went back to the Blue Wing to find Charles Cora and get satisfaction. He soon found the gambler and asked him to step outside, and both left the smoky room, walking shoulder to shoulder. They went around the corner and onto Clay Street. Richardson then backed Cora against a brick wall. With a hand in each of the pockets that contained the derringers and breath that must have smelled like a distillery, Marshal Richardson told Cora that he wanted satisfaction for the insult right then and there. Many of Richardson's best friends—men who wanted Charles Cora's blood before that night was over—were to admit later that, given the situation, Cora had only two alternatives: either to kill Richardson or to let Richardson kill him.[2] He chose the former, pulled out his own derringer, and shot the Marshal in the chest from a distance that couldn't have been more than a yard.

While the dying man was being carried into Keith's drugstore, on Montgomery Street, Sheriff David Scannell arrived and took Cora into custody and away from an angry mob that had gathered immediately and that was threatening to lynch him. About a hundred of them did, in fact, march on the jail in an effort to get Cora, but Scannell quickly moved his prisoner elsewhere.

Within a few hours, San Franciscans were arguing in the streets about whether or not Charles Cora was to be strung up. Samuel Brannan, one of the old Committee of Thirteen, was among them. That night he addressed a large crowd at the Oriental Hotel and urged that Cora be executed immediately, a statement that got him arrested on charges of disorderly conduct and inciting a riot. The crowd followed Brannan to the station house and threatened to rescue him. The venerated former vigilante was later released on his own recognizance, however, so everyone dispersed.

The law was working perfectly. Charles Cora had been promptly arrested for the murder of Marshal Richardson and was being protected from a mob that wanted to hang him. Since a homicide had been committed, he was being held without bail until the next term of the Quarter Sessions Court, while Belle Cora had already begun searching for good lawyers. Brannan, who had tried to instigate Cora's lynching, had judiciously been arrested to prevent it and then, just as judiciously, released as soon as the situation quieted a bit. But the editor of the *San Francisco Bulletin*, among others, wasn't going to let it go at that.

James King of William, who had put his sheet on the press for the first time on October 8, 1855—five weeks before Cora killed Richardson—came from the District of Columbia and had settled in Sacramento in 1848. His father's name was William, and, following an old Irish custom, he called himself James King of William in order to differentiate between himself and other James Kings. He had worked for the post office and for the banking house of Corcoran and Riggs in Washington, had taken up mining and petty politics in Sacramento, and had finally moved to San Francisco in 1849 to start his own bank. The bank went under in 1853–54 because of unsound land investments, and was taken over by a banking and express company, which offered King a job. He took the position, but when his new employer went out of business in February 1855, he was again in trouble. During his days of relative prosperity, though, James King of William had helped John Nugent, a lawyer, to start the *San Francisco Herald*. Something about journalism had whetted James King's appetite, so in spite of the fact that there were already a dozen newspapers in the city in that autumn of 1855, he had borrowed a relatively small sum and started the *Bulletin*. Seeing what he perceived to be rampant crime and corruption on all levels of city life, the Irish antipapist, whose own brother was an unsavory character, decided to turn his infant newspaper into a weapon with which to fight the forces of evil.

It seemed to James King of William and many of his friends that their new land had always been threatened by the forces of evil. California had been taken over by the United States Army in 1848, during the war with Mexico, and had therefore been under military rule. With the discovery of gold, however, the occupation forces had allowed a degree of civil government to return, through the Spanish and Mexican institution known as the *alcalde*. An *alcalde* was elected by the citizens of his community as a combination sheriff, mayor, justice of the peace, and tax collector. As such, he not only enforced the law, but also, in many cases, created it for the community he governed, and therefore exercised almost unlimited powers. That being the case, there was no uniform system of justice when California entered the American fold; the severity of punishment for robbery, swindling, murder, and other crimes varied from one town or mining camp to another, starting with simple banishment, going through the familiar thirty-nine lashes, and ending with hanging. And, if that kind of fluctuating justice wasn't bad enough, there also sprang up the infamous institution known as miners' courts, in which whole mining camps voted on the spot whether an accused man was to be executed and carried out the sentence within a matter of minutes.

California in those days was virtually wide open, and fortunes were up for grabs. There were two basic occupational areas in and around the gold camps in 1849–50: one was pulling the gold out of the earth, and the other was trying to take it away from those who had pulled it out of the earth, by fair means or foul. Taking a miner's gold was done most easily and honestly, of course, by selling him bread, boots, or whiskey at incredibly inflated prices. Or it could be accomplished by stealing. Both methods were practiced with fervor. The prospectors who streamed into the gold fields early in 1849 were accompanied by a horde of bakers, butchers, tailors, pimps, lawyers, gamblers, blacksmiths, loan sharks, gunsmiths, prostitutes, doctors, thieves, teamsters, barbers, journalists, land speculators, counterfeiters, and others who, legally or otherwise, wanted a piece of the action. They literally came from just about everywhere—not only from eastern American cities, but also from Europe, South and Central America, and even Australia and other British colonies in the Pacific. University-educated quacks from England, illiterate Indian peasants from Ecuador and Mexico, charlatans from Paris, impressed sailors from Lisbon, and convicts from Sydney mingled on virtually every tent-lined street, in every loud saloon, and in every two-bit hotel and brothel in north-central California, to compete for the little bags of gold dust and nuggets that were being tossed around like coins at a carnival. They stole from the prospectors and, in turn, had what they stole stolen from them, as thousands of bags of the precious metal changed hands daily.

By early 1851, a crime wave permeated San Francisco, in the wake of two years of gold fever. That spring, gangs of hooligans were roaming the streets picking fights and stealing. Robbers and burglars had developed the technique of setting fire to the buildings they hit as a way of throwing off investigators or creating diversions. There was a real fear, that spring, that one day the whole city would go up in smoke. A group of Australian cutthroats known as the Sydney Ducks was terrorizing merchants and other businessmen. Thefts, robberies, burglaries, and murders had become everyday occurrences, swamping the rickety judicial system and often confounding law-enforcement officers. And there were areas of San Francisco, that spring, that even the police wouldn't enter.[3]

The formation of the first of the two great San Francisco vigilante organizations resulted from all those problems, but if its birth could be attributed to any single incident, it would have to be the robbery of a clothier named Jansen on the evening of February 19. It wasn't a unique occurrence, by any means, but it was the one that pushed the concerned middle and upper classes of the city to their saturation point.

It started when a man came into Jansen's shop, examined hats, shirts, and overalls, and then told the proprietor that he wanted to buy a dozen blankets. Jansen got the blankets, and while the man looked them over a second man entered the store. Suddenly the first man hit Jansen, and, joined by the second, beat him severely, took $2,000, and left him for dead. The shopkeeper crawled for help, the police arrived, and a search for his attackers and robbers was started, based on the descriptions he gave. The police thought they knew the name of one of the robbers after Jansen got through talking to them; he was James Stuart, an escaped murderer, they theorized.[4]

The next day an Australian who gave his name as Thomas Burdue was arrested, and the following day, February 21, another Australian, named Wildred, was picked up. Both were taken under guard to Jansen's home and were identified by the bandaged storekeeper as the men who had attacked and robbed him. By the time they had been returned to jail, a large crowd had gathered and was threatening to take them from the police and hang them, just the way criminals were hanged by miners' courts in the gold fields. Burdue and Wildred were taken before a judge, who heard preliminary evidence, including sworn testimony from one witness who said that he had been playing cards with Wildred at the time of the robbery. Someone else corroborated the story. When the judge adjourned the trial until the following Monday, one of the spectators shouted, "Now's the time," and the men in the gallery rushed at the prisoners, knocking over chairs, tables, and the railing. A few even managed to get their hands on the two Australians before they were beaten back by the sheriff and some deputies. The crowd began chanting, "Shame, shame."

Between 6,000 and 7,000 San Franciscans are said to have gathered around the courthouse that night to organize a committee to make sure that the prisoners remained properly guarded, since jail breaks, often accomplished with the help of jailers who were paid by friends of the prisoners, were common. The crowd finally dispersed, but met again the next morning, when majority and minority reports were read. Some of the city's most concerned citizens had obviously stayed up throughout the night in order to produce something that would give their angry but unorganized neighbors a sense of direction. Sam Brannan, a former Mormon elder turned real-estate and land speculator, was one of them. The majority report recommended appointing a Committee of Thirteen to act as the Australians' judge and jury that very afternoon—to try them with the co-operation of the regular court if possible, but to try them one way or the other. Brannan's minority report called for immediate execution.

"Why should we speak to juries, judges, or mayors?" Brannan asked the crowd. "Have we not had enough of such doings in the last 18 months? It is we ourselves who must be mayor, judges, law, and executioners. These men are murderers and thieves; let us hang them."[5]

Meanwhile, printed handbills were circulated and nailed up along San Francisco's main thoroughfares.

Citizens of San Francisco! The series of murders and robberies that have been committed in this city, without the least redress from the laws, seem to leave us entirely in a state of anarchy. When thieves are left without control to rob and kill, then doth the honest traveller fear each bush a thief. Law, it appears, is but a nonentity, to be scoffed at; redress can be had for aggression but through the never-failing remedy so admirably laid down in the code of Judge Lynch. Not that we should admire this process, but that it seems to be inevitably necessary. Are we to be robbed and assassinated in our domiciles, and the law to let our aggressors perambulate the streets merely because they have furnished straw bail? If so, let each man be his own executioner. Fie upon your laws! they have no force. . . .[6]

John Nugent used the columns of his *Herald* to promote the formation of a vigilance committee.

We are here without jails, without penitentiaries, and without a police sufficiently strong for the circumstances; and cojoined with these deficiencies we have a bankrupt city and an incompetent council. On whom must we depend for relieving the town from the desperate and abandoned scoundrels who now infest it? There is clearly no remedy for the existing evil but in the strong arms and stout souls of the citizens themselves. . . . Let us then organize a band of two or three hundred Regulators, composed of such men as have a stake in the town, and who are interested in the welfare of the community. . . . If two or three of these robbers and burglars were caught and treated to lynch law, their fellows would be more careful about future depredations. . . .[7]

Later that month or early in March, a merchants' night patrol was organized by about a hundred men who had property to protect. They divided into street patrols and worked various districts of the city once a week on eight-hour stints. They did the same thing, in fact, as the Maccabees were to do in the Crown Heights section of Brooklyn exactly 113 years later when confronted with a similar problem. The merchants' patrol was the true nucleus of the vigilante group, which was about ready to move on the criminals.

Samuel Brannan and William T. Coleman were meanwhile urging the creation of a popular tribunal that would try the two Australians *in absentia*—both Wildred and Burdue, whom they knew to be James Stuart. The assemblage agreed. There were apparently many among Brannan's and Coleman's supporters, though, who didn't have their hearts set on a double lynching. In one of those amusing quirks that sometimes have plagued vigilante leaders, the counsels provided for Wildred and Burdue proved so effective that the people's jury failed to get a conviction. No matter. Wildred and seven others were soon to escape from the city jail, anyway. But Burdue, who everyone still assumed was James Stuart, was tried in district court, found guilty, and sentenced to fourteen years in prison. There is no evidence that anyone noted the supreme irony of the popular tribunal's having failed to get a conviction, while the regular courts did so quite effectively. The final irony, however, was yet to come. Before sentence was executed, it was decided to send the man they thought was Stuart back to Marysville for arraignment in the murder of the sheriff there. A Marysville court, in turn, found him guilty of killing Sheriff Moore and sentenced him to die. On the eve of Burdue's execution, however, the real James Stuart was captured. Burdue, severely shaken, was released— and he went even poorer than he had come, since all the money found on him at the time of his capture had been turned over to Jansen as compensation.

The merchants' night patrol turned into the first Committee of Vigilance of San Francisco in Samuel Brannan's office at about that time—in early June 1851. When that meeting was over, a constitution had been drawn up and signed by 716 men, all of whom also listed their places of business and home addresses. Revenue was to come from merchants' donations plus a $5 subscription from each member. Everyone was assigned a number and referred to only by it. Admission to meetings, Hubert Howe Bancroft reported, "was much the same as at a Freemason's lodge; the applicant, if unknown by sight to the door-keeper, called his name and number and was identified by the sergeant-at-arms."[8] Those who didn't show up at a meeting were fined.

There is no doubt that Bancroft favored the San Francisco Vigilantes. While his two-volume account of their doings is by all odds the best and most complete of its type, it suffers from some of the same slanting that marks other histories of vigilance organizations, in California and elsewhere. Yet, probably without realizing it, Bancroft has told us more about his subject than even he seems to have grasped. He paints a compelling picture, for example, of brave and ordinarily retiring men who have been pushed beyond endurance and who finally band together as a last desperate resort to achieve the common good. Certainly the rhetoric of the speeches, conversations, notices, manifestoes, bylaws, and newspaper articles he dug up and applied to his work repeatedly make that impression. But when we come right up to the painting and look closely at it we begin to discern that it is a picture painted over another picture. With a little concentration, we can see isolated but revealing parts of the original showing through.

Of the righteous and anguished characters, for instance, Bancroft says: "The vigilance system was one of popular espionage, the most extensive and complete a liberal government has ever seen. Every man was a spy on every other man. Opposition was intimidated by the watchful eye and silent tongue. Often a bad man did not know his bedfellow, or when or where to speak his mind." Bancroft was clearly talking about frightening the city's dangerous element when he made that observation; he was bragging that the Vigilantes were so secretive and observant that no criminal could safely confide in a stranger without risking the possibility that what he said would get back to the avengers. But look at the anecdote he uses to make the point.

One day a group of men, gathered in the bar-room of the Union Hotel, stood talking somewhat too loudly and vehemently against the "stranglers," when Mr. Ryckman stepped in for his luncheon. After listening attentively for a few moments, though without appearing to notice them, he stepped up to one of the chief speakers, a wealthy, influential man, whom he well knew, and called him aside, saying he wished to speak a word with him. When they were alone, Ryckman drew from his pocket an imprint of the watchful eye, the emblem of the organization, and showing it to him, said: "The Committee will see you at their rooms this evening at eight o'clock."

"My God, Ryckman! what do you mean? Surely you are not one of them?"

"I mean what I say," answered Ryckman. "These men are staking their lives and fortunes for the general good, and they shall not be vilified in my hearing behind their backs. If you have any charges to make, and will substantiate them, they will listen to your accusation against themselves, or any one of their number, as dispassionately as they will listen to my accusation against you. Good-day. You will be there at the appointed hour."

As Ryckman moved off, his quondam friend seized hold of him, and in the most piteous terms begged him to recall the order for his arrest promising respectful prudence for the future. With some further words of admonition, to this at length Ryckman was constrained to yield assent, and so left him.[9]

The first thing we notice about this remarkable vignette is the fact that Ryckman's wrath and indignation are directed not at one of the cutthroats who are the Vigilantes' sworn enemies, but at a "wealthy, influential man" who is, or was, Ryckman's friend. And that wealthy and influential man apparently finds the Vigilantes so distasteful that he refers to them as "stranglers" in conversation with others of his class, who are at least listening to what he says, if not agreeing. We can assume from this that there was some sort of opposition to the Vigilantes among the respectable elements in San Francisco—from men who did not feel that conditions, bad as they may have been, justified summary justice. We also note that Ryckman is threatening to level charges at the man before the Vigilantes and has ordered his appearance before the Committee. On hearing this, the man reacts with emotions that remind us of the Reign of Terror in Paris in 1793, not of citizens banding together altruistically to ensure the well-being of the good folk. And of what, exactly, does Ryckman plan to accuse the man? Being a troublemaker? Bad-mouthing the organization? If the Vigilantes are as beleaguered by thieves, arsonists, and killers as they say they are, it's illogical that they'd want to waste precious time intimidating or possibly taking some punitive action against a member of their own social and economic class whose only crime is disagreement with their philosophy. Illogical unless the Committee of Thirteen feels itself on such shaky ground, where community consensus is concerned, that it must squash opposition within its own establishment before getting a free hand with the lower elements.

Finally, and perhaps most interesting when considering the vigilante reaction as a whole, there is Mr. Ryckman himself. G. W. Ryckman, homeowner, businessman, husband, father, and ordinary citizen, always subject to the vagaries of society and the amorphous pushing and tugging of his equals, emerges after the formation of the Committee of Vigilance as a man exhilarated by his new power. In one account after another of the San Francisco Vigilantes, their secret nature is stressed; repeated mention is made of identification numbers for members, doorkeepers taking passwords, and all the other delightful and exciting falderal that goes with fraternity and secret-society participation. Yet Ryckman can't resist exposing himself (and in theory, therefore, betraying the organization) by pulling the loudmouth aside in a public place and whipping out his little card with its watchful eye. Yesterday the two men were friends and perhaps business acquaintances of equal stature. But today lackluster G. W. Ryckman carries in his pocket a little card whose potency he can feel, a little card licensing him to help decide who will live and who will die in the city of San Francisco. For a man who has spent all his life as one more anonymous head within the citizen herd, such sudden power is intoxicating. It has made G. W. Ryckman arrogant and therefore very dangerous. That is the picture beneath the picture.

John Simpton, another Australian, was the committee's first victim. He was accused of having stolen a small safe from a Mr. Virgin's shipping office and trying to row across the bay with it. Simpton was captured on the water, but managed to toss the safe overboard before his pursuers pulled alongside. He was marched from the wharves to the California Fire Company's bell tower, while the Committee of Thirteen organized a court. Sam Brannan acted as judge and members of the committee as associate judges. In all, there were seventy Vigilantes in the place, as well as witnesses to the crime. A special committee had been appointed to turn up witnesses for the culprit, but they don't seem to have done so. Prosecution witnesses meanwhile identified the Australian as the man they had seen running down the street with the safe under his arm, and they were followed by others who related his former crimes. "This was easily done," Bancroft reports, "as there were those present in the gathered multitude without who knew him well, and his acts were bold and recent."[10] He does not list them, however.

Then nervousness set in. "It was one thing for a half-drunken rabble to take the life of a fellow-man," Bancroft explains, "but quite another thing for staid church-going men of business to do it."[11] William A. Howard watched for several moments as doubts spread across the faces of his fellow committee members. Finally he stood, laid his revolver on the table, and looked at them. When he spoke, it was with slow, clear enunciation.

"Gentlemen, as I understand it, we are here to hang somebody!"[12]

The committee couldn't have agreed more, and Howard's straight-to-the-point declaration strengthened its resolve, started the momentum. G. W. Ryckman told Simpton the verdict: he was going to be hanged in the plaza before dawn.

A sizable crowd had gathered at the execution site by 2 A.M., when Simpton was brought out. Benjamin Ray, the chief of police, worked his way through the gawkers until he got to the procession. When he thought he was close enough, he tried to get a hand on Simpton in order to rescue him. He was roughly pushed aside. A noose was then slipped around the condemned man's neck, as he stood under the gallows that had been erected for him.

"Every lover of liberty and good order take hold," shouted Sam Brannan. About twenty-five did. They jerked the rope so hard that John Simpton's neck broke the instant he left the ground. But, not satisfied with having killed the Australian, they hoisted his body all the way up and left it hanging there, for advertising purposes, until dawn. The $218 pulled out of his pocket was used for his burial.

Before that summer was over, three more victims, including the renowned James Stuart, had swung from Vigilante ropes, and many others had been run out of the city. Lawmen like Ray had made halfhearted attempts to intervene, but for the most part seemed content to let the city's power structure have its way, first, because their work was being done for them, and, second, because no civil servant wanted to cross the notables who led the Committee of Vigilance. By the end of June 1851, the Committee of Vigilance of San Francisco had become famous from coast to coast and was being studied as a model in many towns that had, or thought they had, similar problems. Press comments on what had happened varied with the writers' proximity to the events.

"Where the guilt of the criminal is clear and unquestionable," said the *California Courier* of June 10, 1851, "the first law of nature demands that they be instantly shot, hung, or burned alive. . . . We must strike terror into their hearts."[13]

"It may be that the imperative necessities of self-preservation have driven the people to these extremities," said the *New York Herald* on September 19. "We trust that law and order may soon be reestablished and assigned to some effective guardianship under the regularly constituted tribunals of the country."[14]

With four executed and many others either deported or simply chased out of the city, San Francisco's criminal element quieted, so the Committee of Vigilance met in full session on September 16 and adopted a resolution suspending meetings indefinitely. It did not disband, but simply became inactive and appointed a forty-five-member watchdog council to keep a shadow organization going, in case it was needed, and to try to raise enough cash to pay the debts resulting from having sent thirty-five men back to Sydney and one to Panama.

Although some daring robberies continued, violent crime eased, and the town began to solidify its legal and political infrastructures. During the period between mid-1851 and late 1855, in fact, the whole complexion of San Francisco changed. The fields of tents and shacks surrounding its heart gave way to buildings and streets and to a far more diversified economy than had been possible when forty-niners ran all over the place with their little bags of gold. The disappearance of most of the gold prospectors was most probably directly responsible for the lessening rate of violent crime, although the Committee of Thirteen would probably have given another reason.

But throughout the period between 1851 and 1855 the staunchest of San Francisco's solid citizenry began to perceive a new danger—political prospectors. The system seemed to be getting rotten with corruption, starting in the upper political echelons and spreading downward into the city's administrative bureaucracy and courts. Taxes during that time increased to an astounding $4 of every $100, but the municipal treasury was somehow always empty. Creditors were paid by the city in scrip, which had a market value between 20 per cent and 30 per cent on the dollar. Firms doing business with the interior or the East Coast were losing money to banking houses in their own city and, therefore, were continually putting off their creditors. The architects of that state of affairs, or so it seemed, were the Irish political transplants from New York. Their basic tool was understood to be an ingeniously designed ballot box with false sides and bottom.

"The impudent vagabonds of low extraction who had seized the reins of government," writes Bancroft, "ruled the staid adherents to eastern morals as though they possessed some inherited right to such domination. With this doctrine they seem to have been impregnated, like Thracian mares, by the wind. But the very imprudence of their pretensions drew them on to swifter destruction. There are never lacking men as fond of power as the bear is of honey, who often get stung by thrusting their nose into a hornet's nest. It was the governing element in the community which most of all required governing."[15]

The object of Bancroft's multiple metaphor and of William T.

Coleman's growing anger was the eastern Irish liberal Democrats who had been moving into San Francisco's politics from the beginning of statehood, in 1850, but who by 1855 and '56 were posing a serious threat to the old establishment. Calling those men crooks is an oversimplification. They were transplants from the tough wards of Boston and New York and had learned on the streets that, since nobody was going to give them anything, they were going to have to take what they wanted.

The history of the United States has included a persistent bending or circumventing of establishment rules by whatever group has been shut out by them at a given time. That, in turn, has made for a state of constant adjustment and eventual accommodation (the Civil War being the most wrenching example). The Irish had their day at this nasty game. Where most of the San Francisco Irish politicos came from—the back rooms of Tammany Hall—politics was played hard and according to radical rules, not those laid down by the Anglo establishment to ensure its own survival. The young Irishmen who had found their way into Tammany Hall in the mid-1840s had taken refuge there from the racial and religious prejudices they had run into on the outside. The immigrants who flooded into New York and Boston, particularly after 1846, ran into determined and often vicious nativist bigotry, which shut them out of nearly all sectors of society and certainly out of the political one, since the Anglo-Saxon Protestants abhorred the thought of being governed by a pack of potato-picking papists. "Irish need not apply" was the recurrent last line on job advertisements, and the beating up of Irish youngsters eventually reached the proportions of an acknowledged outdoor sport.

So the "Micks" reacted cynically. They formed their own gangs and, like other minorities that have been forced to run the American social gantlet, became determined to rip off what no one was going to let them earn by honest means. They were shunned by other political groups, but not by the society of Saint Tammany, which facilitated their naturalization, provided relief, and offered a chance at a piece of the political, and therefore the financial, action. The young Irishmen often intimidated the opposition at the polls, packed primaries, committed fraud, and did anything else necessary to get a hand on the ladder. And, once in power, they fell back on the politician's traditional method of operation: the rewarding of friends and the punishing of enemies. Friends were handed jobs in government and business, and, in many instances, they paid monetary tribute for their plums. Enemies were smeared and extorted, because they had to be undermined and destroyed. The object of all this was simple: to maximize economic power, because having it was the only sure way they thought they could protect themselves from their entrenched enemies. That was the way the game was played in New York and Boston, and that was the way it was carried, by coach and clipper ship, to San Francisco's ripe precincts. But in California the leaders of the rough-and-tumble Irish urban proletariat ran into two formidable enemies, not just one: the Know-Nothings and the Vigilantes.

The Know-Nothing party evolved in the late 1840s as a nativist reaction to the Catholic flood. Know-Nothings saw the Catholics (especially the Irish, but also Germans and Italians) as streaming into their country, settling in enclaves, and exercising a great deal of political power, while, in many cases, not even being able to understand the language or the country they were infesting and corrupting. And since they were Catholics, the Know-Nothings assumed, they owed their first allegiance to the pope, not to the president. Where the nativists were concerned, this spelled subversion, and Irish power and corruption in New York and elsewhere only confirmed to the Know-Nothings that the papists were out to ravage America. The Know-Nothings, by the way, took their name from the fact that their movement was in the beginning secret and endorsed political slates accordingly. When asked whether he was a member of the movement, a man who was would answer, "I know nothing." The Know-Nothings surfaced in 1854, called themselves the American party, and carried elections in four New England states, Maryland, Kentucky, and California. They did not carry San Francisco, however, which by then was coming under Irish Democratic control.

The San Francisco Democrats were led by David Broderick, but, far from being a monolithic machine, they, too, were factionalized. One of the factions belonged to James P. Casey, who had come from New York in 1853 and had worked his way up as an assistant county treasurer and supervisor. James O'Meara, a journalist, knew Casey and described him as intelligent, neat, and having taken pride in a reasonably clean record in public office, which compared favorably with that of any of his successors. But Casey did stuff ballot boxes and engage in some fraudulent counting. Broderick stuffed ballot boxes. The Know-Nothings stuffed ballot boxes. Everyone stuffed ballot boxes, in fact, because everyone knew that everyone else did it, and it was therefore the only way to win elections. And winning elections opened the way to the public treasury. The Know-Nothings who went to the state capital on the American ticket in 1854 had jumped on the coffers. They used the money to overinvest at home and elsewhere and soon ran up debts they were unable to cover. With the constitutional power to create a state debt not exceeding $300,000, they produced one totaling $12 million. Funds that had been appropriated for land reclamation disappeared. Everybody had wanted to get in on it, because by 1854 everybody had understood that the real gold fields weren't around Sutter's Mill but in city halls and the state legislature. By the winter of 1855–56, then, San Francisco's urban proletariat and its Know-Nothing-oriented establishment had their horns locked, not over crime and corruption, but over which of them was going to get a crack at all that money.

James O'Meara, writing more than thirty years later, said that the crime rate in San Francisco in 1856 was substantially lower than it had been earlier or would become afterward. The courts, he said, contained many good and reasonably honest judges, and, although juries were packed regularly, that was the fault of the merchants who were to form the leadership of the second great Committee of Vigilance, not the fault of their Democratic opponents or the criminal class. The very same businessmen who joined the Vigilantes in 1856 didn't like serving on juries, explained the newspaperman, because time was money. Important civil and criminal cases usually dragged on, and the businessmen hated leaving their affairs while being locked up in some interminable trial. So if they couldn't get excused from jury duty they would pay their fines and leave the job to professional jurymen, all of whom were otherwise unemployed and always ready to be bribed. "The initial fault was attributable to themselves; the jury-packing they complained of was the direct consequence of their own neglect of the essential duty of the State, in the preservation of law and order; and they cannot reasonably or justly shift the onus from themselves upon the Courts."[16]

Further, while complaining that elections were a mockery of justice, with ballot-box stuffing, false counts, repeaters, and bullying, "more than one member of the Vigilance Executive Committee had thorough knowledge of all this, for the very conclusive reason that more than one of them had engaged in these frauds. . . . One of the Executive Committee had served his term of two years in the Ohio State Prison for forgery; here in San Francisco he had, during two city elections, been the trusted agent and disburser of a very heavy sack in the honest endeavor to secure the nomination, and promote the election, of his principal to high office; yet this pure man was honored by his associates of the Committee, and became singularly active in pressing the expatriation of some of the very 'ruffians and ballot-box stuffers' he had patronized and paid. He had learned that 'dead men told no tales.' "[17]

Which brings us back to that menace James King of William thought he saw after Charles Cora killed Marshal Richardson in November 1855. That menace was not just crime and corruption, but urban-Democratic, proletariat-style crime and corruption, as practiced by assorted Latins and by his newly arrived fellow Irishmen.

"Hang Billy Mulligan!" was the caption over a *Bulletin* editorial that ran a few days after Cora shot Richardson. "That's the word! If . . . the Sheriff does not remove Billy Mulligan from his present post as Keeper of the County Jail, and Mulligan lets Cora escape, hang Billy Mulligan, and if necessary to get rid of the Sheriff, hang him—hang the Sheriff!"[18] It was, for James King of William, a relatively restrained editorial.

Not only was James King of William in the habit of blasting the city's trashy and dangerous proletarian elements, much to the delight of his establishment readership, but he also liked to portray himself as a physically fearless knight of the fourth estate, ready—no, eager—to face death in defense of his lofty ideals. "God help my assailant!" he had once printed. Other times he dared those he didn't like to shoot it out with him and gave detailed instructions on the route he took to get from office to home every day. Probably because nobody in San Francisco in the 1850s talked like that unless he was prepared to back up what he said, James King of William had so far gone unchallenged. That, however, was about to change.

In order to further his own political career, James P. Casey had started his own newspaper, a weekly called the *Times*. He chose for his editor John C. Cremony, a respected writer who also edited the *Sun*. In reading the *Bulletin* every day, Cremony began to notice that, while King attacked other officeholders, he never attacked his brother's boss, Milton Latham, the chief of the Customs House. Thomas King, it turned out, worked there. And, Cremony found out after doing a little investigative work, that wasn't all. Thomas Sim King, alias "Slippery Sim," alias "Slant-eyed Tom," alias "the Nipper Kid," alias "Dead House Cove," was something of a black sheep. According to Ned McGowan, a ranking San Francisco Democrat who had met Tom King in Philadelphia in 1845, "Slippery Sim" had been arrested for robbing guests at the American Hotel there and, before that, had officiated in some capacity at his wife's brothel in Washington, D.C., their home town. Mr. and Mrs. King had eventually migrated to brother James's part of the country, and, while the elder King was launching his literary lightning bolts at the vile and debauched crooks in the Irish wards, the young King was landing a lovely job at the Customs House. His wife had by then dropped out of the prostitution business.

This was too good to ignore. Accordingly, Cremony seems to have written a "card," which appeared in the *Times* of May 11, 1856. In those days, a card was a statement of private opinion, usually not written by a staff member, and either unsigned or signed with a pseudonym. Cremony's having been holding down jobs on two newspapers would account for his using the card format. The card began by accusing the *Bulletin* of inconsistency in its condemnation of certain political appointments, and specifically of passing over anything having to do with the Customs House, where Thomas King "holds a lucrative position." The card ended by delicately charging that Thomas King had applied for the office of United States marshal of California but had lost out to a man named McDuffie and that the *Bulletin* had been slamming McDuffie ever since.[19]

Brother James, noting from his editorial chair that the city's high saloon society was laughing at him and his kid brother, decided to answer Casey's dirt with some of his own. The Broderick faction of the Democratic organization, which didn't like Casey, had some time before given James King an affidavit stating that Casey had once served time in New York's Sing Sing prison. It was, indeed, true. But the circumstances, which King ignored or failed to pursue, were extenuating. Casey had gone back to the apartment of a girl he had been living with, but with whom he had broken up, and reclaimed his furniture while she was out. Since he had paid the rent for the place, he was let in by the landlady and was soon driving off with his possessions. When the girl got home, though, she discovered that her former lover had thrown a few of her things on the wagon, too, so she went to police court and filed a complaint. James P. Casey was then arrested and spent the next eighteen months in Sing Sing. He came to California right after his parole. King probably knew all that, but, if he did, he ignored it in favor of publishing any damning evidence that would show what a scoundrel Casey was. Which brings us to the day of the big confrontation.

Having been warned of King's plans, Casey, who was very touchy about his stint in jail, went to the *Bulletin* office early on the afternoon of May 14, 1856, and demanded that King withhold the story. Bancroft, reconstructing the dialogue from the testimony of two people who were in the next room, gives it this way.

"What do you mean by that article?" [Casey] demanded.

"What article?" asked King.

"That which says I was formerly an inmate of Sing Sing prison."

"Is it not true?"

"That is not the question. I don't wish my past acts raked up; on that point I am sensitive."

"Are you done?" asked King. "There's the door: go! Never show your face here again."

Casey moved toward the door, which was open. There he paused a moment and burst forth again:

"I'll say in my paper what I please!"

"You have a perfect right to do so," returned King; "I shall never notice your paper."

Striking his breast with his hand, Casey now cried, "If necessary I shall defend myself!"

"Go!" exclaimed King, rising from his seat.

Casey immediately went down the stairs.[20]

At a few minutes before five o'clock, and with the *Bulletin* containing the story about Casey just off the press, James King of William left his one-story office building and started along his well-advertised route home. ("If we are to be shot or cut to pieces, for heaven's sake let it be done there," he had crowed in an editorial the previous December. "Others will not be injured, and in case we fall our house is but a few hundred yards beyond, and the cemetery not much farther.")[21] He walked up Merchant Street until coming to Montgomery, and then north to the corner of Montgomery and Washington, where, as was his habit, he went into a cigar store. He had just come out, intending to follow Washington Street home, when he heard James Casey, standing about forty feet away, shout, "Prepare yourself." A moment later Casey fired a single ball, which hit James King of William on the left side of his chest and came out on the other side.

"Oh God! I am shot!" screamed the wounded editor. Casey, who had taken the precaution of making out his will earlier that day because he thought King was as tough as he said he was, walked closer, his five-shot revolver still in hand. He saw King stagger toward the Pacific Express office, so he turned and walked away. "Seeing he did not fire and believing him a dung hill, I did not shoot again," Casey said later.[22]

While the stricken man was being helped into the express office, then undressed and helped onto a mattress, and was having his own pistol taken away, James Casey was being arrested by Deputy Sheriff Lafayette Byrne and a butcher named Peter Whiteman and taken to the police station, about a block away. Deputy Sheriff Byrne took a derringer from Casey, but let him hold on to the pistol that had been used on King. It was cocked.

The streets quickly filled with people shouting "Hang him, hang him; he'll get clear if the officers keep him."[23] With an angry mob close behind, Casey was rushed through the police station's front door. Someone inside, probably Sheriff Scannell, took the Colt from Casey, while City Marshal Hampton North and Fire Engineer Charles Duane ran with him out the back. They jumped into a carriage and were off to the sturdier county jail, on Broadway, where Charles Cora had been languishing for six months, after killing Richardson. Cora's trial had ended in a hung jury, largely because his common-law wife had bought the best available lawyers, and he now waited to be retried. He wouldn't have much longer to wait. Within three hours of James P. Casey's having shot James King of William, the largest vigilante organization in history had been formed and armed and was looking for blood.

Two organizations, in fact, gathered on the night of May 14, 1856: the Committee of Vigilance of San Francisco and a large, well-armed, Law and Order group, composed largely of proletariat-Irish moderators who expected trouble and who were preparing to defend the county jail. As twilight came, the streets of downtown San Francisco started filling with citizens rushing to different destinations. The sounds of angry muttering and the clatter of carriages could be heard and, beyond, the ominous pealing of the 1851 bell on top of the California Fire House.

At six-thirty, while there was still some light, Mayor Van Ness, standing bareheaded in front of the county jail, addressed a surging, deeply angry crowd. Behind him, strung out across the building's entrance, stood deputies and citizen volunteers clutching muskets with bayonets fastened. It was electric.

"You are here creating an excitement which may lead to occurrences this night which will require years to wipe out," said the Mayor. "You are now laboring under great excitement, and I advise you to quietly disperse. I assure you the prisoner is safe. Let the law have its course and justice will be done."

"How about Richardson?" someone shouted back.

"Where is the law in Cora's case?" another wanted to know.

"Down with such justice. Let's hang him."[24]

Another group of armed citizen volunteers appeared, along with the San Francisco Blues and other military companies, until by ten o'clock 300 men guarded the jail. Dirt was thrown at them, while Thomas King and others harangued the mob. A mounted battalion composed of the California Guard, the First Light Dragoons, and the National Lancers arrived at eleven-thirty to reinforce the Law and Order volunteers and the foot soldiers. By midnight, those who wanted to storm the jail saw that it would be impossible without great bloodshed, so they began to break up and drift into the night.

Samuel Brannan and other alumni of the committee of 1851 had not wasted time staying on the street. They had spent that evening meeting at a warehouse that belonged to one of them, drawing plans for the new vigilante organization. William T. Coleman, who was elsewhere, was put up for president. Coleman and a friend, anticipating all this, because it had been talked about for several weeks, were composing a call to arms for distribution to the newspapers, and trying to find a suitable place for an extremely large body of men to call their headquarters. It would turn out, of course, to be Fort Gunnybags. Since the basis for the new organization had been laid out in rough detail beforehand, developments immediately after James King of William's shooting went smoothly. The birth announcement of the second Committee of Vigilance of San Francisco appeared the next morning in four newspapers.

THE VIGILANCE COMMITTEE

The members of the Vigilance Committee, in good standing, will please meet at No. 105½ Sacramento street, this day, Thursday, 15th instant, at nine o'clock A.M.

By order of the   Committee of Thirteen[25]

Two hours after the meeting began, Coleman had formally accepted the presidency on condition that he be given absolute obedience and secrecy. He was smoothly enrolled as Number One and then chose his Executive Committee of twelve, giving the oath to the first six and letting someone else take it from there. More executives were to be added in the coming hours. A constitution, which had already been prepared, was duly ratified. Its preamble said, in part:

WHEREAS, It has become apparent to the citizens of San Francisco that there is no security for life and property, either under the regulations of society as it at present exists or under the laws as now administered, and that by the association together of bad characters our ballot-boxes have been stolen . . . and thereby our elections nullified, our dearest rights violated, and no other method left by which the will of the people can be manifested; therefore, the citizens whose names are hereunto attached do unite themselves into an association for the maintenance of the peace and good order of society, the prevention and punishment of crime, the preservation of our lives and property, and to insure that our ballot-boxes shall hereafter express the actual and unforged will of the majority of our citizens; and we do bind ourselves each unto the other by a solemn oath to do and perform every just and lawful act for the maintenance of law and order, and to sustain the law when faithfully and properly administered.[26]

"Just and lawful" acts, of course, were a matter of interpretation, as was the faithful and proper administration of law and order. In the same issue of the *Herald* that had carried the call to that first meeting, there had appeared an editorial condemning the Vigilantes. It had been written the night before by John Nugent after he agreed to publish, without charge, William Coleman's short announcement. Nugent had supported the committee of '51 but was emphatically against its successor because he didn't think it was needed.

We see that a number of highly respectable merchants—some of them our warm friends—have called a meeting of the old Vigilance Committee for nine o'clock this morning. We wish to be understood as most unqualifiedly condemning the movement.[27]

John Nugent's "warm friends," the crusaders for unbridled democracy, reacted to his editorial by pulling every copy of the *Herald* they could find off the newsstands or away from newsboys and burning them. They then launched an advertising boycott. Nugent's paper, which that morning had been the fattest in the city, was to be severely crippled within two weeks.

Throughout the rest of the fifteenth and into the sixteenth, the Committee of Vigilance moved from its temporary headquarters, at 105½ Sacramento, to the more spacious rooms down the street, at number 41. Guards were posted, officers were elected, men were assigned to combat units, sandbags were stacked, flags, drums, and the rest of the stuff were hung on the walls, cannons were found and dragged onto the premises, and close-order drilling was started among the growing legion of the curious, the naïve, the impressionable, and the malcontented who showed up to collect their secret identification numbers, ranks, and muskets. The Executive Committee, which also was growing by the hour, had meanwhile decided that James P. Casey was definitely going to swing for the murder of James King of William—a remarkable show of resolve, since King was still alive.

Fort Gunnybags was visited on the night of the sixteenth by Governor James Neely Johnson and his militia general for northern California, William Tecumseh Sherman. Besides commanding a sizable portion of the state's home guard, Sherman at the time was the manager of a Saint Louis banking house's branch office in Sacramento and therefore a solid establishmentarian. The Governor proposed to Coleman that Casey be tried in a court presided over by a Judge Norton, apparently well known as a neutral, and that the Vigilantes have the privilege of monitoring the selection of a jury. Fine, said Coleman. But then he added the proviso that some of his men be allowed to enter the county jail to ensure that Casey remained in custody. It's inconceivable that Governor Johnson and General Sherman didn't understand that the problem was not keeping Casey in jail, but keeping out the people who wanted to kill him. The Governor nonetheless agreed to Coleman's terms and, in so doing, as much as signed Casey's order of execution.

On Sunday, the eighteenth, Governor Johnson, General Sherman, hundreds of members of the Law and Order moderator faction, at least as many Vigilantes, and other citizens of San Francisco looked on while a regiment of Vigilantes advanced on the county jail. A cannon was rolled up and pointed at the door, behind which stood 106 armed Law and Order men, the Sheriff, and a group of deputies. The leader of the Vigilantes ordered the Sheriff to turn over Casey and Cora. Scannell refused. After several long minutes of threats and counterthreats, the Sheriff backed down, the heavy door swung open, and the Vigilantes stepped inside. Coleman and another member of the Executive Committee led their men into the cell block and shortly emerged with James P. Casey. The avengers of the city's good and defenseless folk loaded Casey onto a carriage and took him directly to Fort Gunnybags; Charles Cora followed an hour later. Left behind, in another cell, was Rod Backus, the young cousin of a prominent auctioneer, who had murdered a German he had never seen before because a prostitute Backus liked had told him that the German had insulted her. Backus had simply gone out and shot the German in Stout's Alley; he had shot him from a distance of twelve feet. But Rod Backus was left unmolested by the leaders of the anticrime crusade when they took Casey and Cora away.

The trials took place in secret inside Fort Gunnybags. Both were complicated, Cora's because even the Vigilante jury was hung on the question of his guilt, getting a bare majority for execution when two-thirds was required, and Casey's for the very obvious and undoubtedly embarrassing reason that there had as yet been no murder. That knotty problem was reconciled at 1:45 on the afternoon of the twentieth, however, when James King of William finally died—some said because of medical incompetence. Casey was promptly pronounced guilty and sentenced to hang, and, in order to make it a more spectacular double execution, the two-thirds rule was suspended and Charles Cora was given the same sentence. "Had they confessed to their following that they could do no better than an authorized court," said one of the chroniclers of the incident, referring to the Executive Committee, "they would have had to quit."[28]

Vigilantes tend to have a definite flair for the dramatic, and those in San Francisco in 1856 were no exception. They lynched Casey and Cora early on the afternoon of Thursday, May 22, while James King of William's funeral procession was passing along Montgomery Street. And the hangings were as impressive, in their way, as the editor's funeral. Both prisoners spent the morning talking with friends, while the guards around the committee rooms were strengthened, companies of infantry were sent out to form a block-long line in front of Gunnybags, and cavalry was paraded up and down the nearby thoroughfares, undoubtedly to discourage any last-minute attempt by the Law and Order group to rescue the prisoners. The Law and Order crowd, by the way, was heavily Irish. Other Vigilantes, as well as curious spectators, lined the roofs for a good view of the show, while the crowd on Sacramento Street kept watching the windows and chatting excitedly, the way people tend to do before the curtain goes up at a hit show. The planks extended three feet beyond the windows from which they had been pushed, and soon afterward beams came sliding out over either plank from the roof. There were nooses at the ends of both beams. By the time they were ready to walk their planks, Casey and Cora had said good-bye to their friends, seen priests, and taken care of their final affairs. One of Casey's had been the writing of a short note.

San Francisco, May 22, 1856, half after twelve

To John Nugent:
you have not Judge me to gratify the publick may god bless you. If you will pleas to see Estell, Farley, Alderman, Peckham, and others, you may yet satisfy the Publick you are right. I am innocent of murder or an attempt. Farewell. For my mother sake save my name in New York.

James P. Casey[29]

At 1:15 a white paper was dropped from one of the upper windows, signaling the guard facing the crowd below to present arms (they had been taught how to do that). Casey's and Cora's shackles were taken off and were replaced by cords. A white handkerchief was placed over Charles Cora's head and tied around his neck. Before another could be laid over Casey's head, he asked for permission to address his audience, and did so standing on his plank—the left plank. His face was pale and his eyes bloodshot. Cora remained silent under his handkerchief a few yards to Casey's right.

"Gentlemen, I am not a murderer. I do not feel afraid to meet my God on a charge of murder," Casey said, his voice quivering.

"I have done nothing but what I thought was right. Tomorrow let no editor dare to call me a murderer. Whenever I was injured I have resented it. It had been a part of my education, during an existence of 29 years. Gentlemen, I forgive you this persecution. Oh, God. My poor mother. Oh, God."[30]

Casey stepped back and was hooded and roped. As Sterling Hopkins, the hangman, drew the handkerchief down over Casey's head, he whispered something in his ear, causing the young Irishman to struggle violently for a moment, as if trying to tear open the cord binding his hands so he could get at his executioner. A minute later, though, the traps were sprung, the hinges folded, and the Italian gambler and the Irish politician dropped about six feet. Cora fell like a sack of potatoes and stayed that way, probably because his neck had broken instantly. But James P. Casey, feisty to the last, jerked around for several seconds as he strangled in front of the silent crowd. Then he went limp.

Encouraged by its success, the Committee of Vigilance now moved to consolidate its power and break the back of David Broderick's Democratic organization. After the double execution, Governor Johnson and General Sherman seem to have come to understand that the committee was in control of San Francisco, but it was too late to do much about it. General John Ellis Wool, the United States Army's commander of the Department of California, was a Vigilante sympathizer, but couldn't have acted against them, anyway, without authorization from Washington. And the War Department's official policy was to let states take care of their own problems, particularly where potential combat with citizens was involved. Wool agreed to give Sherman arms for the militia to use against the Vigilantes, if that should have proved necessary, but, after considering the matter, changed his mind. Captain David G. Farragut, the acting commodore of the Navy's Pacific Squadron, likewise did nothing, pending orders from Washington. The preponderance of strength in the summer of 1856 therefore belonged to the Committee of Vigilance. And that strength was used.

Between midnight and 3:00 A.M. on June 21, ten to twelve Vigilantes allegedly boarded the sloop *Julia*, anchored off San Pablo Point, and relieved its crew of 113 muskets and cavalry swords destined for Governor Johnson. At a trial for piracy instigated in September by the Law and Order party, the boarders were quoted as having said that they came by order of the Vigilance Committee and that they were trying to prevent the weapons from falling into the hands of the militia or the Law and Order group. A jury found the suspected leader of the "pirates," a fellow named Durkee, not guilty. According to the *San Francisco Morning Globe* of September 13, a crowd of 4,000 cheering San Franciscans, led by a band, greeted the news outside the United States circuit court. William Blanding, the United States district attorney who prosecuted the case, was soon dismissed by Attorney General Jeremiah S. Black for being sympathetic to the Vigilantes. Blanding hotly denied the charge, but to no avail. Not for the last time, Washington was frustrated and embarrassed by vigilante activity, but could do next to nothing to prevent it; the thirty-one states, after all, were sovereign and therefore jealously guarded their right to control their own affairs.

By the end of July, two more men had been publicly hanged, and another, Francis Murray "Yankee" Sullivan, had died in his cell of mysterious stab wounds, while awaiting a Vigilante trial for deportation. The hanged men, Philander Brace and Joseph Hetherington, had been found guilty of murder. The deportation list included William Mulligan, Martin Gallagher, Charles Duane, Wooley Kearny, John Coony, William Carr, T. B. Cunningham, Terence Kelly, James Hennessey, John Lawler, William Lewis, Francis Murray, Thomas Mulloy, Jack McGuire, William Hamilton, John Crowe, and Alexander Purple. All were sent to New York or Hawaii. Still others, including Ned McGowan, Broderick's onetime judge and police chief, fled before capture. No one knows exactly how many were thrown out of California or sneaked out any way they could.

By the end of August, then, David Broderick's organization had been smashed. And on that note the San Francisco Committee of Vigilance laid down its muskets and put away its drums and cannons. Although the Executive Committee wanted its military arm available in a kind of reserve capacity, marching soldiers weren't going to be needed for the next phase of the vigilante reaction—serious politics.

The committee's last meeting was held on August 18, 1856, followed a few days later by a grand review, staged near South Park, in which the entire Vigilante army paraded behind snapping flags and drawn swords. It was an awe-inspiring sight. Then there was an open house at Fort Gunnybags. Thousands of men, women, and children wandered through the Vigilante museum to see the trick ballot boxes, cells, unused nooses and those that had held the necks of Cora, Casey, Brace, and Hetherington, unit banners, fifes, drums, and that pervasive watchful eye. Commemorative medals would eventually be struck for display on desks and mantels, use as watch fobs, and presents for grandsons entering manhood. The great San Francisco committee, after all, had become famous, as newspapers throughout the United States and even in Europe showed.

The *Washington Star* praised the committee, saying that it had resorted to "the first law of nature, to the right of self-protection." The *New Orleans Delta* agreed, charging that "in New Orleans the murderer would remain unpunished. . . . But in San Francisco it is different. The people are stronger than the bullies and the gamblers, and accordingly the respectable citizens, the merchants and property-holders, turned out and demanded the New Yorker who murdered King from the hands of the sheriff, and have probably hanged him before now. They did right."

"When assassins of influence are enabled to twist the legal meshes so as to suit their own operations," said the *New York Sunday Times*, "when they can openly put those to death, with the bowie-knife or the bullet, whose honesty they fear or whose presence is embarrassing, what can a community do but fall back on its natural rights, and personally maintain that standard of peremptory justice which the exigency demands and the authorities are too corrupt to enforce?"

Expressions of distaste came from the *New York Commercial Advertiser,* which said that "the thing is radically wrong. Once let it be established that private citizens, whatever their number and respectability, may take the administration of justice into their own hands . . . and a despotism ensues more oppressive and cruel than that of any individual sovereignty." And, perhaps most poignantly, the *New York National Democrat* noted that "if the same energy which prompted the formation of the Committee and organized the armed force that assaulted the jail had been directed to strengthen the regular course of justice as public opinion can do, there would have been no need for the outbreak."[31]

The Committee of Vigilance of San Francisco went on to bigger things, after spending the period between August 18 and the fall elections turning itself into a finely honed political machine. Having broken and scattered the opposition, the committee held what amounted to a self-constituted nominating convention. Vigilance candidates running under the banner of the *ad hoc* People's party were victorious across the board; they were entered in virtually every municipal contest and won all of them. The People's party also sent representatives to the state legislature. Not long after the beginning of Vigilante political supremacy, business taxes were lowered to the point where some schools were forced to close. The establishment had managed to hang on.

6

Montana: 3-7-77—
"You are as good
as dead"

HENRY PLUMMER probably would have made it big back east, where society was more sophisticated than it was in Montana during the Civil War, and where public servants had more subtle and complicated ways of bilking those they were paid to serve. Plummer might have become the mayor of Providence, the chief of police of New York, the most powerful political boss in Baltimore, or even a senator from any of those places. He undoubtedly would have made a lot of money awarding municipal contracts to friends and relatives, taking bribes, and masterminding sophisticated shakedowns. He might well have ended his life as the founding father of a great moneyed dynasty and perhaps even have built a college dormitory on a New England campus to perpetuate his name forever. Plummer Hall.

As it turned out, though, Henry Plummer vented his genius for organized crime in the wilds of what is now southwestern Montana, where people tended to accumulate wealth with their hands and solve their problems with ropes and guns, not with writs and attorneys. And Henry Plummer was one of them, too, although surely a cut above most. He was at the same time the leader of a large and disciplined band of road agents that plundered and killed residents of the area and the sheriff paid by those very people to protect them from desperadoes. You might, therefore, say that Plummer's civic responsibility was to catch himself, while his livelihood depended on his eluding himself. Plummer managed to reconcile that contradiction quite nicely for a while, but then the people who had been victimized or thought they were going to be victimized by the outlaw-lawman decided to stop him. Depending on the size of his bank account and the quality of his connections, Henry Plummer might have gotten ten to twenty years in Providence, New York, or Baltimore and probably would have been paroled after five for good behavior. When they caught Plummer in Bannack, early in January 1864, however, they just took him out and hanged him, on a gallows he had built for someone else. The men who hanged him knew that what they were doing was illegal, of course, but none of them worried about it very much. After all, the instant he died there was no longer a sheriff within a hundred miles.

Very few people except the Indians who lived there really cared about Montana until 1858, when gold was discovered. Lewis and Clark had passed through in April 1805, on their way to the Oregon country, and were followed by a scattering of fur trappers, "black robe" Catholic missionaries using Iroquois interpreters to bring Christ to the Sioux, and a few pioneers who felt they couldn't breathe in the congested rural areas of Illinois, Ohio, Kentucky, Tennessee, and elsewhere. Those people really needed room, and they found it in Montana's mountainous central and western reaches, where 10,000-foot peaks rose out of thick pine forests and canyons with sheer drops of 500 feet or more held in winding rivers of white water impossible or nearly impossible to navigate. Montana was then, as it still is, a hard land of bitter winters, often tortuous terrain, and people spread far enough apart so that they tended to function individually, rather than as members of groups. It was, in short, ideal country for bandits.

Gold was discovered in 1858 by James and Granville Stuart, and, while abolitionists and proslavers were squaring off for their war in the East, prospectors began moving into the territory with their picks, pans, and mules. Four years later, while the Northern and Southern armies were pounding each other senseless and communities on the fringes of the fighting were splitting over whether to throw in their lots with Washington or Richmond, a big strike was made on Grasshopper Creek, in the Beaverhead country. The town of Bannack was created in a matter of weeks and became filled with people from all over the war zone who preferred being rich to getting killed, plus others, from the Pacific region, who had gotten to California too late to find much besides fool's gold. One of the richest lodes in history was found at Alder's Gulch in 1863, and that was the reason for Virginia City, another town of canvas tents and rough log cabins, which rivaled Bannack in size, minimal creature comforts, and crime. Montana in 1862 and '63 was northern California all over again, but with a significant difference: there was no port city through which filtered the dressy dudes—doctors, lawyers, politicians, poets, teachers, importers, and others—carrying eastern sophistication and the attendant concept of white-gloved social stability. They were the ones who had carried silk ties, sauerbraten, and Socrates to San Francisco. But they weren't in Montana in the beginning of the 1860s, at least in numbers that mattered, so the country—at that time part of the sprawling Idaho Territory—was raw from men and women pushing one another and the Indians out of the way, by any means possible, so they could get at the gold.*

Bannack in 1862 was a boom town of tents and cabins of various sizes, separated by dirt streets and usually permeated by the sounds of raucous shouting and laughter, music of sorts, and gunfire. Saloons and hurdy-gurdy dance halls opened in the afternoon, as the miners got off work, and closed as dawn approached. "Tangle-leg," "Forty-rod," "Lightning," "Tarantula-juice," and other respected labels were uncorked and poured by the gallon every night, at 25 cents to 50 cents a shot, while "orchestras" that were noticeably strong on fiddles and uprights, but very weak elsewhere, screeched and pounded through the roll-your-own tobacco haze. Men who were hitting pay dirt in the

---

* The fur trappers and traders and the missionaries, who respectively wanted Sioux, Cheyenne, and other tribes' pelts and souls, treated them decently. But, since the miners didn't need the Indians, they treated them badly and often brutally. The miners' invasion of the Sioux Black Hills reserve in 1876 was to lead to the battle of the Little Big Horn and the sensational annihilation of five companies of the Seventh Cavalry.

mountains gladly paid hurdy-gurdy girls $1 in gold for a dance and refreshed their high-stepping partners with a bubbly liquid alleged to be champagne and costing $12 a bottle (also payable in dust or nuggets). Thomas J. Dimsdale, a wide-eyed and impressionable Oxford-educated Englishman who had come to Montana by way of Canada and who chronicled the bloodshed that had by then already started and was to build to a crescendo during the winter of 1863–64, described the hurdy-gurdy girl as a first-class dancer and a delight to behold. "She is of middle height, of rather full and rounded form; her complexion as pure as alabaster, a pair of dangerous looking hazel eyes, a slightly Roman nose, and a small and prettily formed mouth."[1] She was probably also the owner of more dust and nuggets than most of her grizzled customers had.

Gold then, as now, was more valuable than paper and was therefore more welcome than greenbacks, which were popularly known as "Lincoln skins," after the politician in Washington. In the early 1860s, Alder Gulch gold was commonly called "Virginia dust" and was worth $18 an ounce because of its purity. A man paid for his drink by allowing the bartender to take a pinch of dust out of his bag. Most bartenders therefore had long fingernails. In the late '60s, one man bought a saloon in Virginia City, burned it down, and hired two assistants to sift through the ashes while he stood guard, day and night, with a shotgun. Ten days later, the story goes, he owned $10,000 in dust that had dropped through the cracks in the floor.

In the autumn of 1863, sugar was selling for 60 cents a pound in Bannack and Virginia City. Raisins and potatoes were $1 a pound; eggs cost $1.50 a dozen, were scarce, and probably were never fresh. Who would want to collect eggs when almost everyone else was collecting gold? Butter cost about $3 a pound in the winter of 1864, and the newly published *Montana Post* went for 50 cents a copy. In 1865, coaches were making the bone-rattling, 475-mile trip from Salt Lake City to Bannack and Virginia City in four days; the fare was $225 (one way), with twenty-five pounds of free baggage and the excess pegged at $1.50 a pound. Passengers were prohibited from carrying considerable quantities of gold on the coaches, because of the threat of highwaymen, and therefore had to use the express service for transporting their riches.[2]

The judicial system in the Montana mining towns paralleled that in California in 1848–49, and even included miners' courts copied directly from those around San Francisco and Sacramento. And, as had been the case during California's first days, as well as elsewhere on the frontier, due process amounted to an in joke. "No matter what may be the proof," Dimsdale complained, "if the criminal is well liked in the community, 'not guilty' is almost certain to be the verdict of the jury, despite the efforts of the judge and prosecutor. If an offender is a moneyed man, as well as a popular citizen, the trial is only a farce—grave and prolonged, it is true, but capable of only one termination—a verdict of acquittal."[3]

Montana in 1862 and '63 was on the verge of becoming a separate territory of the United States, from which statehood would be the next logical step. As elsewhere, territoriality and then blessed statehood would work to the advantage of the landed interests, because federal laws would have a stabilizing effect, better judges and lawmen would arrive, serious participation in Washington politics could be started to help the area's communications and transportation, and closer ties with the eastern financial establishment would get under way. All those things would allow the Montana establishment to build on what it already had. The solid citizens of Bannack, Virginia City, Lewiston (which, of course, was to end up in the state of Idaho), and the other mining towns strung along the gold-strike area were therefore looking forward to a closer relationship with the United States of America and were conscious of the fact that they did not yet really belong to it. It seems strange today to read newspaper accounts of Montanans in 1863 who traveled from Montana to the United States. At any rate, concern over their being admitted as a separate territory and then as a state was among the reasons why the notables' frustration grew into desperation when they looked around, in 1863, and saw a country filled with two-bit gunslingers, drunken rowdies, petty thieves, crooked gamblers, what we would call muggers, and a gang of bandits and killers. The gang was worst of all. Its guiding hand belonged to Henry Plummer, their sheriff, a man who, years after his appropriate and altogether timely execution, would be elevated to folk-hero status, along with the James and Dalton brothers and such homicidal maniacs as Wild Bill Hickok, Wyatt Earp, John

Wesley Hardin, and Billy the Kid. Many peoples have produced Jesse Jameses and Billy the Kids; only North Americans would recast their violent lives as ballets, as has recently been done by American and Canadian dance companies.

So far as dapper Henry Plummer was concerned, though, guns were secondary. His strength came primarily from his head, which radiated a charm and charisma to which both men and women responded, and which contained an organizational ability unequaled in the annals of western outlaws. Henry Plummer stood about five feet ten inches and weighed between 150 and 160 pounds, making him trim but not lean. He had solid features, blue eyes, and chestnut-brown hair barely tinged with red. He also sported a mustache, which was always carefully trimmed. A daughter of Sidney Edgerton, Montana's first governor, met Plummer in Bannack when she was thirteen and later described him this way: "Plummer looked like a gentleman, that's what he looked like. He looked more like a gentleman than any man in Bannack. He never wore buckskins and his clothes were always clean and pressed. He kept his hands clean, too, and I never saw him when he seemed to need a shave. Of course, I saw him only when he was, you might say, on his good behavior; but I can remember that his voice was low and pleasant and that he never used any of the slangy talk of the miners or their rough expressions. He had a bow and a pleasant smile for every woman he met on the street, and the same for men. He had the reputation of being the best dancer in Bannack. Everybody liked him."[4] Well, not exactly everybody.

Plummer's origins are uncertain, but have been narrowed to either Boston or somewhere in Connecticut, where he apparently learned baking and gambling, both of which were honorable professions in nineteenth-century America. He turned up in Nevada City, in eastern California, in 1852, undoubtedly having been lured by the gold strikes, but instead of mining, he opened the Empire Bakery with a partner named Henry Hyer. He had made enough friends by 1856 to be elected town marshal, but not enough to get him to Sacramento as a state assemblyman running on the Democratic ticket the following year.

While serving as marshal, Plummer had an affair with a Mrs. Vedder and was caught in the act by Mr. Vedder, who attacked

131

Vigilante!

him. Marshal Plummer shot and killed the enraged man, and was promptly arrested, tried, and found guilty.* An appeal to the state supreme court was successfully made, however, when it was demonstrated that before the trial one of the jurors had loudly let it be known that hanging was too good for the likes of a home wrecker such as Henry Plummer. He was therefore re-tried in Yuba County and sentenced to ten years in the peniten-tiary, but was then pardoned by Governor John P. Weller after friends and admirers of the suave marshal convinced Weller that Plummer was dying of tuberculosis. Weller doesn't seem to have checked the story.

When he returned to Nevada City, Plummer opened the La-fayette and United States Bakeries, had another affair with a Spanish or Mexican woman, and severely pistol-whipped some-one during a brawl in a rowdy section of town. Since his victim seemed to have recovered from the beating, charges were not made, but the man did die two years later of complications re-sulting from the incident. A few weeks after the brawl, Plummer and some friends tried to hold up a Wells Fargo stage in Nevada's Washoe Valley, but their debut as road agents was ludicrous. Plummer planned his holdup according to universally accepted procedure. He selected a shotgun because the coach-man would know that his chances of being hit by a cluster of pellets were greater than of being hit by a single ball. Still going by the book when the big day came, Henry Plummer shouted "Hands up" to the driver as he smoothly swung his shotgun in the proper direction. That's when both of its barrels fell off. The incredulous driver, of course, applied his whip and disappeared in a cloud of dust, leaving Henry to pick up his barrels and snap them back onto the piece of wood in his hand. He was duly arrested and tried for attempted robbery, but got another acquit-tal, this time for lack of evidence. The next court appearance came during the winter of 1860–61, when he was tried and con-victed of murdering a man named Ryder during a vicious quarrel over two prostitutes. Plummer's friends came to the rescue again and smuggled pistols into his cell. He used them to walk out of

* Note that, the San Francisco Vigilantes' claims notwithstanding, Nevada City's marshal was dealt with quickly, indicating a relatively efficient law-enforcement and judicial system. It's hard to believe that Nevada City, which was much smaller than San Francisco, was the only municipality in the state that had such a system.

the jail in broad daylight. With lawmen and assorted vigilantes increasingly aware of his presence, though, it was clearly time for Henry Plummer to get out of California.

After a brief stop at Walla Walla, in the Oregon country (where he seduced another married woman and sent a rumor back to California describing how he had been hanged with a confederate), he pushed on to Lewiston, which wasn't very far from Bannack and Virginia City. And, like the two Montana towns, Lewiston was the parasite community of Orofino, another important digging area.

It was in Lewiston that Henry Plummer's latent organizational ability flourished. He collected every bandit and cutthroat he could find and turned them into the largest and probably the most efficient gang of highwaymen in American history. Plummer's men numbered between fifty and a hundred at any given time, all of them garden-variety badmen such as could be found almost anywhere in the West at that time. What made their escapades the model for countless pulp stories and dime novels, however, was the fact that Henry Plummer got his collection of semiliterate, mean-minded, often independent saddle bums to obey his instructions. Furthermore, he worked out real plans and pulled them off. The plans were so well worked out and so well executed, in fact, that several of his men became rich enough to buy their own ranches (which they stocked with rustled cattle).

Like any aspiring executive, Henry Plummer started small and expanded as quickly as possible. Toward the end of the summer of 1862, he was big enough to set up two large hide-outs, called shebangs, and a network of smaller ones for temporary use or for times of emergency. One of the shebangs was located about twenty-five miles outside Lewiston, just off the main road to Walla Walla; the other was at the foot of Craig's Mountain, on the other side of town and in the direction of Orofino and, beyond it, Bannack and Virginia City. Plummer's men were therefore able to hit traffic coming and going. The strongholds commanded the thoroughfare linking several of the most important towns in the Idaho-Montana gold-mining belt. Operating out of them, Plummer's boys pounced on mule trains, coaches, express riders, and individuals on horseback or in carriages, picked them clean, and disappeared into the mountainous terrain protecting the shebangs. First in Lewiston and then in Bannack, Plummer would get information on gold shipments or wealthy travelers moving through his area and relay what he had learned to his men in the shebangs, and the deed was as good as done. He used the card table to get information in Lewiston; in Bannack, he used his badge. Coaches carrying gold were given special secret marks that were visible from hundreds of yards and were hit accordingly. Information was sent to the shebangs by gang members who wore their bandannas tied with a distinctive kind of sailor's knot that everyone in the gang would recognize. Plummer planted an "innocent" in every major mining camp in the district to keep him advised of large shipments and any individuals who had struck it rich. "Innocent," in fact, was the gang's recognition word. For two years, starting in the winter of 1861–62 and continuing throughout 1863, serious crimes were an almost daily occurrence in and around the mining towns.

"The number of robberies and murders committed by the banditti will never be known," wrote Nathaniel Pitt Langford, one of the men who formed the first Montana vigilante group and the author of a book about its exploits. "The danger which every man incurred of being robbed or killed was demonstrated by numerous escapes made by horsemen who had been assaulted and fired upon, and escaped by the fleetness of their horses. It was fully understood that whoever passed over either of these roads would have to run the gauntlet in the neighborhood of the shebangs, and people generally went prepared. . . . The country itself, about equally made up of mountains, foot-hills, canyons, dense pine forests, lava beds, and deep river-channels, was as favorable for the commission of crime as for the concealment of its perpetrators."[5]

The Grasshopper strike that created Bannack in 1862 attracted Plummer and elements of his Lewiston gang, who simply moved their sector of operations a bit to the east. There was a great deal of crime in and around Bannack when Plummer and his men got there, so his main task in the beginning was settling in and taking over. This he accomplished with formidable efficiency. Before long, good old Henry Plummer, the Lewiston gambler who made friends wherever he went, was directing attacks against the miners and merchants in the area and then offering sage and sympathetic advice to the victims, many of whom began turning to him before turning anywhere else. Within a few months of his arrival in Bannack, Henry Plummer's ingratiating personality, courtly manner, good looks, and better-than-average education had won him many friends and admirers among the town's respectables. His accomplices—bandits and killers like Charley Reeves, Billy Bunton, Cyrus Skinner, Jack Gallagher, Bill Hunter, and Steve Marshland—treated him with easy familiarity in public, but never with comradeship. Only one man among the outlaws who drifted into Bannack late in 1862 posed a threat to Plummer. The man's name was Jack Cleveland, and he was not to remain a threat for long.

Cleveland had once been friends with Henry Plummer, but since quarreling over a woman they had become enemies. Cleveland had known Plummer in the Nevada City days, in Oregon, and in Lewiston. He therefore knew about the murders of Vedders and Ryder, about Plummer's criminal activities in Oregon, and about the gang in Lewiston. And, as Henry Plummer and others knew, Jack Cleveland liked to drink, and when he drank he talked a lot. Even sober, though, Cleveland made no secret of why he had come to Bannack. "Plummer's my meat," he liked to brag. When the threats were carried back to the handsome man about town, the likable target of that loudmouth's foul tongue, he would answer with something like "I'm not looking for trouble, but he knows where to find me if he wants me bad enough." Henry Plummer seemed like such a nice young man. But behind his demure expression there was a brain that knew Jack Cleveland had to be taken care of before it was too late. It was only a matter of waiting for the right moment.

The moment came on the morning of January 14, 1863, as Plummer and some others sat around the wood-burning stove in Goodrich's saloon sipping hot Tom and Jerrys and talking about the bitter weather. It was too early in the day for poker, roulette, or faro, so they just sat passing the time in idle conversation. Then the door was thrown open, letting in a gust of cold air and Jack Cleveland, who was already drunk but who nevertheless headed right for the bar. Ivan Moore, Jeff Perkins, Henry Crawford (who was going to be the next sheriff), and Henry Phleger were sitting near the stove with Plummer. George Ives, a young punk from Wisconsin who liked horses, specialized in robbing coaches, and had a habit of asking shopkeepers for small "loans" at gunpoint, lounged against the bar. Another man was dozing in a barber's chair in the corner.

"I know 'em all," said Cleveland, as he swallowed a drink. "I know every son of a bitch that's come over here from the other side of the mountains. They're trying to freeze me out, but I'll get some of 'em yet. I'm the chief around here, and I'll fight any son of a bitch that says I'm not." Henry Plummer watched Cleveland and the two Navy Colts hanging from his gun belt and undoubtedly thought about the ones he was carrying.

Then Cleveland recognized Jeff Perkins, who, he thought, owed him $40. He told Perkins to pay him the money. Perkins answered quietly that he had paid his debt at Fort Hall. "If you have, it's all right," said Cleveland, who nevertheless pulled one of the large revolvers halfway out of its holster and said again that Perkins owed him the money. Plummer saw his chance. He told Jack Cleveland to let the matter drop. As the drunken man turned toward the new voice, Perkins, who was unarmed, slipped out of the saloon to get his own guns after whispering to Henry Crawford that he was going to return and kill Cleveland. Jack Cleveland again turned and saw Perkins walk quickly out of the place.

"There he goes," Cleveland shouted. "He's afraid of me. All you sons of bitches are afraid of me, but I ain't scared of a damned one of you." He was standing in the middle of the room now, facing Plummer and keeping his back to the bar. Plummer was still sitting on one of the benches near the stove. He must have figured that this chance to silence Cleveland was as good as any he was about to get; his former friend was drunk, nasty, and threatening to hurt or kill somebody.

"I'm tired of this," Plummer said at last. He stood, drew one of his revolvers, and fired twice, hitting Jack Cleveland in the torso. Cleveland pitched forward, landed on his knees, and started groping for his revolvers while begging Plummer not to shoot again—not to shoot while he was down. "I won't," answered Plummer dryly. "Get up on your feet." Cleveland obliged, whereupon Plummer fired two more rounds, one of which went into the wall above the barber's chair and the other into Jack Cleveland's head, just under his left eye. He went down again.

While Jack Cleveland, who was dying, was taken to Henry Crawford's cabin by Crawford and Phleger, George Ives and Charley Reeves, guns in hand, escorted Plummer to his own cabin, where all waited for word of Cleveland's death. It came a few hours later. Several times that day, however, Henry Plummer was to ask Crawford whether Jack Cleveland had said anything about him before he died; each time, Crawford assured Plummer that Cleveland hadn't so much as mentioned his name. But Henry Plummer was not entirely convinced, and he therefore decided that at the appropriate time Henry Crawford would have to be taken care of, too.[6]

The residents of Bannack were still talking about Jack Cleveland's death when, five days later, there were more killings—this time, really tragic ones. Earlier in January, Charley Reeves, who was developing into one of Plummer's finest and most dependable killers, had bought a squaw belonging to the Sheep Eater tribe of Bannack Indians, part of which was camped on a low rise at the south end of town. Reeves treated the woman brutally, so she left him on January 18 and went back to her people. Reeves tried to retrieve her. He tried to convince her, in the presence of an old chief, that she should return to his cabin, and when she refused he became violent. The old chief finally threw Reeves out of his tepee.

Reeves and another of Plummer's band, named Bill Moore, walked into Goodrich's the next morning, laid two shotguns and four revolvers on the bar, and started drinking. The cowardly whites in Bannack might be afraid of Indians, they said, while putting away several glasses of whiskey, but they weren't. They weren't afraid of a few Sheep Eaters. Finally, both men left the saloon, went to the Indian encampment, and fired into the chief's tepee, wounding an Indian. But that wasn't enough. They returned to Goodrich's for three more drinks apiece, picked up another drunken gunman, named William Mitchell, and again marched on the Indians. All three satisfied themselves by punching holes in the chief's tepee with their revolvers. They made a lot of holes. When they stopped shooting, the old chief, a lame brave, an infant, and a Frenchman named Cazette, who had become curious and gotten too close, were dead, and two other bystanders were seriously wounded. When the three gunmen were told that they had killed a white man, Bill Moore replied that "the damned sons of bitches had no business there."[7]

Even the hardened residents of Bannack were appalled by the slaughter of Cazette and the three Indians. A mass meeting was held that night at which it was decided to capture Moore, Reeves, and Mitchell and put them on trial. When members of the citizens' group went to collect the three, however, they found that they had already fled. And so, it turned out, had likable Henry Plummer, although the townspeople thought he was only missing. The angry men of Bannack, having seen one helpless white and three Indians murdered and the killers slip through their fingers, decided to send a four-man posse in pursuit. That tiny posse was the embryo of the vigilance committee that was to form the following December and become one of the deadliest organizations of its kind in American history.

Plummer had left Bannack ahead of his men, probably to arrange a hide-out for them. In their haste to get out of town, though, Moore, Reeves, and Mitchell had not bothered about horses, but had gone on foot. All four were tracked from horseback over mountains covered with snow, making the tracking easier, and were finally located in a willow grove on the bank of the Rattlesnake River, about twelve miles from Bannack. After some shots had been exchanged, the men in the posse saw that the advantage lay with their quarry among the trees, so they decided to bargain. It soon became apparent to everyone that they were stalemated; those in the posse would get mauled trying to rush the willow grove, but those inside didn't have a prayer of getting out on foot in that weather. Henry Plummer and his men therefore agreed to return to Bannack with the posse, provided they were guaranteed a jury trial. That suited the posse just fine.

Plummer was the first to go on trial—Plummer and his agile mind. He explained that he had run from Bannack because he thought the posse wanted to hang him for killing Jack Cleveland. He explained in the most passionate way that, since the townspeople were in an ugly mood because of the tepee incident, he'd thought he hadn't had a chance and had therefore panicked. Plummer then called witnesses who testified that he had killed Cleveland in self-defense. He was acquitted after his succession of honest witnesses recounted how they had heard Cleveland threaten to kill him and how Cleveland had been mean drunk the morning Plummer gunned him down. All that was perfectly true. And, besides, nobody had really liked nasty Jack Cleveland, anyway, while in January 1863, everyone in Bannack wanted to like likable Henry Plummer.

It was clear and cold the next morning when Moore, Reeves, and Mitchell went on trial. All work in Bannack and the surrounding area came to a halt as perhaps 400 inhabitants, most of them carrying shotguns, revolvers, rifles, or knives, assembled at the log building where the trial was to be held. Honest people who were quietly determined to see justice done stood shoulder to shoulder with dozens of Plummer's men, who fired their weapons in the air and threatened the town in general. That prompted some of the exasperated honest element to start shouting for a miners' court, and since everybody knew what that meant, the rowdies quieted down. It was by then well understood that trial by jury was infinitely preferable to trial by a miners' court, since the relatively small number of jurors could be held accountable for their verdict, while the mob in a miners' court would vote anonymously and in numbers for the death penalty and would have no fear of reprisal. After a few hours of bickering, Nathaniel Langford convinced those who wanted a miners' court that the prisoners had been promised a jury trial and that jury trials were fairer, anyway.

When order was restored, J. F. Hoyt was elected judge and George Copley the prosecutor, and since it was an auspicious moment to take care of other civic business, Henry Crawford was elected sheriff. Next, a jury was chosen by majority vote, and William C. Rheem, a noted lawyer around Bannack, was picked as defense counsel. Rheem was told that every question he wanted to ask would first have to be submitted to the prosecutor, and, that having been agreed, William Mitchell went on trial and was promptly found innocent. Although he had accompanied Moore and Reeves to the Indian settlement, it could not be proved that he had actually fired his gun. Mitchell was, however, banished from Bannack (but would continue to skulk around town, anyway).

The setting for the trial of Moore and Reeves should be told by Nathaniel Langford, who was present.

The guilt of Moore and Reeves was fully established. This result was foreseen by their friends; and while the trial was in progress they sought by threats and ferocious gesticulations to intimidate the jury. Gathering around the side of the enclosure occupied by the jury, they kept up a continued conversation, the purport of which was that no member of that court or jury would live a month if they dared to find the prisoners guilty. Occasionally, their anger waxing hot, they would draw their pistols and knives, and brandishing them in the faces of the jurymen, utter a number of filthy epithets, and bid them beware of their verdict. Crawford was an object of especial hate. Their abusive assaults upon him and threats were so frequent and violent that at one time he tendered his resignation and refused to serve, but upon the promise of his friends to stand by and protect him he retained his position.

The jury were occupied in their deliberation until after midnight. No doubt was entertained, from the first, of the guilt of the prisoners, but the exciting question was whether they could afford to declare it. They all felt that to do so would be to announce their own death sentences. They knew that the friends of the prisoners fully intended to have life for life. They had sworn it. One of the jurymen said that the prisoners ought never to have been tried by a jury, but by a miners' court, that he should not be governed in his decision by the merits of the case, but that, as he had a family in the States to whom his obligations were greater than to that community, he should have to vote for acquittal. After much conversation of this sort, which only served to intensify the fears of the jurymen, a vote was taken which resulted as follows: not guilty, 11; guilty, 1.

The Court met the ensuing morning, when the verdict, under seal, was handed to the judge. He opened and returned it to the foreman, with a request that it be read aloud. An expression of blank astonishment sat upon the faces of every person in the room, which was followed by open demonstrations of general dissatisfaction, by all but the roughs, who, accustomed to outrages and long immunity, hailed it as a fresh concession to their bloody and lawless authority.[8]

And that's exactly what it was, the jury's recommendation that Moore and Reeves be banished notwithstanding. The result of the first formal clash between the law-abiding residents of Bannack and their predators, held in a popularly constituted court of law, was a ringing victory for the outlaws. Henry Plummer's gang had decisively defeated the law-and-order faction on its own turf. Langford points out that until the verdict of that trial came in no one in Bannack actually knew the relative strengths of the opposing sides. But a sentence of mere banishment for murdering an old Indian, a crippled one, a papoose, and even a white man left no doubt in anyone's mind where the power was. The four men who had risked their lives in a hail of lead to bring in Plummer, Moore, Reeves, and Mitchell understood that they had obviously done so for nothing.

For its part, the Plummer group decided at a meeting right after the trial that even a sentence of banishment had been impudent and that everyone connected with the trial (except the defense attorney) would therefore have to be killed in order to leave no doubt whatever as to who controlled the district. The murders were to be accomplished by provoking quarrels and then shooting in "self-defense" or by simple assassination. Henry Plummer won Sheriff Crawford, which was perfect, since Crawford not only was the embodiment of whatever law existed in Bannack, but also was thought by Plummer to be carrying the secrets of his shady past. Five months after that trial, no more than seven of the twenty-seven who had participated as judge, jurymen, prosecutor, or witnesses, would be left alive in the territory.

During the weeks immediately following the Plummer gang's decision, its leader tried repeatedly to draw Crawford into a gun duel or get some of his men to do it. The Sheriff skillfully avoided all of them, however, because he knew he was a rotten shot and would therefore most likely get killed. Although a number of townspeople noticed that Plummer was always trying to instigate a gunfight with their sheriff, they put it down to a case of bad blood existing between the two. But Crawford reached his saturation point the day someone told him that Plummer had become so angry that he planned to shoot him in his doorway. Sheriff Crawford went and got his own rifle, rested it on a log coming out of the corner of a building, and let Henry Plummer have it. The ball struck the gentleman outlaw on his right arm; it went in at the elbow and stopped at the wrist.

"Fire away, you cowardly ruffian," shouted Henry Plummer, straightening and looking Sheriff Crawford in the eye, as a crowd gathered. (In addition to his other qualities, Plummer was a born actor—a real crowd pleaser.) Crawford took him at his word, though, and fired again. The second ball missed, so Plummer, who was incapacitated anyway, turned his back and walked bravely to his cabin with his entourage.

Sheriff Crawford now understood that he was a marked man— that there would be no more challenges to duels, but that he could expect to get bushwhacked at any time. Accordingly, he got out of Bannack as fast as he could. He rode 280 miles to Fort Benton, over the most obscure trails he could find, with three of Plummer's men following. He reached the fort ahead of his pursuers, though, stayed there until spring, and then got on a riverboat for the United States. The Bannack–Virginia City area was without a sheriff.

And who would make a better sheriff, suggested Henry Plummer, than Henry Plummer? The residents of the district were getting hit every day by an extremely well organized band of robbers and killers, who not only stole what they had from behind bandannas, but who then came to town to eat and drink with their victims. No one in Bannack had a clear idea of who among them was a good guy and who was a bad, but they rightly supposed that the local nasties were also outlaws. That tended to make the honest citizens very jumpy, particularly since many who had been involved in the Moore-Reeves trial had a way of disappearing or turning up murdered. Furthermore, the banished bandits had soon returned to Bannack and were actually walking around as if they owned the place. Who among the decent people was going to throw them out again? Who was brave enough, intelligent enough, and likable enough to stop the robbing and killing and bring safety to the district? Henry Plummer, that's who. So Henry Plummer was elected sheriff, and everyone who voted for him rested a little easier.

The crime rate didn't lessen during the summer and fall of 1863; it got worse. In fact, it got much worse. Plummer appointed two of his best lieutenants, Buck Stinson and Ned Ray, as deputies in Bannack, and a third, Jack Gallagher, as deputy sheriff for Virginia City. Bannack's chief deputy, a man by the name of Dillingham, was a holdover from the Crawford days and was therefore honest. Dillingham wasn't to last long, either.

Week after grueling week, the people of Bannack and the surrounding region watched their new sheriff ride out of town with his deputies in apparent pursuit of road agents only to return in a day or two without prisoners. Not only that—and this was really mystifying—the biggest and best robberies seemed to happen while their sheriff was in the hills on his tracking missions. And every time a particularly awful robbery or murder occurred and the people of Bannack muttered about the temptation of taking matters into their own hands, the way folks did in California and elsewhere, their sheriff would counsel against it. Patiently, like a wise uncle talking to demented nephews, Sheriff Plummer would assure the people of Bannack that he completely understood how they felt but that they had to understand the terrible implications of vigilantism. Vigilantes were really anarchists, and anarchy was a black thing; it was a menace that, once started, would be difficult or perhaps impossible to stop. Did they want the reputation of being a pack of crazed, lynch-happy killers, who showed complete contempt for the legal process? Did they want the government in Washington, which was almost ready to bless them with territorial status, to think they were a bunch of bloodthirsty anarchists? No, advised Henry Plummer. The law and the judicial process had to be allowed to take their courses, and the people of Bannack would end up better for it in the long run. But they had to be patient. Very patient.

Dillingham, the head deputy, was, of course, in a better position to follow Plummer's comings and goings than anybody else in Bannack. And, since he was a reasonably intelligent man, it soon became clear to him that his boss was a scoundrel. Dillingham would overhear Plummer, Stinson, and Ray discussing clandestine meetings that were held outside of town and to which he was never invited; he would hear certain names that belonged to men who ended up being robbed or murdered or who simply vanished. And, when Dillingham wanted to pursue a case, he was usually told to take it easy and leave the work to his superior. All that made Deputy Dillingham angry, so when he overheard one day that a man named Dodge was going to be robbed he told the intended victim about it. Dodge then started boasting around town that Dillingham had warned him that road agents were planning to hit him. Possibly Dodge wanted to show off his connections or perhaps he wanted to show the people of Bannack that their lawmen had an intelligence system that worked. In any case, he sealed Dillingham's fate.

Three of Plummer's men, including Buck Stinson and one Charley Forbes, gunned down Dillingham in front of the Virginia City Hall of Justice. It was a carefully selected execution site, because Deputy Sheriff Gallagher immediately rushed out of the building, grabbed the killers' weapons, carried them back in, and reloaded them. Then Jack Gallagher arrested his friends and held them for trial.

It was a mass trial, not a twelve-man-jury trial, since by now a growing number of people in the district had dark suspicions about their sheriff's role in their continuing catastrophe and were afraid that a twelve-man jury would either be packed or be intimidated to the point of uselessness. The problem with a mass trial, however, was that it was unwieldy. Three presidents presided, and a blacksmith named E. R. Cutler was given the job of public prosecutor. Charley Forbes's defense was built partly on the fact that he was good-looking and educated and partly on the fact that his revolver, like those of the other defendants, had been fully loaded at the time he was captured. It was therefore impossible to tell which man had actually fired the fatal shot. A majority of the jurymen nevertheless voted in favor of hanging them all. Then the defense questioned the fairness of such a vote and called for a vote on *that*. Those who thought the vote and the whole trial should be condemned as unfair carried the motion by the simple expedient of allowing each man on their side to vote several times. Deputy Sheriff Gallagher at last grew tired of all that fancy legal maneuvering, pulled out his Colt, and shouted, "Let them go." And all three did just that. They got up and left. The disbelieving citizens followed them outside and watched the accused ride down the street until they were out of sight.

After the trial of Dillingham's murderers, writes Thomas J. Dimsdale, life became even worse for the beleaguered people of Bannack and Virginia City. Wounded men could be seen lying in the streets, there were shootings and knifings every day, and everyone except the outlaws became terrified of traveling. Here is the way Dimsdale justifies what was about to happen.

Let the reader suppose that the police of New York were withdrawn for twelve months, and then let them picture the wild saturnalia which would take the place of the order that reigns there now. [He apparently chose to ignore the well-publicized draft riots in Manhattan.] If, then, it is so hard to restrain the dangerous classes of old and settled communities, what must be the difficulty of task, when, tenfold in number, fearless in character, generally well armed, and supplied with money to an extent unknown among their equals in the east, such men find themselves removed from the restraints of civilized society, and beyond the control of the authority which there enforces obedience to the law?

The administration of *lex talionis* by self-constituted authority is, undoubtedly, in civilized and settled communities, an outrage on mankind. It is there wholly unnecessary; but the sight of a few of the mangled corpses of beloved friends and valued citizens; the whistle of the desperado's bullet, and the plunder of the fruits of the patient toil of years spent in weary exile from home, in places where civil law is as powerless as a palsied arm, from sheer lack of ability to enforce its decrees—alter the basis of reasoning, and reverse the conclusion. . . . The question of the propriety of establishing a vigilance committee depends on the answers which ought to be given to the following queries: Is it lawful for citizens to slay robbers or murderers, when they catch them; or ought they to wait for policemen, where there are none, or put them in penitentiaries not yet erected?[9]

The mountain people of Montana—ranchers, miners, merchants, and professionals—in 1863 were far from being the worldliest group in America, but they didn't live in a vacuum, either. All had recently come from somewhere else, usually in the United States of America, and most knew how to read newspapers—even old newspapers, which were passed around the mining camps until they yellowed, turned brittle, and finally disintegrated. They therefore thought of vigilantism exactly the way the people in Shelby County, Texas, and elsewhere did—as a necessary fact of life, an entirely reasonable last resort when a social situation had degenerated to the point of being intolerable. It was a reaction every bit as normal to the nineteenth-century frontiersman as forming wagons in circles or not forgetting the sourdough. All the people in Montana knew about what had happened in San Francisco, Los Angeles, Monterey, San Diego, and elsewhere during the 1850s. And almost everyone in the Bannack–Virginia City area knew somebody over at Lewiston, where a 900-man vigilance committee was at that moment working its dauntless way toward a total of thirty-one executions. No matter where a Montana mountaineer came from, then, he was well acquainted with the recourse to vigilance and with the tempting possibilities it offered. In fact, by the time the snow started to move in from the northwest during that winter of 1863–64 the noose was foremost on his mind.

The actual momentum of the first great Montana Committee of Vigilance started, ironically enough, at the funeral of the first man in the Bannack–Virginia City area to die of natural causes since the settlement of the district. His name was William H. Bell, and he died of mountain fever at about the time Henry Plummer was elected sheriff. While still on his deathbed, Bell had asked that he be given a Masonic funeral, and, obeying his wishes, every Mason in the district came to pay homage. Many of those men, all of them respectables who had a stake in law and order, hadn't known that others were members of the brotherhood until the day William Bell was buried. In addition, few of them would have risked their lives at an open meeting except under the seemingly innocuous pretext of a funeral. As Nathaniel Langford, who conducted the ceremony, recalled:

A large congregation had assembled. Near by, and surrounding the grave, stood the little band of brethren, linked by an indissoluble bond to him for whom they were now performing the last sad act of office. . . . How strange it seemed to see this large assemblage, of other townspeople all armed with revolvers and bowie-knives, standing silently, respectfully, around the grave of a stranger, their very features—distorted by the lines which their hardened lives had planted—now saddened by a momentary fleeting thought of the grave and immortality.

Nor was this all. They learned from what they saw, that here was an association, bound together by bonds of brotherly love, that would stand by and protect all its members in an hour of danger. They saw each brother drop the evergreen as a symbol of the surrender of him they mourned, to the eternal care of a high power. And while the brethren, as they regarded each other in the light of their strong obligations, felt that in each of themselves there was a power equal to the necessities of their exposed condition, we may reasonably suppose that the ruffians who had marked them for ultimate destruction felt that a new and formidable adversary had thrown itself across their bloody pathway.

The ceremonies were conducted to a peaceful conclusion, and the assembly quietly dispersed. But from this time onward, the Masons met often for counsel. Among them there was no lack of confidence, and very soon they began to consider measures necessary for their protection. These meetings were carefully watched by the roughs, but they were quietly told that the Masons met to prepare for organizing a lodge. This threw them off their guard, and they continued in their lawless course.[10]

And, most ironic of all, handsome and likable Henry Plummer actually managed to convince the Masons, during the early spring of 1863, to elect him to their organization—a decision that would give him the distinction of being the only member of the lodge to get killed during the coming slaughter.

December 1863 was the month in which the Masons and Plummer's band began meeting head on, and once the momentum had started events moved quickly. They began with the murder of a young German named Nicholas Tiebalt, who had accepted money from a rancher for some mules but had never returned with the animals. He was discovered shot in the head nine days later. Tiebalt's murder was particularly atrocious because he had been dragged by a lariat around his neck, while still alive, to the clump of bushes where his killer wanted to hide him. When his frozen body was discovered, there was still sagebrush in his fists, indicating that he had struggled all the way. Nicholas Tiebalt's corpse was loaded onto a wagon and brought into the tiny hamlet of Nevada, where it was left on display for half a day.

That evening twenty-five men, meeting in private, simply decided that they could stand no more and that they would go after Tiebalt's killer. They started at ten o'clock, tracked and rode all night in the subfreezing weather, and shortly before dawn captured a suspect named John Franck, better known around there as "Long John." Franck swore that he hadn't murdered Tiebalt and, under the threat of being hanged where he stood, fingered George Ives. The young Wisconsin stage specialist was promptly taken by surprise, brought into Nevada, and put on public trial on December 19. The only evidence Langford cites is Franck's testimony. "Long John," continuing to read the faces of his questioners very accurately, said that Ives had told him how he had murdered Tiebalt: "'When I told the Dutchman [sic] I was going to kill him, he asked me for time to pray. I told him to kneel down then. He did so, and I shot him through the head just as he commenced his prayer.'"[11] That was the Masons' case. Defense witnesses who tried to provide alibis were ignored because of their association with the accused and with other known criminals. After an angry confrontation similar to those at previous trials, but with the citizens' group this time heavily armed and in no mood to back down to anyone, Ives was sentenced to be hanged that evening.

He was executed by moonlight, while people from all over Alder Gulch, some sitting on roofs and nearly all cradling rifles, watched. Ives was strung up at the end of a forty-foot pine tree that had been wedged into the space above a crossbeam near the ceiling of a cabin. Standing on a wooden dry-goods box, Ives kept insisting that he was innocent and in turn blamed Alex Carter, another bandit. Tough. Dozens of miners cocked their guns, just before someone said, "Men, do your duty." Another kicked the box out from under George Ives, causing his neck to snap. They left him swinging there under the pale winter moon.

The idea of forming a vigilance committee had been incubating since Bell's funeral, but Ives's execution—tangible proof that resolute and armed men could strike back effectively—clinched the matter. They had started, and now they would not stop. The following night—December 20, 1863—five men met in a shop in Virginia City and signed a vigilante oath. Four were from Virginia City, and one, Wilbur Fisk Sanders, was from Bannack. They seem to have agreed on only two matters that first night: that a vigilance committee was going to be formed and that its oath and organization were going to have to be laid out quickly. The names of prospective vigilantes were brought up at that first meeting, and those men, together with the original five, held a second meeting two days before Christmas. It was at that meeting that twenty-four signed the following oath, whose authorship was deliberately omitted and never mentioned.

We the undersigned uniting ourselves in a party for the Laudible purpos of arresting thievs & murderers & recovering stollen propperty do pledge ourselves upon our sacred honor each to all others & solemnly swear that we will reveal no secrets, violate no laws of right & never desert each other or our standard of justice so help us God as witness our hand & seal this 23 of December A D 1863.[12]

As was usual when anything in writing was concerned, the oath doesn't mention the fact that those signing it knew they were going to go out and kill people, so it says that arrests were to be made. More interesting, though, is the part about not revealing secrets, meaning identities. The San Francisco committee of 1856 had used similar phraseology in its manifesto, but the identities of its leaders had been more or less an open secret; one even gets the feeling that they basked in the publicity. And why not? That group pitted about 6,000 armed pseudo soldiers against a relatively small and militarily inferior opposition. But Montana was different. The night they signed that document, the Vigilantes were outnumbered on the order of about three to one, by an organized, practiced, and deadly opposition, besides having to consider the dedicated free-lances who were always drifting into the territory to knock off an occasional express rider or ambush a miner. They understood that, especially where the gang was concerned, swift retribution was the rule; the aftermath of Moore's and Reeves's trial had proved as much. So when chroniclers say that vigilantes have usually preferred anonymity because of fear of reprisal they're quite right,

But there was another wrinkle. The Montana Vigilantes knew

that territorial status would tighten law enforcement and judicial procedures, and they had no wish to be known in their communities as hangmen or even to risk legal prosecution by the survivors of the gang they were planning to decimate. Langford, who was one of them, was therefore careful to leave out their names, while at the same time listing those of every criminal he could think of. Dimsdale, whose own classic book grew out of a series of articles he wrote on the subject for the *Montana Post*, also knew the Vigilantes intimately, but they warned him not to use their names. Given the fact that he believed not only in their cause, but also in the possibility that he could become accident prone for ignoring their warning, he did as he was told and was rewarded with the kind of inside information close to all newsmen's hearts.

While the Bannack and Virginia City Vigilantes were still organizing under Wilbur Sanders, "Captain Jim" Williams, Paris S. Pfouts, John S. Lott, John X. Biedler, and others, word came of a new massacre. Lloyd Magruder, an Elk City merchant and independent Democratic candidate for Congress (which Montanans were thinking about late in 1863), had been robbed and murdered; $14,000 in gold had been taken from him while he was crossing the Bitter Root Mountains on his way home from Virginia City. It had been an inside job, too. As it turned out, members of Plummer's gang had hired on to Magruder's pack train, which was supposed to get whatever wares he hadn't been able to sell in Virginia City back over the frozen mountains. Not only had they killed Magruder, it was discovered, but they also had apparently murdered four of his sleeping friends and picked the bodies clean. That was absolutely it where the men of Bannack and Virginia City were concerned. They decided to move on the killers.

Twenty-eight of them, each carrying a pair of revolvers, a rifle or shotgun, blankets, and, of course, enough rope, rode into the intense cold to track and catch the men who had hit Lloyd Magruder's party. Although severe storms were sweeping over the continental divide and pushing the snow into high and dangerous drifts, the creeks and streams had long since iced, and temperatures at night must have been in the zero range, Dimsdale makes a point of noting that no liquor was taken along. Bundled in thick sheepskin coats, their fingers and faces stinging and their eyes hurting from the wind and dazzling sun coming off the snow, the Vigilantes guided their horses into the mountains.

While moving through Deer Lodge Valley, they came on Erastus Yager, better known as "Red" Yager, because of the color of his beard, and were told that those they were looking for— Alex Carter, Billy Bunton, "Whisky Bill" Graves, and some others —were lying drunk at a place called Cottonwood. After spending twenty-four hours resting and getting warm at a ranch belonging to one John Smith, they moved in on the campsite where the outlaws were supposed to have been, only to find it deserted. As it turned out, a warning note had been written to them by George Brown, in Virginia City, and had been carried by Yager, who had killed two horses doing so. The Vigilantes found Brown's note and somehow learned that Yager had delivered it. So they decided to get Yager, who, they now learned, was twenty miles away, at Rattlesnake. The number of people in those mountains who knew the whereabouts of other people is astounding, especially in view of the weather. At any rate, the Vigilantes camped in a stand of willows for another two days, during which they were caught in another snowstorm, which frightened off some of their horses. They pushed on when it had passed. "Red" Yager was taken at gun point, disarmed, and forced to accompany them as they went after Brown, who was picked up at a ranch close to Virginia City.

Brown and Yager were interrogated and eventually confessed to having written and delivered the warning note. Both were then taken to the Stinking-Water Bridge, where the Vigilantes were to vote penalties. Brown, a suspected petty thief, was at that point openly terrified, but Yager kept his composure as the leader of the Vigilante group told his men to stand on the right side of the bridge if they favored execution and on the left if they wanted acquittal. Everyone stepped to the right. That having been decided, the prisoners were taken to another ranch and allowed to get some sleep. Meanwhile, word had spread, and other Vigilantes began arriving. Brown and Yager were awakened at ten o'clock on the night of January 4, 1864, and told that their time had come. They were going to die. Erastus Yager then started talking his head off.

Langford, who was not there but who was eventually filled in on what happened, recounted the scene in *Vigilante Days and Ways*, originally published in 1890 as an apology for the killing spree that started that night. Even if he faithfully recorded every word of the dialogue between Yager and the Vigilante leader as given to him, he was still getting the conversation from someone who would hardly have been taking notes at the fateful hour but was relying on his memory several years later. It is therefore most unlikely that the following passage accurately represents the exchange between the two men. It's important, however, because it hangs heavy with the usual outlaw contrition—the hallmark of the nineteenth-century vigilante scribe.

"You have treated me like a gentleman," [Yager] said. "I know that my time has come. I am going to be hanged."

"That's pretty rough, Red," interjected the leader.

"Yes. It's pretty rough, but I merited it years ago. What I want to say is, that I know all about this gang. There are men in it who deserve death more than I do; but I should die happy, if I could see them hanged, or know it would be done. I don't say this to get off. I don't want to get off."

"It will be better for you, Red," said the Vigilantes, "at this time to give us all the information in your possession, if only for the sake of your kind. Times have been very hard. Men have been shot down in broad daylight, not alone for money, or even hatred, but for mere luck and sport, and this must have a stop put to it."

"I agree to it all," replied Red. "No poor country was ever cursed with a more bloodthirsty or meaner pack of villains than this—and I know them all."[13]

The dialogue is almost without question a product of some Vigilante's conscience and imagination, perhaps even of Langford's. But the information supplied by "Red" Yager was real and must have brought grim smiles to the men, standing around him. He confirmed what they had suspected for months—that Henry Plummer, their sheriff, was the leader and mastermind of an extraordinarily well organized band of outlaws. Yager then named most of the others.

The gang was bound by a sacred oath, said Yager, and everyone performed his specialty. Disobedience, they had been warned by Plummer, would be punished by death, and so would betrayal. According to the rules, anyone who tried to expose or arrest them was automatically put on an enemies list and taken care of. The aim of the organization, Yager continued, was simply to pick the district clean—without killing, if possible, but by killing without hesitation if necessary. "Innocent" was the password; bandannas and neckties were done in a sailor's knot for identification; and each member wore his mustache or beard trimmed in a certain way, to be doubly sure he was recognizable to the others (which indicates the probable size of the gang). Yager, who admitted to being a member of the group but not to being a murderer, went on to detail a number of coach robberies and other banditry and supplied the names of those who had pulled them.

"Red" Yager and George Brown were taken to a stand of cottonwoods less than a quarter of a mile from the ranch house. It was a dim but starlit night, so lanterns were used to guide the party to the execution site. Standing in the deep snow, George Brown began to beg for his life, pleading with the stone-faced men holding the lanterns and watching him that he had an Indian wife and family back in Minnesota. One stool was placed on another, and Brown was put on them. He was then noosed from a thick branch, and the stools were kicked out from under him. Brown died in a few seconds, and minutes later the process was repeated on "Red" Yager. Before they left, the Vigilantes signed their work; pieces of paper explaining all that had to be said were pinned onto the dead men's clothing.

RED!	BROWN!
ROAD AGENT & MESSENGER	CORRESPONDING SECRETARY

Although Plummer at that moment had no way of knowing that Yager had spilled every one of the proverbial beans, the Sheriff of Bannack nevertheless sensed that his Masonic brothers were organizing and were about ready to close in. He had been around enough to have seen the results of vigilante operations elsewhere and must have been fully aware of what was happening over in Lewiston at that very moment. He had therefore begun making plans to get out of the district, but, cool to the last, he was doing so unhurriedly. The others in the band were, for the most part, already trying to figure the best routes through the snow to Walla Walla and beyond.

The trappings of pseudojudicial procedure much in vogue elsewhere on the frontier, where "prosecutors" and "defense counsels" held half-hour and half-hearted debates beside the gallows before executions, were dispensed with. The Committee of Vigilance this time simply issued execution orders for Plummer, Stinson, and Ray. Both deputy sheriffs were picked up on the night of Sunday, January 10; one was in the cabin of a man named Toland, and the other was stretched out, probably drunk, on a card table in a saloon.

The group sent to take Plummer found him in his cabin preparing to go to bed. He offered no resistance, probably due in part to the fact that his revolver was broken, and was marched to the execution site at the edge of Bannack, where Stinson and Ray were waiting. A set of gallows that had been erected by Plummer the year before was selected as suitable for the Sheriff and his men. Stinson and Ray cursed the Vigilantes all the way to the spot where they were marked to die. Henry Plummer at first begged for his life and then tried to convince his captors that he was innocent. That was the word he used—"innocent"—and it couldn't have been wasted on those who were waiting to see him hang. Finally, he began pleading again, promising that he would leave the country forever if they let him go and even suggesting that they cut off his ears or cut out his tongue, rather than kill him. They responded to his appeals by assuring him, in the calmest possible way, that he was going to hang that night, no matter what he said.

Ned Ray went kicking and screaming. He struggled frantically while Vigilantes held his arms firmly to his sides, hoisted him up with a noose around his neck, and then dropped him. A few minutes later, Buck Stinson was hanging beside his cohort, a few feet above the now thoroughly trampled snow and under a clear sky full of bright stars.

Now it was Henry Plummer's turn. Whereas Ray and Stinson had been considered common criminals and had therefore been killed as quickly as possible, Plummer was another matter. Enough of the charisma remained so that his executioners, resolved as they were, hesitated. "Plummer, steeped as he was in infamy, was a man of intellect, polished, genial, affable," says Langford. "There was something terrible in the idea of hanging such a man."[14] But they did it, anyway. He requested time to pray and was answered by one of the Vigilantes, who, pointing at the pine crossbeam forming the top of the gallows, told him to pray "up there." Henry Plummer then took off his tie, flung it to a young friend as a souvenir, and asked for a "good drop."

They gave him a fine drop. After the noose had been tightly secured and adjusted to the correct length, several of the strongest men in the committee held him as high as they could and then suddenly let go. He died quickly and without much of a struggle, and after the Vigilantes had made certain that he and the others had really expired, they left them hanging there and marched, military style, back to their homes. Plummer and his lieutenants were not cut down until five days later, according to a witness whose letter appeared in the *St. Paul Pioneer* of March 1, by which time all three were "frozen stiff." They were then taken to a vacant room above George Christman's store and, as custom had it, displayed there for three more days.

Although the Committee of Vigilance had formal regulations and bylaws similar to those of the San Francisco committee of 1856 and was even patterned along loose military lines, with captains and lieutenants, it was far smaller and much less rigidly structured than its famous predecessor. It never had more than 110 members, for example, and the majority of those drifted in and out of active service as the weeks passed. Mechanics, merchants, ranchers, and others would abandon their businesses for a few days, or for as long as it took to go out on a strike, and then return to their regular work, while another group mounted an expedition in another direction. Only a few stayed in vigilante work on a full-time basis, and, understandably, they were incredibly tenacious.

The emotions and dispositions of the leaders varied as much as those of the ordinary volunteers. Surviving evidence indicates that "Captain Jim" Williams, the executive officer, was shy and self-effacing. He came originally from a farm in Pennsylvania and had lived in Illinois, Kansas, and Colorado before becoming attracted to the gold at Grasshopper Creek. Sanders, the prosecutor, and one of the most powerful men in the group, seems to have been of normal temperament, as were Pfouts, the president, and Lott, the treasurer. Charles Beehrer and John X. Biedler (referred to only as "X" by Dimsdale), on the other hand, seem to have taken a savage delight in stringing up victims.

Armed with a bylaw stipulating that "the only punishment that shall be inflicted by this Committee is DEATH,"[15] the Vigilantes began scouring the area for members of the Plummer gang the morning after its leader was hanged. Well-armed and moving through snow-covered ravines and pine forests, men from Bannack, Nevada, Virginia City, and elsewhere in the region prowled in search of their prey, which by then was either scattering or making frantic preparations to do so. Montana Vigilantes were to turn up in Denver some weeks later, after having made an astounding ride of at least 600 miles over some of the most difficult terrain in North America. It was a classic long pursuit, which showed just how badly they wanted to take the remnants of the Plummer gang.

"Dutch John" Wagner, who had been "arrested" on January 2 and charged with attacking a pack train, stealing a gray horse from Barrett & Shineberger, and being one of Plummer's men, was hanged the day after Plummer—January 11. The same day, a group of Vigilantes stormed Joe "Greaser" Pizanthia's cabin in an effort to capture him and see "precisely how his record stood in the Territory." The Mexican (hence, "Greaser") shot both of the Vigilantes who made the first rush, wounding Smith Ball in the hip and killing George Copley. A small howitzer was then brought up and used to blow large holes in the cabin, after which six more Vigilantes, from Nevada, charged the place under covering fire from the others. Pizanthia was found lying badly hurt in the rubble, his gun on the floor nearby. Ball, the wounded Vigilante, limped up to the "Greaser" and emptied his revolver into him. Then the body was dragged out of the cabin, hanged with a clothesline, and riddled by Vigilantes and townspeople alike. Others had meanwhile set fire to the smashed cabin; the grisly, mangled corpse was cut down and thrown into the blaze, where it was thoroughly consumed. The following morning, some prostitutes panned the ashes for gold, but found none.

Five more were taken on the fourteenth: "Clubfoot George" Lane at Dance & Stuart's store in Virginia City; Hayes Lyons at a miner's cabin just outside of town; Boone Helm in front of the Virginia Hotel; Jack Gallagher at the Arbor Restaurant; and Frank Parish somewhere else in town. Since the evidence against them was considered so overwhelming that a trial wasn't necessary, they were promptly hanged together from the main beam of an unfinished building at the corner of Wallace and Van Buren.

Steve Marshland was taken by "Vigilanter No. 84" as he lay in bed at a ranch near the Big Hole River. He reacted jovially until his shirt was taken off, showing a recent bullet wound thought by the Vigilantes to have been inflicted in a pack-train robbery.

Marshland was another pleader. He was strung up at the end of a pole that had been planted in the hard ground and rested at an angle over a corral fence—nothing fancy. Since his body started to attract wolves, he was cut down and buried where he had died. Three days later, on January 19, the same group got Billy Bunton at a ranch near Cottonwood. Bunton was also hanged in a corral, and also had to be cut down and buried, since the corral keeper's wife objected to having a corpse dangling on the premises.

George Shears was hanged on the twenty-fourth from a cross-beam in a barn. According to Dimsdale, Shears was brought into the barn by a party led by energetic No. 84, and, after the rope had been tossed over the beam, he was asked to climb a ladder and execute himself, rather than forcing the Vigilantes to cope with a complicated drop problem. "Gentlemen, I'm not used to this business, never having been hung before," Shears is quoted as saying. "Shall I jump off or slide off?" After a moment's thought, one of the Vigilantes suggested jumping, and that's just what Shears did.

The next day was another busy one. Cyrus Skinner, Alex Carter, Bob Zachary, and John Cooper were captured at Hell Gate by eight Vigilantes, and also were hanged from poles resting on a corral fence, this one at the Higgins ranch. Carter and Cooper had been getting ready to leave the area the day before, but an argument over the ownership of a pistol had resulted in Cooper's being wounded. The delay probably cost them their lives.

"Whisky Bill" Graves, who had become partially snow-blind while on the run, was taken by three Vigilantes at an Indian settlement called Fort Owen in the Bitter Root Valley. Since the Indians didn't want any white man hanging around their property, the Vigilantes obliged by taking Graves some distance from the fort. They hanged him by the simple expedient of jerking him off the ground, using a horse and rider pulling a rope that passed over a tree limb. "Whisky Bill's" neck broke instantly. Bill Hunter, the last of Plummer's inner circle, escaped from Virginia City on January 13 and headed east toward the Gallatin River. He was taken while in bed by six Vigilantes on February 3. They promised to take him back to Virginia City for trial, but, instead, hanged him near where they caught him.

A week later, a rancher named James A. Slade got drunk in

Virginia City, threatened to tear the place down, and was arrested by J. M. Fox, the newly appointed sheriff. Once in court, Slade, who had a nasty temper even when sober, tore up the warrant and held a gun to the head of Judge Alex Davis, threatening to kill him if he wasn't freed. Slade apparently calmed after a while and ended up harming no one. The Nevada Vigilante contingent decided that the rancher was a dangerous troublemaker, however, so they hanged him, too. James A. Slade was, in effect, hanged for disorderly conduct, a fact that seems to have embarrassed even Nathaniel Langford.[16]

The first Montana Committee of Vigilance executed twenty-two men in thirty-seven days and sent dozens of others fleeing the territory. By the end of February 1864, the Bannack and Virginia City Vigilantes had lost most of their momentum, but they continued to execute on an *ad hoc* basis throughout the rest of that year and well into the next. When they weren't hanging, they were making their presence felt with threats, especially through the use of the famous "3–7–77" warning, which was widely used throughout the West. Sometimes the mysterious numerical combination was pinned to a victim to tell others that he had been executed by vigilantes. Other times it was left as a clear warning: "You are as good as dead." The recipient of a note with "3–7–77" on it knew that he was being told to get out of the district as quickly as he could or suffer the consequences. The combination appeared in newspaper ads and on broadsides announcing meetings, and was occasionally even scrawled on the ground. No one knows exactly what it stands for. Some have guessed that the numbers are the dimensions of a grave—three feet wide, seven feet long, and seventy-seven inches deep. Others have claimed that it measures the time a marked man was given to get out of the area—three hours, seven minutes, and seventy-seven seconds. Still others have guessed that it was once the identification number of some Vigilante and simply spread. It may even have been the date of some renowned but subsequently lost hanging or other form of lynching—March 7, 1777.

At any rate, the Bannack-Virginia City-Nevada organization's official tally for the period 1863–1865 came to thirty, but vigilante operations in the area and in the rest of Montana continued sporadically throughout the following years and into the 1880s, when the second great Montana group formed. A broadside announcing a meeting at Argenta (about ten miles from Bannack), for example, urged citizens to "Double Up!" and "Let Justice Be Done!!" It was printed in 1867 and carries mysterious and boldly printed combinations of letters (such as "EORLKA"), which may have been intended to mystify the public or intimidate bad elements or simply form a code known only to members of the organization.

There's considerable evidence, however, that not all of the law-abiding residents of central and western Montana cared for what the Vigilantes did. At a bar-association meeting in 1886, Wilbur Fisk Sanders, who founded the Montana Bar and who went on to become a leading Republican politician and one of the state's first two United States senators, showed irritation in a speech he gave to defend the events of 1863–1865. Both Langford's and Dimsdale's classics on the episode reek with justification, not only for the benefit of eastern readers but apparently for Montanans as well. The full title of Dimsdale's book is *The Vigilantes of Montana; or Popular Justice in the Rocky Mountains; Being a Correct and Impartial Narrative of the Chase, Trial, Capture, and Execution of Henry Plummer's Road Agent Band*. It may have been correct, but it was anything but impartial. As it turned out, Mark Twain had met James A. Slade and, judging by his recollection in *Roughing It*, liked him (although he conceded that Slade was often a mean-tempered rascal). Twain referred to Dimsdale's work as "a bloodthirstily interesting little Montana book."[17]

There is evidence that by 1867 many Montanans were on the verge of starting moderator opposition to the scattered executions still going on. An attempt that year by the Helena Vigilantes to revive their organization was met by stiff resistance and this notice in the *Montana Post:*

We now, as a sworn band of law-abiding citizens, do hereby solemnly swear that the first man that is hanged by the vigilantes of this place, we will retaliate five for one unless it be done in broad daylight, so that all may know what it is for. We are all well satisfied that in time past you did some glorious work, but the time has come when law should be enforced. Old fellow-members, the time is not like it was. We had good men with us; but now there is a great change. There is not a thief comes to this country but what "rings" himself into the present Committee. We know you all. You must not think you can do as you please. We are American citizens, and you shall not drive and hang whom you please.[18]

In July 1883—the year before Granville Stuart's monumental thirty-five-victim organization formed in the Musselshell and Missouri river regions—angry residents of Miles City reacted to the possibility of a vigilance committee in their neighborhood by posting warnings in red ink on the doors of the ringleaders: "Notice—Bullard, Burleigh, Ringer, Dear, Van Gasken, Russell and others—murderers—you're marked." That particular note was signed "7-22-82," meaning that moderators knew how to use intimidating number combinations, too. Another simply said, "Stranglers!—Beware! You are known. 7-23-83—11 p.m. No. 1—XX 7."[19]

Dimsdale, who became the editor in chief of the *Montana Post* and territorial superintendent of schools before he died in 1866, at the age of thirty-five, remained awed by his friends among the Vigilantes until the end. Reporting that Wilbur Sanders claimed to have seen "a scoundrel" lurking in the bushes on his way home, Dimsdale warned darkly that "this outrage will demand a hempen solution." Ten days later, on September 19, 1865, he waxed poetic in this Helena item: "The beams of the rising sun fell upon the stiffened corpse of Tommy Cooke . . . with the fatal sign of the vigilantes (3-7-77) and bearing the simple legend 'Pickpocket.' "[20]

And Thomas J. Dimsdale's new-found American friends paid him tribute for his loyalty and admiration. They eventually gave him something that no one back at Oxford, where they didn't have vigilantes, would have dreamed he needed. They presented him with a beautiful silver-plated and gilt pistol with ivory handles. Carved in relief on the handles was the American eagle, grasping in its talons the national shield and the mythical thunderbolts that symbolize swift retribution.

Oh, yes—not long after Henry Plummer's execution his appointment as a United States marshal arrived. He had applied for his new badge at about the time he took his solemn Masonic oath.

7

Missouri: "Don't fool with the wrong end of the mule"

THE BLACK hoods cost 25 cents apiece and were easily worth every penny of it to the tough Baptist mountain men who gathered in Smelter Hollow, in Christian County, in southwestern Missouri, on the night of March 11, 1887, to do their Lord's work.

Even the womenfolk who had patiently crafted the hoods out of flour sacks and old pillowcases wouldn't have pretended that they were really worth that kind of money. Mountain folk in those days, after all, were careful about their money; "sensible," they'd call it. They were sensible for the very obvious reason that they worked hard farming their bony land, raising cattle, horses, and mules, or cutting oak for ties for the St. Louis and San Francisco Railroad, and never had much to show for it. But those who met in Smelter Hollow that night, as well as hundreds of others in that part of the Ozarks, had gladly given their captains two bits each for their hoods. They worked hard and never had much to show for it, and they had to believe in something, so they believed in God and in the black hoods.

Each hood was really a fitted skullcap that came down to its wearer's eyebrows. A black flap hung from there to the man's chest, and into the flap were cut holes for his eyes and mouth. Red thread was stitched buttonhole fashion around each hole, and that border was, in turn, circled with white paint. The paint had also been used to form beards on some of the flaps, starting just below the mouth holes and ending near their bottoms. Every hood was topped with a pair of four- to six-inch horns made of cloth cones stuffed with cork or wooden plugs and tasseled at their tips with more of the red thread. It was the designer's intention to make the men who wore the hoods look as much as possible like gruesome devils. He had undoubtedly studied the Klan and therefore understood the terror that came with seeing hoods and masks in the night. In Saint Louis, Kansas City, or even Springfield, which was nearby, the effect would have been comic. But in the rough and isolated hills of Christian County, and particularly at night, when the Bald Knobbers rode, the effect was absolutely frightening. And that, of course, was precisely the idea.

Smelter Hollow, or "holler," as they called it, was named after the lead smelter that had been there several years before and had then been abandoned when its owners found that the cost of moving ore out of the rugged hills was prohibitive. The smelter had been followed by a sawmill, but it, too, had had to be closed because the Hollow's rough wooded slopes, jutting rocks, and limestone caverns made heavy-wagon movement next to impossible. The sawmill in Smelter Hollow, like many others in the area, had been built to service the railroad, which always needed ties. The St. Louis and San Francisco, in fact, was Christian County's main payroll source in 1887. Mountaineers from all over the district, weary and frustrated by their bony land, had begun chopping oak trees for railroad ties as soon as the company established its spur at Chadwick. They were called tie hackers, and, although none of them prospered, they were usually better off than their kin who had stayed behind the plows.

With the railroad, however, came vice. A few brothels and gambling parlors had opened in Chadwick after the St. Louis and San Francisco brought in the spur. But they and others at nearby Sparta ("Sparty") were practically inconsequential. The real problem—the heart of the trouble—was understood to come from the saloons, where otherwise good men learned to overdrink. The saloons weren't fancy, but they were nevertheless places where mountain men, accustomed to nothing more than passing around a jug, could stand before a real bar, like men in city saloons, and order their whiskey poured right into a glass. It was a treat that easily turned into a habit, so many of the tie hackers and others who came to Chadwick on business began leaving large percentages of their earnings with the bartenders. That, in turn, made their womenfolk unhappy.

Worse, all that public liquoring brought what the serious and determined Baptists around there perceived as moral decadence and a crime wave. There were occasional brawls and individual fights that ended in shootings or stabbings. Livestock seemed to be stolen at annoyingly frequent intervals. And even the ties piled in the railroad yard were sometimes moved from one man's area to another's, with the identification marks of the real hacker changed, in the same way that rustlers elsewhere altered brands. All this was blamed on the railroad, which was seen as a necessary evil, and on the liquored-up miscreants, who were seen as a quite unnecessary one.

Then there were the homesteaders, who came into the hills because they had heard stories about the relative wealth to be had by cutting ties. By 1886, the homesteaders had begun crowding into Christian County in numbers that annoyed the natives, some of whom went all the way back to the 1830s. The natives didn't like that. They didn't like intruders in their hills, and they particularly didn't like homesteaders and, worse, plain squatters. The squatters were moving in, claiming some land, throwing up simple shelters, and then chopping timber, without bothering about legal formalities. In other words, they were living on the land and making some money by depleting it, but paying no taxes. And taxes were taken very seriously by the natives. If it hadn't been for taxes, or so it was said, mountain families could have lived virtually without money. Their little log cabins, built with few nails and little or no glass, had split-log floors and handmade clapboard roofs. Most cooking was done in large fireplaces, since few homes had real stoves and wood for burning was literally everywhere. A few sheep or a small cotton patch provided fiber for spinning and weaving, and there was always enough corn and sugar cane to make bread and even some molasses for "sweetnin'." When corn needed grinding, a farm boy would toss a few sacks on his mule, take them to the local mill, and just leave a bit as payment to the miller. Coffee was "biled" over and over again; once in a while a pinch of fresh coffee was added as a "starter;" when the pot became full of washed-out grounds, the process was repeated with a new starter. Every family had its lean houn' dogs, or "potlickers," which could be depended upon to chase down wild turkeys, deer, and the razorback hogs that ate acorns in the forests and provided bacon, salt meat, and soap. So taxes were the native mountain family's main financial worry, and those of their neighbors who didn't pay any were a source of abiding irritation. It was only natural.

Scattered bushwhackers left over from the Civil War were even more aggravating than the homesteaders or the squatters. Taney, Douglas, and Christian counties had been in a particularly difficult situation during the war, since Taney bordered Arkansas and the other two were just north of it. The White River was the border between Yankee and Confederate sympathizers, and when the shooting began families had fled in both directions, according to their convictions. Because of the peculiarly unstable political conditions at that time, a subclass of bandits and killers had developed, which preyed on both "Northern" and "Southern" communities, moving over the unprotected countryside along the Missouri-Arkansas border and taking full advantage of the military and legal uncertainties. They had shot old men left at home with the women and children and had then picked their homes clean. They had hung around their own communities, in the absence of menfolk who had gone to war, and plundered the homesteads of defenseless neighbors whose possessions they had always wanted or whom they had simply always hated. When a team of horses worth perhaps $200 was stolen, it was tantamount to ruin. When a cabin was burned out, as they often were, it meant that the survivors had to double up with another family, causing social strains and deep embarrassment among the rugged and proud individuals who lived in those hills. So, toward the end of the war, the people of Stone County, which bordered on Arkansas and on Taney and Christian counties, had formed a home guard and begun counterattackings. They had shot dozens of marauders, some in fierce gun battles, and had often hanged loners where they found them. They were still doing it after the war ended—long after the war ended. The chaos of the Civil War, then, taught the southwest Missouri hillbillies an immutable lesson: when they couldn't depend on anyone else, they could band together and get the job done themselves. The war was therefore the seed out of which the Bald Knobbers grew.

Boredom and religion were the soil and the fertilizer. A close reading of American frontier history shows that when settlers weren't "building" the country—when they weren't plowing their fields, moving their cattle, erecting their homes and shops, selling their pots and pans, or pounding their iron into horseshoes, plowshares, and wheel rims—they were bored stiff. In his *Frontier Violence*, W. Eugene Hollon recalls the interviews he had with dozens of elderly people who had settled the Oklahoma Territory during the time when the Bald Knobbers were nightriding in Taney and Christian counties. "When I asked them what they remembered most about the recent frontier, the answer that a great majority gave was the wretched loneliness and almost total lack of excitement in their lives," writes Hollon. "Sam Rayburn once reminisced about his experiences in growing up on the frontier of northeast Texas. He recalled the boredom that he could never escape. Even though he worked in the fields all week, from sunup to sundown, the worst time of all was Sunday afternoon, when he had nothing to do. There were no newspapers to read and no books other than the family Bible, there was no one his age to talk with, and the nearest store was miles away. He usually passed the entire afternoon sitting on the wooden fence in front of the unpainted family house, gazing down the country road in the hope that someone would ride by on horseback, or, even more exciting, in a buggy."[1]

Life in the Missouri Ozarks in the 1880s was better than that, but not much better. Springfield, the largest town in the Taney-Douglas-Christian County district, had at least three competing newspapers by the winter of 1885, when the Bald Knobbers were formed: the *Daily Herald,* the *Leader,* and the *Republican.* Since many hillbillies either couldn't read at all or else did so falteringly, however, the papers' entertainment value was minimal. Furthermore, very few in the Ozarks were interested in what "furriners" did in places as far away as Springfield, Jefferson City, and Kansas City. They always had their own problems, without looking for other people's, and isolated mountain life tended to turn most of their vital interests inward.

Given that situation, plus their constant financial worries, spending perfectly good money on books was, with one exception, out of the question. The exception, of course, was the Bible.

No matter how badly the head of a household read, his family owned and regularly used its Bible. The Baptist church formed the bedrock of mountain morality and laid the basis of whatever social cohesion existed outside of family and clan. It initiated believers, guided the spirits of young and old, and sent off the grateful dead with solemnly comforting pageantry. Along with sex, drinking, and an occasional turkey shoot, it provided almost all the entertainment in the hills. Its God was a stern one, who demanded in His followers the appearance and substance of fidelity but who nonetheless occasionally winked at transgression. Drinking in public places on Sunday, for example, was evil; getting blind drunk behind one's own door was acceptable. Wife beating was cruel and was the sure sign of a confirmed bully—unless the wife really needed beating, in which case she was being helped. Killing violated the Lord's will—unless there was a good reason for it. The Bald Knobbers who murdered Charles Green and William Edens on the night of March 11, 1887, were accompanied by John Mathews, who not only took part in the killings but also prayed for the group's success. Mathews was a devout deacon. The nightriders, good Baptists to the last man, in effect had their own chaplain.

The Bald Knobbers didn't start in Christian County; they ended there. They started in Taney County, either during December 1884 or, more likely, in January of '85. And they started with reasonably effective judges and sheriffs all over the place, and certainly in Springfield, which was pretty large at that time. The founder of the Bald Knobbers, interestingly enough, was a "furriner," named Captain Nat N. Kinney. If Kinney had nothing else to recommend him as a vigilante leader, he had true size. The fifty-year-old native Virginian was more than six and a half feet tall and weighed 275 pounds. He was described by admirers as being powerful and handsome, with dark hair and deep blue eyes. "The finest specimen of humanity I ever saw," his friends liked to say when describing him. His enemies' descriptions have not survived.

Kinney was born in Virginia, but he didn't stay there very long. He went west as a boy, became a young captain in the Union Army during the Civil War, and after that worked as a frontier agent for the Post Office Department. Rumor had it that during his postal service he killed several men who were resisting arrest for holding up stages. It may have been true, because Kinney eventually left government service to become a detective for the Atchison, Topeka, and Santa Fe Railroad, and it didn't hire the faint of heart. He then drifted eastward to Springfield, where he opened a saloon that seems to have become popular enough to allow him to retire to Taney County in 1883.

After picking out a piece of good grass-covered land that already had a house on it, the Captain moved down his wife, their two children, and a daughter by a previous marriage. His son by that former marriage moved onto adjoining property. The Kinney home was soon made bigger and nicer than any of the others in the neighborhood; rooms were added, and an "elegant" carpet, plush red chairs and a settee, real oil paintings, and the first piano in Taney County were shipped down from Springfield. Georgia, the Captain's younger daughter, could even play that piano. Then Captain Kinney brought in the region's first Merino sheep, Red Durham cattle, and blooded horses. Everyone else owned plain old houn' dogs, but Kinney showed them a greyhound, a terrier, and other real breeds. He also lost no time in making friends with Colonel Alonzo S. Prather, one of Taney County's leading Republicans and for several years a representative in the Missouri legislature. Captain Kinney's older daughter eventually married Colonel Prather's boy, which was fitting.

Captain Nat N. Kinney, his gun belt resting on a table, was soon delivering sermons and teaching Sunday school in the Oak Grove schoolhouse, which was turned into a "church house" each Sabbath. He liked to lead the congregation in the singing of "Ninety and Nine," one of his favorite old hymns, and then deliver lessons on Moses, another born leader. After church, the Kinneys would bring a dozen or so friends back to their home for dinners that usually included chicken or roast meat, beans, potatoes, pies, and cakes, all spread on a long table around which the hosts and their guests gave profound thanks for the bounty that had been provided. The ladies would then gossip, and their men would discuss more important matters, such as how the weather was affecting their crops, who was likely to win the next election, or how to gun-break a horse so it wouldn't shy at the sound of a shot fired close to its head. Within a relatively short time, then, Captain Nat N. Kinney, Mason, man of God, champion of decency, and Taney County's stoutest cultural pillar, had become the local squire and, therefore, the resident wise man and unofficial guardian of the interests of his friends and neighbors. And it wasn't too long after that when Captain Kinney thought he began to perceive a serious crime problem. The Captain was later quoted as having observed:

"So far as I could learn the history of Taney county has been a record of lawlessness and disregard of social proprieties. When I came here some four years ago it was common for men to live with women to whom they have never been married. Why, one old Mormonlike neighbor kept six women. Then the county was $42,000 in debt, and had not even a plank to show for it. The money had simply been stolen. That wasn't all. Over thirty men had been shot to death in the county since the war and not one of the murderers had been punished by the civil authorities.*

"Well I had come here to lead a retired and quiet life, but I could not refrain from expressing my opinions of such things, and I cannot refrain now. The consequence was that men came to me and said: 'Kinney, you had better look out. These people don't like your talk, and you had better go slow or you will get it in the neck.'

" 'Well,' I said, 'I have some experience in that line myself and I say these things should be condemned, and I propose to condemn them.' The best men in the county gradually drifted to my side, and it became a war between civilization and barbarism."[2]

The barbarians who provided the main catalyst for the formation of the Bald Knobbers weren't really thieves, bandits, or professional killers at all, but, rather, that species of mean-minded roughneck who is a cautious bully when sober and a vicious grudge holder when drunk. Al Layton, a rough young mountaineer, was typical of the type. On the afternoon of September 23, 1883, he shot and killed James M. Everett, the popular owner of a general store and saloon in the town of Forsyth; he also wounded Everett's brother, Barton. The Everett brothers were liked by the people around Forsyth, because they had extended a lot of credit during and immediately after the drought of 1882 and had even sent wagonloads of bacon, beans, corn, and other staples into the hills to families that had been "burned out."

James Everett and young Layton had been playing a game called pigeonhole in the back of Everett's saloon when both decided they were thirsty. Each had therefore gone to the bar and taken a drink. Layton had then walked outside and gotten into a

* That averaged about one and a half murders a year—hardly an epidemic.

fight with some workmen who were headed for the saloon, and, hearing the commotion, Everett had gone out, grabbed Layton, and started wrestling with him. The wrestling match had then gradually moved into the saloon, with Al Layton finally getting the best of the proprietor. But Layton hadn't let Everett get up. The disturbance had eventually attracted Barton Everett, who, rifle in hand, had ordered Layton to get off his brother. Layton had done as he was told, but as he had gotten up he had pulled out his revolver, fired once, and killed the man he had beaten—popular Jim Everett. He had then run behind a door, gotten off another shot, and hit Barton in the arm. Al Layton had ridden out of Forsyth as fast as he could after the shootings, but had been promptly captured by lawmen, put on trial, and exonerated (probably because one Everett had jumped him on the street and the other had ordered him off his opponent while pointing a rifle at him).

The point, however, was that Al Layton was a yokel and a ruffian, while the Everett brothers were liked by the other notables in the community. So, all through the winter and well into the spring of 1884, small knots of aroused citizens, usually seated around Captain Nat N. Kinney's dining-room table or in his parlor, spoke somberly about the need to take the law into their own hands. They spoke about the need for a law-and-order league. Everett's murder wasn't the only thing bothering them, either. Petty thievery was on the increase, it seemed, and so were apparently senseless depredations against their property. One farmer had found several of his cows with their tongues either cut off or pulled out, causing them to starve. In an area where money was tight and beef relatively expensive, it's curious that, rather than stealing the animals, the culprit had mutilated them.[3]

No one knows exactly when the first law-and-order meeting took place, probably because there was a series of small meetings before the first big one. Vigilante groups often germinated in a casual conversation between two or three men, then perhaps among five, and finally a formal meeting would be called. Pinpointing dates is therefore usually impossible where first meetings are concerned. Captain Kinney presided at the preliminary meeting, however, and it was decided there and then to start the league. That group, composed of heavily bearded property owners, sitting on boxes, kegs, and every stick of furniture in the Everett brothers' supply room, reviewed the crime situation in

their county. Kinney reminded them of the number of unpunished criminals who wandered through the hills threatening the
lives and possessions of decent people. He explained, as he had
on many other occasions, that he was at heart a very peaceful
man, but that there came a time when even the most peaceful of
men had to defend themselves or suffer the direst of consequences. Everyone finally agreed to form an organization composed exclusively of taxpayers and landowners. J. J. Brown, a
lawyer, was appointed to draw up a secret oath, but Kinney
himself decided to write the customary constitution and bylaws.
The password and secret grip came later.

The monumental meeting took place, according to most participants, in January 1884. One member said years later that it
had taken place on the previous Fourth of July, because he remembered a great deal of "speaking and flag-waving," and
another set the date as sometime in April 1885. There was almost
unanimous agreement, however, on the site of that meeting. It
was held at the top of one of the broad, treeless hills that stick up
around the southwest Missouri countryside like bald heads rising
from fringes of green hair. In that part of the country, in fact,
such hills were given the name "bald" to describe their lack of
any vegetation taller than grass—Big Bald or Snapp Bald was the
way some referred to the hill where the law-and-order faction
held its first formal meeting, but to most it was known simply as
Bald Knob. It was picked because no one could approach its top
without being seen by the members of the league.

In what was described as a "blood-stirring oration over the
bloody shirt of J. M. Everett," Captain Kinney explained the
purpose of the group as passionately as he could and appealed to
those around him to join. "What will become of our sons and
daughters?" he asked. "Our lives, our property, and our liberty
are at stake. I appeal to you, as citizens of Taney county, to say
what we shall do. Shall we organize ourselves into a vigilant
committee and see that when crimes are committed the laws are
enforced? Or shall we sit down and fold our arms and quietly
submit?"[4] Everyone voted not to quietly submit.

Those present at the earlier meeting in Everett's storeroom,
including Colonel Prather, Captain P. F. Fickle, Captain J. B.
Van Zandt, Barton Everett, J. A. De Long (the Forsyth newspaper publisher), and others, had assumed that everyone at the
mass meeting would vote the group into formal existence and

had therefore worked out the initiation ceremony beforehand. All the charter members were told to split into groups of thirteen, join hands, and repeat the secret oath as lawyer Brown read it.

Do you, in the presence of God and these witnesses, solemnly swear that you will never reveal any of the secrets of this order nor communicate any part of it to any person or persons in the known world, unless you are satisfied by a strict test, or in some legal way, that they are lawfully entitled to receive them, that you will conform and abide by the rules and regulations of this order, and obey all orders of your superior officers or any brother officer under whose jurisdiction you may be at the time attached; nor will you propose for membership or sanction the admission of anyone whom you have reason to believe is not worthy of being a member, nor will you oppose the admission of anyone solely on a personal matter. You shall report all theft that is made known to you, and not leave any unreported on account of his being blood relation of yours; nor will you wilfully report anyone through personal enmity. You shall recognize and answer all signs made by lawful brothers and render them such assistance as they may be in need of, so far as you are able or the interest of your family will permit; nor will you wilfully wrong or defraud a brother, or permit it if in your power to prevent it. Should you wilfully and knowingly violate this oath in any way, you subject yourself to the jurisdiction of twelve members of this order, even if their decision should be to hang you by the neck until you are dead, dead, dead. So help me God.[5]

It was, of course, a college-fraternity sort of initiation, which must have left a majority of the half- or uneducated hillsmen awestruck, just the way an especially good preacher might have done with a hellfire-and-brimstone sermon. Notice should be taken of the typically military structure of the organization and the references to "lawful" brothers; there was, of course, nothing even remotely lawful about the group. More important, in this case, there was the insistence on obeying orders even to the extent of turning in a relative who committed a crime. Considering the importance of the family unit and the clan in Ozark society, Captain Kinney and J. J. Brown were demanding unprecedented loyalty. And, to further cement his vigilance committee, Captain Kinney devised a grip and passwords for use at night. The "captain" of the organization was supposed to be the first to arrive at a night meeting; each new arrival would approach with a long, unvarying whistle. "Who goes there?" the captain would then ask. "Bell," answered the newcomer. "Whose bell?" "My bell" or "Your bell" was the correct reply.

In the beginning, some members covered their faces with handkerchiefs or other pieces of cloth, while others never bothered. The grotesque black hoods would come later, and so would turning clothes inside out to further impede identification, particularly in Christian County about a year and a half later. With their moral justification, rules, loyalty, and chain of command firmly established, Captain Kinney and his chief lieutenants didn't have to worry about dress, though. They found themselves in the immensely invigorating position of having a large group of armed and obedient men at their complete disposal. They could now do what they really wanted to: they could strike.

Five miles north of Forsyth stood the tiny hamlet of Taney City, named more for the convenience of the postal authorities than as an accurate reflection of its size. The place was built around a general store and post office operated by an English couple named Dickenson. John T. Dickenson, very naturally, patterned his store after its British counterparts, right down to having a bell attached to the front door that would announce customers and bring him out from the living quarters in the back. The Dickensons were another popular couple in Taney County, at least among the better people, partly because of their refined English ways. On the other hand, they tended to do things that struck ordinary mountain folk as just plain "quare." Like drinking tea. Except for strong brews made of herbs and bark and taken for medicinal purposes, the mountain folk rarely drank tea, preferring their "biled" sludge. They also never ate mutton, the smell of which they hated, and therefore ridiculed anyone who, like the Dickensons, had a taste for roast lamb, mint sauce, and aromatic tea. That was one reason why Frank and Tubal Taylor had it in for the Dickensons; it was a reason most of their kin and friends would have understood. But the other reason concerned credit, or the lack of it, since John Dickenson had refused any to the Taylor boys after Frank had apparently ignored a month-old debt. When he asked for more credit and was turned down, Frank Taylor simply picked out a pair of shoes and left Dickenson's store with them under his arm. But the Englishman was not easily intimidated. He went to Forsyth, where, it should be noted, a grand jury was in session, and swore out a complaint against Taylor. After having been arrested within hours (which also is noteworthy) and having posted bond, Frank Taylor walked out of the Forsyth jail and into a store across the street, where he bought a heavy leather mule whip. He was quoted as boasting that he intended to wear it out on old John Dickenson.

According to most of the residents of nearby Forsyth who were around at that time, the Taylor brothers and a few friends paid the Dickensons a visit that night. The couple were awakened by shouting and pounding on their door. The shopkeeper lighted a kerosene lamp, but refused to open the door, so the Taylors and their friends smashed it open and went for him. Hearing the disturbance, Mrs. Dickenson grabbed a stove poker and rushed to the aid of her husband. Both of them were then shot—Dickenson in the mouth and right shoulder, and his wife in the back of the head. Their attackers, leaving them for dead, got out of there as fast as they could. One of them, however, dropped the mule whip near the broken door.

Both law-enforcement officers and the Bald Knobbers started looking for the Taylors the next day. Sheriff J. K. McHaffie was in the singular position of being not only the county's chief lawman, but also one of the founding "brothers" of the vigilante organization. When the Taylors sent word to McHaffie three days later that they wanted to give themselves up, of course, they could have had no idea whom they would be surrendering to. They had heard that the Dickensons were alive and therefore probably assumed that the trouble they were in would soon blow over. Their friends, assuming no such thing, kept going and were never seen again in that part of the country. Their friends would therefore continue living.

Among some of the more obvious elements of the situation that angered Captain Kinney and his friends was the suspicion that the Taylor boys had turned themselves in to collect the $500 reward offered by the county for their capture. So, the night the Taylors were put in jail, several dozen masked horsemen rode into Forsyth and pulled up in front of the flimsy building. Curious townspeople who were still up at that hour were warned to "Git back," while horses were hitched and sledge hammers applied to the jail door. Considering the small size of the town and the racket the Bald Knobbers must have made while smashing in that door, it's interesting that Sheriff McHaffie wasn't embarrassed enough at least to make a show of protecting his prisoners. No one seems to have questioned his absence, though.

Frank and Tubal Taylor were dragged whimpering and plead-

Membership certificate #3593 of the 1856 Committee of Vigilance of San Francisco. The watchful eye is uppermost.

Courtesy of William E. Burrows

This letter, written on San Francisco Committee of Vigilance stationery, was sent by a member of the organization to a brother in the East. One side shows Fort Gunnybags and the watchful eye seal. "at present the Villigance Comittee is doing the most," the writer reported. "every good citizen is a soldier   just imagine three thousand men armed to the teeth and Drilling by Moon light (your humble servant among them with a Musket on his shoulder) and you will have some idea of the scenes of san Francisco." The letter belongs to John McCarty of Cape Elizabeth, Maine.

Sharpshooters of the great San Francisco committee posed for this portrait within hours of the organization's reformation. They are a captain, three lieutenants, and two privates (standing left and center). Note the rudimentary uniforms, *de rigueur* display of swords, and the fact that one of their first acts was to be photographed.

William T. Coleman's
San Francisco Committee
of Vigilance
medal #1.

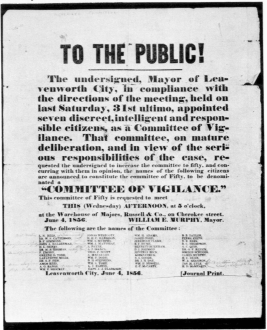

This Leavenworth, Kansas broadside, distributed in 1856, is notable for its listing of not only the names of those on the vigilance committee, but also for bearing the official sanction of the mayor. This open attitude suggests that the members of the committee thought they had little or nothing to fear from the law.

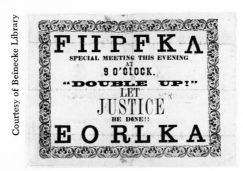

This broadside, posted in Argenta, Montana in 1867, includes mysterious letter combinations used either as a code or simply to intimidate the opposition. The broadside appeared three years after the death of Henry Plummer and in a town which was a short ride from Bannack, indicating that Vigilantes continued to be active in the area long after they were needed.

James Daniels, a vagrant, was captured by Montana Vigilantes in 1866 after he killed a man during a card game. Daniels was turned over to the authorities, convicted of manslaughter by a jury, and sentenced to three years in prison. After a few weeks behind bars, however, a petition by 32 respectable citizens prompted a reprieve. The Vigilantes' answer was recorded in this rare photograph.

Although Montana's two biggest vigilante actions occurred in 1863-64 and in 1884, smaller operations were a continuous fact of life in the territory. This double execution took place at Helena's "Hanging Tree" in 1870.

A mob, led by vigilantes, breaking into the New Orleans parish prison on March 14, 1891. Minutes later, nine of the Sicilians inside were shot to death, and two others were dragged onto the street and hanged. The illustration, by W. R. Leigh, appeared in the February 1896 issue of *Scribner's Magazine*.

In September 1975 a posse comitatus tried to keep union organizers out of tomato fields in California. These two vigilantes, one with a revolver, are shown wearing their badges (inset).

Francis Gillings, organizer of the vigilante group, was arrested in the tomato fields after a scuffle with sheriff's deputies during which his shotgun went off. Gilling's 14-year-old son, Dennis (rear) and two other posse members also were taken in by the lawmen. Their "posse" was organized the previous February; by September, when the confrontation occurred, twenty-two similar groups had sprung up.

ing out of the jail and taken to Swan Creek, about two miles north of Forsyth. There, under a large spreading oak, they were tried by a twelve-man Bald Knobber jury, were found guilty of attacking the Dickensons (everyone by then knew that the couple were recovering), and were hanged. With other miscreants foremost in their minds, the executioners slipped a note into the pocket of one of the corpses: "The Payton boys are next on the docket. Don't fool with the wrong end of the mule. Bald Knobbers."

A coroner's jury, meeting the next day, returned a verdict that as far as it went, was a model of accuracy: Frank and Tubal Taylor had met death by hanging at the hands of about a hundred unknown men. And that was it. Except that some people in Taney County began talking about "an eye for an eye," which, of course, hadn't been the case at all. And some, that very day, started muttering about the need for a counterorganization, because they considered the punishment inflicted on the Taylors to have been excessive. Moderator opposition to vigilantes, as we have seen, was frequent in nineteenth-century America. But rarely was it mentioned so early in a vigilante campaign, and it is safe to judge from that that there was considerable disapproval of Captain Kinney and his nightriders almost from the beginning. Within a few months, the anti–Bald Knobbers, also known as the Militia or the Slickers, would be actively opposing the group.

Meanwhile, bundles of switches began appearing on the doorsteps of "undesirables," as warning that if they didn't get out of the county immediately they could expect severe floggings or worse. The switches were the unmistakable equivalent of "3–7–77." Fires on the top of a knob in the middle of the night told frightened mountain families that the Knobbers were riding, and volleys of bullets smashing through windows confirmed the worst fears of those who had been singled out for eventual punishment. A reign of terror had started in Taney County.

Many Bald Knobbers were to say later that they never terrorized innocent people—that those who did were not under Captain Kinney's control. Laying aside the obvious questions of who decided guilt and innocence and the nature of the crimes the marked persons were guilty of, there's probably at least some truth to the claim. Evidence suggests that many of those who rode with Nat N. Kinney became infatuated with their power and made occasional sorties on their own. As with many other vigilante organizations, there was an element within the Knobbers that cloaked personal vendettas under the guise of popular justice. And the tendency was especially pronounced in the Ozarks, with that area's feud system. It was that trait of sheer personal revenge that was most often the catalyst for the formation of organizations that were antivigilante. How could the innocent victim of a grudge reprisal complain to the vigilante leadership when that leadership was secret? The only effective way of stopping splinter attacks was to gather one's own supporters and hit back. But, time and again, doing so was interpreted by the vigilante leaders as a threat to their organizations at large, so they, in turn, hit back, too. That was the usual genesis of a full-scale regulator-moderator war.

In spite of increasing antagonism and opposition to the Bald Knobbers, Kinney and the other leaders began encouraging similar groups in adjoining counties; Stone, Barry, and Douglas counties soon started Bald Knobber operations. It was the group in Christian County, however, that was to prove the most fateful. The Christian County Knobbers were organized in September 1885, after one of Kinney's lieutenants rode over and explained to some people in the neighboring district what the Knobbers were all about. Punishing the forces of evil, especially during those long, monotonous mountain evenings, seemed like a fine idea. So many of the men in the eastern reaches of Christian County started their own chapter, under the leadership of a farmer named "Bull Creek" Dave Walker and the oldest of his nine children, a seventeen-year-old named Bill. Whether Nat Kinney ever set foot in Christian County isn't known, since most of his group's records were deliberately destroyed. It isn't even known for sure if his brother Knobber was acting on orders when he delivered the word to Christian County or whether he was acting strictly on his own. What is known, though, is that as late as the 1930s surviving members of the mother chapter bitterly resented having their own activities in any way linked with those of the Christian County branch. What they had on their minds, though few of them would even mention it, was that night raid against the Greens and the Edens and its aftermath.

The Bald Knobbers in Taney County reached their peak during the winter and spring of 1886, as they left their switches behind doors, flogged or shot at undesirables, and tried to put down increasingly determined opposition by people who had become frightened and angry enough to organize. Captain Kinney shot and killed a young hillsman named Andrew Cogburn in a duel in front of the church house early in March. Cogburn, it seems, didn't like what Kinney stood for. But when he heard that a warrant had been issued for his arrest, on a charge of disturbing the peace, and that it had been given to Kinney to serve, he came into Forsyth, with a friend named Sam Snapp, looking for trouble. And he found it, too. Those who defended Kinney, both in and out of print, were quick to point out (as they always did) that Cogburn and Snapp were "rowdies" and that Cogburn had provoked the Captain into shooting. The jury that exonerated Kinney (which, it was charged, was crammed with Knobbers) seems to have believed that story. Yet Cogburn's reaction to word that a supposedly ordinary citizen like himself had been given, and had accepted, the responsibility of arresting him had made him understandably angry. Just who the hell was Nat N. Kinney to go around arresting folks, in place of the sheriff?

Captain Kinney may have been exonerated by the jury in Forsyth, but his having killed Andrew Cogburn proved to be the beginning of the end for the Taney County Knobbers. Charging that Kinney had killed Cogburn in cold blood, the anti-Knobbers sent a representative to Jefferson City to complain to Governor John S. Marmaduke and to suggest that a regular militia be set up to deal with the situation. Newspapers outside the Ozarks began getting the first details of the hooded bands riding through Taney County, and thousands of eager readers began following the exploits of the mysterious nightriders. That mortified many Taney County residents. Editorials denounced Knobber activities, and charges were made that they were all Republicans who attacked only Democrats (which tended to be true, but more because of economic motives than strictly political ideology), or that they were just settling old Civil War scores (which was nonsense). One anonymous letter appeared in the *Springfield Daily Herald* on March 6, 1886, and summed up a widespread feeling among Taney County people.

The killing of Joe [*sic*] Cogburn by Captain Kinney is but an outburst of the malice and hatred deep-seated and long-cherished in the hearts of an organized clan, whose motto is "rule or ruin." They scruple not at the most shameless schemes nor the darkest deeds of rapine and murder to redress imaginary injuries or to accomplish their diabolical aggressions upon the victims of their design.

When four or five hundred desperate men organize for the perversion of law and the frightening into silence of good citizens while they insult the dignity of law and order; when howling mobs run riot through the land, fire deadly volleys into houses, among helpless women and children, and force peaceable men to the alternative of deserting their homes and families or living perpetually under the menace of outlaws and assassins, the time has come for prompt and decisive action on the part of those who are in favor of law and order. . . . In 1885, during the April term of circuit court at this place, while a man was on trial for his life, the officers of the law were shocked one morning on finding two halters suspended, one in the grand jury room and one over the judge's seat in the court room, a peremptory demand for the verdict of guilty and a sentence of death. It was during the same month and year that the Taylor boys, who were charged with an assault on old man Dickenson, were forcibly wrested from the custody of the law by a mob, taken to the woods two miles from town and hung until dead. When the bodies were cut down by citizens a card was found in the vest pocket of one of the dead boys warning others in the following suggestive language: "The Payton boys are next on the docket. Don't fool with the wrong end of the mule. Bald Knobbers." . . . The unsuspecting victim of their malice is hounded and harassed until forced in defense of his own life or the protection of his home to shed blood or otherwise transgress their inflexible law. He then falls a victim either to lynch law or to perjury before the tribunals of the court. . . . In justice to the better classes of our citizens the present deplorable state of affairs calls loudly for forcible reform.

Citizen of Taney

Not, apparently, the hand of a godless and illiterate rowdy.

Having been petitioned by both sides, having read an increasing number of newspaper stories and editorials about the escapades in Taney County, and even having gotten reports that a miniature Civil War was brewing down there, Governor Marmaduke decided to send Adjutant General J. C. Jamison to Forsyth to investigate. Even before the General got there, however, Kinney called a mass meeting of his men, at which he justified their actions to them, denounced the militia plan as a potentially explosive one, and went on to push through a resolution intended to calm Governor Marmaduke. Its six paragraphs doggedly deplored lawlessness in the county, but stressed that the Bald Knobbers would thereafter "protect and defend the legal officers of the county in preserving the peace and enforcing order, and the mandates of the courts of the county, and will hold ourselves always in readiness to assist the civil authorities."[6] It was signed not by Nat N. Kinney, but by his friend, Alonzo Prather.

Although there doesn't seem to be anything around today to prove it, the situation in Taney County on the day of that resolution, March 10, 1886, suggests that Kinney had good reason to believe that events were closing in on him and his nightriders and that it was only a matter of time before angry and well-organized neighbors, and possibly even troops or lawmen sent in from the capital, ripped the Bald Knobber organization apart. Kinney's malleable attitude thus made it much easier for General Jamison to tell the Knobbers and others, in Forsyth on April 9, that his boss, Governor Marmaduke, intended to "enforce obedience to the civil law" and that it would be better for everyone if the Bald Knobbers disbanded, because they had "outlived" their usefulness. Jamison was able to report to Marmaduke that the suggestion had been accepted.

Kinney, Prather, and the other Taney County leaders who were present, with 500 of their men, on the village green when Jamison implored them to disband agreed to do so and immediately adopted a resolution that said so.

Whereas, there no longer exists any necessity for the continuance of the Citizens Committee in Taney County, as peace and quiet prevail supreme, and protection to everyone is guaranteed by the civil authorities; therefore, be it resolved. . . .[7]

The resolution was a face-saving one; its drafters were saying, for what they thought was the record, that they had done such a good job that they no longer were needed. They were also calling themselves a "Citizens Committee," which not only was less sinister than "Bald Knobbers," but also suggested broad community support. With that resolution drafted and signed, Kinney, Prather, Van Zandt, Fickle, De Long, and the others shook hands and parted, at least organizationally. For all practical purposes, and with the exception of a few minor sorties during the next couple of years, the Taney County Bald Knobbers ceased to exist. But the final, and by far the most infamous, chapter in the history of the Missouri nightriders was to be written in Christian County nearly a year later. On the day the Taney County group was disbanding under the thinly veiled threat of official force, their successors around Chadwick and Sparta were just warming up.

Captain "Bull Creek" Dave Walker's men started dispensing God's vengeful will in the approved way. They smashed whiskey barrels and beer kegs, broke bottles and spilled their contents, destroyed gambling equipment, chopped up rudimentary casinos and brothels or burned them down, and lashed scores of the devil's disciples to trees for barebacked whippings with hickory rods. In every case, whether the evildoer was a liquor seller, gambler, brothelkeeper, wife beater, or just plain troublemaker, he was severely flogged and given twenty-four hours to either get out of the region or stay there suspended from an oak.[8]

Captain Dave had gotten his commission in the Seventy-second Missouri Infantry during the Civil War and had separated from the service in 1864 with a reputation for coolness and bravery under fire. He then returned to Christian County, where his parents had settled after leaving Kentucky, and married Sarah Shipman. He followed that by planting crops and offspring as often as possible. Bill, the first of the nine, had the makings of a good man, according to his friends. That may have been true, but he also had a fair complexion and what were taken in those parts to be the soft features of a girl. He had a full head of dark hair, for example, but not so much as a whisker. In a land where almost every man had a beard, a mustache, or both, young Bill had to go barefaced. His appearance doesn't seem to have bothered his father or any of their friends, but it very likely bothered Bill quite a bit.[9] Perhaps to compensate for what he took to be his physical inadequacy, he gladly accepted a position as his father's lieutenant in the Christian County Knobbers. Having unsuccessfully tried tie hacking and clerking, Bill Walker found a suitable outlet for his abilities among the Knobbers. He was eventually to be attacked as ruthless and vicious by neighbors who didn't like him and his organization, but he tended to think of the enthusiasm with which he flogged bad people as stemming from his keen interest in high morals. Besides, being a leader of the Bald Knobbers gave Bill Walker his first taste of power, and power definitely agreed with him. So, of course, did doing good.

Doing good, or at least trying to, didn't necessarily mean beating and banishing debauched neighbors. Sometimes the Christian

County Knobbers rode for more complicated reasons. At two o'clock one cold morning in February 1866, for instance, about 200 of them got the owner of the timber company that supplied ties to the railroad out of bed and informed him that he was going to either raise the price he paid for the ties or see his commissary burned to the ground. Nearly 600 Knobbers worked for that company and bought food and other provisions from the company store, which paid them 20 per cent more if they took merchandise instead of cash. In an interview several years later, Robert E. Lee, the son of the owner of the company, and a distant relative of the Confederate general, said that the hooded men told his father to "hike the price and tell the inspectors ter be easier" or his commissary would go up in flames. Company inspectors had to pass on the size and quality of ties before a hacker could get paid for them; many of the oak slabs apparently were judged substandard, either because they really were or because the firm was trying to get them cheaper. J. L. Lee, however, stood his ground that cold February night and refused to be intimidated.

"You can burn my commissary and burn my ties. You can even take my life," the timberman told the hooded horsemen, in his most soothing tone. "After you do that, you won't find that you have accomplished what you hope for. I'm paying you as much as I can and am treating you as well as I can on the inspection. Here is something you must take into consideration—you are feeding your wives and children out of the commissary. If you burn it, where will you get anything to eat? After that, where would you find employment? If that happens, nobody else would be brave enough to come into these hills to employ you."[10] The Knobbers took a few minutes to put their horned heads together and finally decided that they got the message. They apologized to their employer and galloped back into the night, total failures in the art of the shakedown.

The first spectacular action, at least by Christian County standards, took place that summer, when 300 Knobbers, all wearing their black hoods, rode into Chadwick and poured 180 gallons of beer and whiskey through the floor boards of a few selected saloons. That escapade went down in mountain lore as the Chadwick Raid. The second spectacular action happened on the night of March 11, 1887, and it was the last.

It was a cold night, and, because it had been drizzling earlier, the ground and bushes were soaked. As the Knobbers wandered to their secret rendezvous at Smelter Hollow, however, the moon came out and provided enough light so they could barely see where they were going. Some came on horses and some on mules, but most walked, either along the St. Louis and San Francisco tracks or on top of the muddy ridge paralleling them. At a point about two miles from Sparta, they turned onto a secluded road that led into a dark oak forest. Now one or two of them who had brought kerosene lanterns with reflectors lighted them, so they could lead the others deeper into the trees. Finally, individually and in small groups, they began arriving at the Hollow. Those who had gotten there first had already cut long hickory switches and laid them in little bundles against exposed tree roots. They were thinking about laying them across exposed backs in a little while, though they weren't really sure whose backs they would be.

As the men from the Chadwick and Sparta companies drifted in, they gave the password and then stood around waiting for something to happen. William Newton, a twenty-six-year-old, who lived three miles southeast of Sparta, near the Walker place, came into the secret circle. Bill Walker was "sparkin' " Newton's sister. John Mathews, the deacon, was there, with his son, James, and Wiley, his nephew. Bud Ray, a smooth-shaven young man, like Bill Walker, and the leader of one of the Knobber contingents, had already come and gone. He had been disappointed by the small turnout and had decided that it wasn't a promising evening. The tedium of waiting around was broken by the initiation of William Abbott, who was ordered to stand in the center of a circle of Knobbers. He was then asked whether he could identify anyone around him. Abbott said he could not.

Now, however, some of the twenty-six Bald Knobbers who had bothered to trudge through the mud and wet foliage talked about going home because of the absence of so many of their brothers on that cold and uncomfortable night. Someone mentioned Bucky Bill's whiskey, undoubtedly looking forward to wrecking his place and giving him a good whipping. Captain Dave explained that a report on Bucky Bill had been expected but hadn't been made, so he didn't know for sure whether the man had whiskey or not. Some others tried to assure the elder Walker that they would find some liquor if they looked for it, but they were talked out of trying. Another black hood suggested whipping a farmer named Baty, whose crime consisted not of wife beating, overdrinking, or gambling, but of denouncing the Knobbers themselves. And Baty wasn't the only one, either. As had been the case in Taney County, an opposition group had already been formed by mountaineers who had had enough of the Knobbers' seemingly arbitrary and always terrifying night visits. They were called Slickers in Christian County, and they were, of course, intolerable to the Knobbers. Like other vigilante groups, whatever mandate they claimed to have rested squarely on citizen support, so serious opposition by their neighbors struck at the very heart of their existence and therefore had to be extinguished before it extinguished them.

A fire had by then been built to warm the group, and, as it reflected on their frightening hoods, they deliberated over whether to get Baty. They finally decided against it. With that the meeting really began to seem pointless, so at about ten o'clock Captain Dave reluctantly told his men to break up and go home. Five or six got on their horses and promptly disappeared into the brush cover. The rest started walking or riding slowly along the forest road toward the railroad right-of-way and the nearby dirt highway that connected with Chadwick and Sparta. They still wore their hoods.

As they came to the end of the dark trail and approached the muddy ridge near the tracks, someone got an idea—an inspiration. Not far away, secluded in the heavy timber, was the cabin of the William Edens family. Although the reason for deciding to hit his homestead has never been clearly established, it has been supposed that Edens's transgression, like that of farmer Baty, was "talkin' agin" the Knobbers. On the night following the elections the previous November, in fact, Edens and a relative had been whipped for the offense. Some recalled that either Charles Green, Edens's son-in-law, or William Edens himself had shot and killed a dog, while bringing a load of timber to Sparta, and then had openly wisecracked that he had knocked off a Knobber. Comparing anyone in the Ozarks to a dog was an unmistakable challenge, and when Bald Knobbers were the ones being compared it definitely was "fightin' talk." One of the hooded men who had administered that flogging in November had even warned Edens that any more insults against the sacred and God-fearing brotherhood would be answered with rope.

Now, having remembered quite clearly their grudge against

Edens, those who were left of the twenty-six decided to pay him a visit and reinforce the lesson given four months earlier. The Knobbers' frustration, after more tramping through the wet woods only to find William Edens's cabin deserted, can be imagined. They were still carrying their hickory switches and all, and itching for a godly errand to carry out with them, but close inspection showed beyond doubt that the place was empty. Some nights, the Walkers and their followers probably reflected, nothing went right. Disheartened and now deeply frustrated, the Knobbers walked back to the road wondering where their intended victim could be. And about then somebody thought of William Edens's father, James. The younger Edens might likely be spending the night over at the old man's place, and if they were lucky they'd find that smart-aleck son-in-law there, too.

As it was to turn out, that guess would mark a drastic change in the fortunes of the Bald Knobbers. Old James Edens was, indeed, sheltering his son and his daughter-in-law, Emma, and Charles Green and his sixteen-year-old wife, Melvina. Green had carried Melvina over from their own cabin the day before. She had come down with measles in January, at about the time she had her second baby, and had spent most of the time since then close to death. Early in March, though, Melvina had taken a turn for the better and had been brought to her grandparents' cabin, so that both her ma and her grandma could help complete her recovery. The one-room cabin therefore held eight people that night, including Charley's and Melvina's two children, one of them a two-month-old. The patriarch and his wife were sleeping on a high oak bed while the Knobbers were bearing down on them through the darkness outside, some running as quietly as possible and others guiding their horses under low branches while trying to stay on the trail. Charley, Melvina, and the children were sleeping in the only other bed, while William and Emma Edens shared a "shakedown" pallet on the floor. The men were in their long underwear and shirts, and the women had on heavy nightgowns. It was still very cold at night in the Ozarks. The tiny flame from a small lamp flickered on the mantel, over still-glowing coals that had heated the family's dinner. It was about eleven o'clock, which explains why no one in the little cabin heard the hooded men vaulting quietly over the unpainted fence out front and running around to the back door. Some of the raiders, excitement unquestionably welling inside them, moved to the front door and waited, giving the others plenty of time to get around back. None inside heard anything until it was too late.

The cabin had a small four-pane window just to the right of the front door, but, because of the hour and the practiced stealth of the squirrel and turkey hunters outside, none inside saw the hooded face appear at that window and look excitedly in at them. None heard the others bringing up railroad ties and axes with which to break down both doors. None heard the frenzied whispering as still others clutched hickory switches, slicing them through the damp air and against imaginary backs. None heard a sound until the windowpane shattered. There were few window-panes in Christian County in 1887, so getting to break one was a real treat. The glass exploded inward.

"Git up! Git up, or we'll kill every damned one of you," shouted one of the black hoods. A tremendous banging on the front door and then, again, "Git up, God damn you, or we'll kill you!"

"Pap," screamed William Edens, sitting up. "Git up! The Bald Knobbers are here!" The women screamed. Both Edens men and Charley Green, probably still foggy with sleep, began searching frantically in the near darkness for their pants and guns. More panes were smashed, and three bullets came through the empty space where they had been. The front door gave way to a heavy railroad tie, its timber shattering, and the rear door was broken apart at almost the same instant. Men wearing the black hoods with flapping horns and white-rimmed eye and mouth holes were now running into the room from both directions. Old lady Edens grabbed her husband's revolver, but it was too late. As James Edens tried to take it from her, three men caught him.

"He's got a pistol," screamed one of God's avengers. "Shoot him."

But they didn't shoot him. Somebody hit him on the head with an ax. James Edens fell onto Emma, his daughter-in-law, who fell backward, with the bleeding old man on top of her. He seemed to her, even in the poor light, to be dying for sure. As Emma Edens wriggled out from under her father-in-law, another Knobber pointed a gun at her and squeezed the trigger. The bullet barely missed her head.

Charles and Melvina Green, who had been sleeping on that bed beside the window, bore the brunt of the initial attack. He was shot through the head while swinging out of bed and was killed instantly. His recuperating wife was meanwhile fighting off a Knobber who had pounced on her. As she tore loose, another of the raiders pointed his shotgun at her, but they were so close that she was able to push his gun up as it went off. The shot nicked her little finger and the muzzle blast set her nightgown on fire. But, on fire or not, Melvina Green continued to struggle with the man holding the shotgun and even managed to tear away enough of his hood so she could see his face. There wasn't so much as a whisker on it.

William Edens, who had managed to get to the center of the room before most of the Knobbers crowded in, was hit where he stood. Seeing that her son had been shot, old lady Edens rushed to him, and when she realized that he was dead she collapsed beside his bleeding body.

Captain "Bull Creek" Dave Walker, who was to testify at his murder trial that he hadn't been in the Edens cabin during the onslaught, recalled running up to the place and shouting "What does that shooting mean?" He was to explain at the trial that when he got no coherent answer from his frenzied men he commanded, "Boys, for God's sake, stop that shooting."[11] Whatever he did or did not say, however, it must have been clear to him at that moment that the situation was desperately out of control. As he started for the cabin, he saw his men rushing out. His son, supported by two others, was in the lead. The reason young Bill Walker needed assistance quickly became apparent: his pants were on fire, and he had taken a bullet six inches above the knee. He was helped to the road in front of the cabin, where the fire was smothered and where he was allowed to slump to the ground. Bloody tracks led back to that dark cabin, and inside, two widows were wailing and already beginning their agonized calls for help.

While Captain Dave was deciding that his boy was going to have to get out of Christian County in a hurry and the other marauders were disappearing into the darkness, George W. Green, Charles's father and a close neighbor of the James Edenses, was rushing toward the place—toward the place from which the gunfire had come. As he ran down the road toward the cabin, he was stopped by one of the retreating Knobbers. "I've killed one damned Slicker tonight," said the voice behind the red-and-white-trimmed hole, and "I'd just as leave kill another." When he was asked where he was going, George Green answered meekly that he was "goin' but a little ways." He was allowed to continue, since the Knobber, too, was in a rush. Green would testify that the voice belonged to one of the Mathewses—either to Deacon John or to his nephew, Wiley.

The elder Green, followed by his wife, who had taken longer to dress, found his son sprawled on the bloody oak floor between the beds. Melvina had put out the fire on her nightgown and then had fainted. Now she lay near her bloodied husband. Old lady Edens had fainted, too. James Edens was found to have survived a bullet wound in the neck and an ax blow on the head.

Hillsmen began arriving at the Edens cabin at about sunrise. They found two black hoods near the house, both of which would substantiate the story the survivors were going to tell the authorities. Sheriff Zack A. Johnson and the county prosecuting attorney, Almus Harrington, arrived in a buggy at about noon, and so did J. P. Ralston, the coroner. While curious neighbors continued to poke around the cabin and grounds, Johnson and Harrington delicately grilled the women. The first question, of course, was whether anyone had gotten a look at a Knobber's face. It was a good question, rewarded with a good answer.

"I jerked a mask from one's face—aṭ least I tore it," said Melvina Green. "He had no beard. It was Bud Ray."[12]

Bud Ray was arrested within hours and taken to the small jail in Ozark, even as the wounded Bill Walker was on his way to refuge with kin in Douglas County. Under questioning, Bud Ray admitted to having been at the Smelter Hollow meeting, but insisted emphatically that he had gone home early and was unsaddling his horse when he heard the shooting. While an angry mob gathered outside the little jail and talked about revenge, Ray was asked for the names of the others who had attended the meeting the night before. He understood quite clearly that there was far more than a flogging charge against him, and in the face of that reality he quickly decided that all the secret grips, whistles, oaths, and passwords were inconsequential. So he talked. In fact, he named each of the other twenty-five Knobbers who had met at the Hollow, including William Abbott, the hapless initiate, who had taken his vow just in time to be implicated in the murders. The Sheriff then swore in about a dozen deputies. Before that day was over, the lawmen were combing the district for every man on the list.

Before he was taken at his Bull Creek farm, Captain Dave Walker whispered to relatives that word should be sent to his son to move from Douglas County to other kin in Arkansas. Captain Dave thought that crossing the state line would offer more protection. He was wrong. After leaving the instructions for Bill, "Bull Creek" Dave went peaceably to the jail in Ozark. The three Mathews men who had been at the meeting also were brought in, and so was C. O. Simmons, the pastor of the Chadwick Baptist church. Parson Simmons, in fact, was arrested right after he finished singing a hymn, in his fine bass, at the Edens-Green funeral. Within thirty hours of the start of the man hunt, it should be noted, all the Bald Knobbers named by Bud Ray were behind bars except for Bill Walker, and Sheriff Johnson was even then developing a plan for catching him, too.

Like all good rural sheriffs, Zack Johnson knew the goings on of the people in his jurisdiction. He knew about their births and deaths, their arguments and feuds, the success or failure of crops and business enterprises. He knew who tended to drink too much, who had done well or badly in school, who liked to beat up on their women. And he even knew who was "sparkin'" whom. Men like Johnson thought that a good peace officer should know those things. He therefore knew that Bill Walker had been keeping company with pretty Lois Newton, the sixteen-year-old sister of William Newton, one of the Knobbers who had already been captured and indicted for the double murder. Now Lois and William had an older brother named Joseph, and Joseph, Zack Johnson figured, would be understandably upset by William's predicament. He might even be upset enough to find out where his sister's sweetheart was hiding, in order to save his younger brother. No matter that Bill Walker and Joe Newton were supposed to be friends and eventual in-laws; the responsibility of kinship would come first. Zack Johnson was right. He quickly persuaded Newton to find Bill Walker.

When Joe Newton finally caught up with Walker in Arkansas, the young fugitive was very glad to see him—a familiar, friendly face. With seeming anxiety, Newton explained to the Bald Knobber lieutenant that all hell had broken loose back home; that people were stirred up, that their friends in the Knobbers were locked in jail and charged with murder, that the papers around the state were playing up the double killing as if nothing else were going on in the world, and that the law was searching relentlessly for the only Knobber who had gotten away. Newton then suggested to Walker that the only really safe course was for both of them to keep moving, maybe even to Mexico or South America, where Bill could make a new start. The Knobber enthusiastically agreed. That having been decided, Joe Newton further suggested that they make their way back up to West Plains, Missouri, and catch a freight headed for the Southwest. Apparently unaware that that route would lead him back into the jurisdiction of Missouri lawmen, Bill Walker again agreed, and both of them started the trek toward West Plains. Along the way, they picked up another Christian County man who had escaped from jail there a few months earlier and who was delighted for the company of the two kindred souls from back home.

When the three reached the outskirts of West Plains, Newton suggested that they make camp and rest for a few days. They did. Then he suggested that, since he was the only member of the trio who wasn't wanted, he was in the best position to go into town for food. The logic seemed faultless. Within an hour of Joseph Newton's arrival in West Plains, this telegram was sitting on Zack Johnson's desk:

Z. A. Johnson, Ozark, Mo.
COME TWO
J.D.N.[13]

Newton estimated how long it would take Johnson to get to West Plains, and when he thought he would be able to find the Sheriff there he again left camp, this time on the pretext of trying to find out when the next train was due from Memphis. He told his companions that they wanted to be on that train. After meeting Johnson and a deputy in town and making plans, Joseph Newton returned to camp, told Bill Walker and the other man that they would be going in later that day, and waited. All three walked into West Plains at the appointed time, went to the railroad station, and started looking for the train from Memphis. Instead, they found Zack Johnson, his revolver drawn, and were taken in handcuffs to a hotel, where they were kept until they were put on the midnight train for Ozark. Johnson played his part perfectly, even to handcuffing Joe Newton and telling him he was under arrest for aiding fugitives from justice.

Those who had been taken during the first thirty hours had in the meantime been thoroughly questioned and, in some cases, had provided thorough answers. A few no doubt hoped for leniency; others, lacking experience at being grilled by lawmen, became confused under close interrogation. They had begun implicating one another within hours of being captured, and Charley Graves even took Sheriff Johnson to a secluded place where the nightriders had stashed four hoods and a lantern. Eight days after the roundup, fifteen Bald Knobbers had been sent to the Springfield jail on murder charges, while those suspected of lesser crimes had been freed on bail. The people of Christian County had several times voted down a bond issue for a new jail to replace the flimsy and cramped one they had. The necessary money was voted after the Edens-Green killings.

The Knobbers in Taney County had no sooner quieted down when the newspapers in southwest Missouri had fresh grist for their columns. "If found guilty, the extreme penalty of the law should be meted out to them," said an editorial in the *Springfield Daily Leader*. "Bald Knobism must be crushed out in southwest Missouri, let it cost what it may."[14] The grand jury, probably well aware of the editorial rage and also flinching at the prospect of having the rest of the country picture southwest Missouri as a nest of hooded, nightriding sadists out of the mold of the Ku Klux Klan, adjourned on April 27 after indicting eighty men on nearly 250 charges of murder, whippings, intimidation, and, interestingly enough, pouring out perfectly good Chadwick whiskey. The *Daily Leader* used one paragraph the next day to praise the grand jury's decision and slice through the Knobbers' Fundamentalist balderdash.

The inquiries have been thorough and it is thought that the society of masked regulators, who caused a reign of terror in this vicinity is totally annihilated, although at an awful cost to the community. Many old gray heads will be brought to the grave through the errors of a son blindly following desperate leaders, seeing only fun and frolic in midnight whippings.

The trial began, in Ozark, on Monday, August 23, 1887, and ended the following April, after one of the most colorful and spirited legal clashes in Missouri history. Journalists from as far as Saint Louis were there. So were hill people who feared and despised the Knobbers, others who openly admired them, and the families and close friends of the accused.

If the people of Christian County shared just one thing at that point, it was embarrassment. The picture of fiercely proud Ozark hill people, rugged individualists who made a fetish of pride and independence, has been overdrawn. They were, however, at least as aware of a communal black eye as any other Americans, and they resented it just as much. Now they looked around and saw reporters scouring their community for bits of local color, recollections of actual Knobber attacks, and all manner of description of their lives and customs, as if they were some species of freak. The one telegraph line out of Ozark was a conduit for "hot copy" about them that would appear in newspapers most of them would never read. But they knew that the "furriners" with the notebooks were describing them to the city people as a bunch of backward bumpkins who had produced a secret society of moral fanatics and nightriding terrorists and lunatics.

The prisoners who were accused of relatively unimportant crimes, such as unlawful assembly, were given small fines. Knobbers who had pleaded guilty to involvement with the organization but who could satisfactorily prove that they had had nothing to do with the murders were fined a bit more heavily. The presiding judge, given the choice of housing the culprits in the local jail, and therefore feeding them at county expense, or of getting as much money out of them as they could afford to pay, wisely chose the latter. He fined twenty-four of them amounts ranging from $12 to $50 and put them under bond.

It's important to mention here that while the Christian County trial was going on another Knobber trial was taking place in Jefferson City, the state capital. And that affair was being watched, too. The trial at Jefferson City had been started by federal prosecutors who were charging the nightriders there with intimidating homesteaders and with trying to use terror to frighten them off their land. The tactics, according to the federal lawyers, amounted to a violation of the Homestead Act.* One homesteader testified at the federal trial that a gang of Knobbers, most of them from Christian County, had whipped him at two o'clock in the morning and, because they had heard that other Knobbers were getting in trouble for warning victims to vacate their land, had used "reverse English" and told him to stay. He said he had gotten out fast. According to his statement, the

* The Homestead Act, which went into effect on January 1, 1863—the day Lincoln issued the Emancipation Proclamation—opened vacant lands to the public for agricultural settlement. As originally written, any citizen or intended citizen over the age of twenty-one could get title to 160 acres of public land by establishing residence, cultivating part of it, and paying $1.25 an acre after six months.

Knobbers had told him that they were flogging him because he didn't support his wife. He went on to testify, however, that before the whipping Amos Jones, a son-in-law of Captain Dave Walker, had tried "two or three times unsuccessfully" to buy his homestead.[15] Other witnesses said that Captain Dave himself had led the foray.

This testimony in federal court adds an interesting dimension to the Bald Knobber story, although it is another familiar one in the history of vigilantism—that of wielding an armed citizens' group for the accumulation of wealth. It is precisely what the San Francisco committee of 1856 did, in a far more sophisticated way, by forcing the political and economic opposition into exile and then, in effect, staging a political *coup d'état*. The accumulation of good land, then, seems to have been one of the motives for Knobber activity, along with moral fervor and the pervasive craving for entertainment.

Captain "Bull Creek" Dave Walker, his son Bill, and John and Wiley Mathews were sentenced to hang after several other Knobbers and the survivors of the March 11 slaughter testified in grim detail about what had happened that night. Dave Walker's defense—that he hadn't been in the cabin at the time of the murders—was dismissed by the jury on the ground that, present or not, he had been responsible for the acts of those under his command. The verdict was taken to the state supreme court on appeal. It was upheld. It was taken to Governor David R. Francis, who was to serve as ambassador to Russia during World War I. Francis, after weighing petitions by both sides, decided not to substitute life imprisonment for the gallows, as defense counsel had requested. He did, however, agree to set a stay of execution, from April 19 to May 10. Meanwhile, John and Wiley Mathews escaped through the efforts of a friendly and enterprising jail employee. The Bald Knobber chaplain was picked up the next day, after having spent the night huddling in a near-frozen field (he was turned in by a farmer). Wiley was never found. Some said he went to England, others that he never left the country.

Three days before the new date for the hanging, Governor Francis sent word to the defense lawyers that their request for another stay had been denied. His motives undoubtedly were political. On the one hand, there was growing sentiment in southwest Missouri to spare the lives of the three remaining prisoners.

But, on the other, the Governor read the papers and he therefore understood that many in his state and across the nation saw the Walkers and John Mathews as dangerous lunatics and, even worse, as dangerous lunatics representative of Missouri mountaineers. To commute the death sentence, Francis must have calculated, would be to show the outside world that he sanctioned cold-blooded murder. Francis had ambitions that went beyond the governorship, and he was not about to be derailed by a trio of Christian County crackers. And that was that.

The scaffold was positioned so that an opening to it could be made in the brick wall of the new Ozark jail. The condemned men could therefore walk right through and, because only one trap was to be used, all fall at the same instant. Zack Johnson figured it would be better if they all went at the same time, although he wasn't really sure, since these were to be the first legal executions in the county. Sheriff Johnson, in fact, had never even seen a hanging and for a while considered sending for a professional hangman. The prisoners talked him out of it, though, explaining that they preferred to die at the hand of a sympathetic "friend," rather than that of some stranger. It was another in their string of mistakes.

Nor was that Zack Johnson's only problem. The night before the executions were to take place, Bill Walker decided that he wanted to be baptized. Since the Sheriff had no intention of taking one of his celebrated prisoners to the nearest creek on the eve of his execution, particularly after Wiley Mathews's escape, he decided to move a bathtub into the jail. Finding a bathtub in Christian County in 1889 was no easy matter, but one was finally located and brought in, and while a large group of the devout sang and prayed Bill Walker was properly cleansed and purified. He spent most of the remainder of the night singing, praying, and playing "Home, Sweet Home" and "Swanee River" on his harmonica, while his father sobbed and worried about the family, but repeated his innocence. Outside, a small group of the morbidly curious watched the jail. They, in turn, were watched by twenty-five deputies whose Winchesters glinted in the moonlight.

The three stepped out of the jail and onto the trap at 10:00 A.M. on May 10, 1889, each in a new black suit and each fortified with a big breakfast and a shot of port to steady his nerves. The trial jurors, some witnesses, and about a dozen reporters stood nearest to them and, beyond, the crowd that hated or loved them. Each man made a short statement explaining that he was innocent and adding that he was fully prepared to meet God. Dave Walker complained to Zack Johnson that the rope around his neck was too tight, so the lawman loosened it. All three now stood there looking out at the crowd, with the ropes in place.

"Friends," said John Mathews, nearly in tears, "how many of you will help my poor wife and children who are the sufferance when I am gone?" Hands went up. "Thank God there are many." Zack Johnson put a black hood over each of their heads. Then he stepped in front of the scaffold and pulled the lever that activated the trap door he had designed and built. The crowd gasped.

Dave Walker dropped so low that his feet touched the ground; he seemed to be slowly strangling. His son had fallen even lower; he had fallen so low, in fact, that he was on his knees. Bill Walker began to moan as blood started gurgling out of his mouth. His father had meanwhile been lifted and dropped again, on a shortened rope. He struggled violently and then was still. When they tried to pick up Bill, though, the noose slipped off, and he pitched forward on his face.

"Oh, Lord," whimpered Bill Walker, "be merciful to me and relieve me of this anguish."

While his father and John Mathews were being cut down, Bill Walker was lifted back up and seated on the trap. Zack Johnson sat beside him and tried to steady him. He was still throwing up blood under his black hood.

"Let's hurry and get it over," he begged the sheriff.[16]

Two deputies held up the agonized vigilante lieutenant, and Zack Johnson again slipped the noose around his bloody neck. Again the trap was sprung, and this time the shortened rope did the job. He was cut down sixteen minutes later and laid beside his father and the Deacon. Then the black death hoods, which had probably been made by Zack Johnson's wife, and which weren't really worth two bits apiece, either, were removed and thrown away.

8

Louisiana: "Arrest every Italian you come across"

THE WHISTLING boy should have put David C. Hennessy on his guard. Had the popular young New Orleans Superintendent of Police become suspicious when the boy appeared out of the mist ahead, whistled loudly, and then darted off, disappearing into the shadows made by the street lamps, it would very likely have saved his life. Had it crossed David Hennessy's mind that the whistle was a signal to the men waiting up ahead, with their shotguns ready, he could have turned and hurried back to the corner of Rampart and Girod, where he had just left his friend Captain William O'Connor, of the Boylan Police Agency. Or he might have pulled out his revolver and taken cover in the doorway of the nearest of the residential buildings that lined Girod. At the very least, Hennessy might have shouted for help, although doing that would have been out of character for him. But, strangely, he ignored Asperi Marchesi as the fourteen-year-old spotted him and whistled and then ran as fast as he could. Italian urchins are fast on their feet.

It was close to midnight on Wednesday, October 15, 1890, and it was Superintendent Hennessy's last night on earth. Earlier that evening, he had gone to City Hall to attend a meeting of the Board of Police Commissioners. He had then returned to his office at the central police station on South Basin Street, stayed there for a little more than an hour talking with colleagues, and finally left with Captain O'Connor at about eleven-fifteen. There had been a great deal to talk about, both at City Hall and at police headquarters, and, as usual, much of it was about all the Sicilians in New Orleans and the crime they had brought with them from the Mediterranean. Hennessy and some of his colleagues had been directly involved in the capture of the notorious Giuseppe Esposito, back in '81, and had seen him sent to New York in irons and then deported to the old country for a sentence of life imprisonment. David Hennessy was well acquainted with the Provenzano-Matranga banana vendetta, and with the majority of the brutal crimes that had been committed in New Orleans since 1878 and attributed to the Mafia Society. As much as anyone else in New Orleans police circles, in fact, David C. Hennessy could be said to be an expert on the workings of the mysterious and sinister organization. He was a Mafia specialist, and that's why it was ridiculous for him not to have understood what the whistling boy was doing on that misty street at that hour of the night.

David Hennessy lived with his widowed mother at 275 Girod Street. Although it wasn't a particularly nice block, his mother had been there so long that she had become attached to it, so her thirty-two-year-old son had told his friends that he would remain there until she died. Then, he said, he would move to a better neighborhood. The Superintendent usually walked along Basin Street to get to the house, but when it rained the sidewalks on Basin became muddy, so he would use South Rampart, instead. On the night of one of the most sensational murders in New Orleans history—a murder that has yet to be solved—Hennessy and O'Connor walked up South Rampart because of the sporadic rain. Chatting all the way, they crossed Gravier and Perdido and, just before reaching Poydras, came to Dominic Virget's celebrated oyster saloon. Virget's had a pleasant ambiance and very good oysters, so Hennessy invited his friend to have some, and William O'Connor accepted. Hennessy was always good company. He was a tall, intrepid-looking man, with a ruggedly handsome face, well-oiled black hair combed into a long curve over his forehead, and an amicable disposition. So both men, talking all the while, had a half-dozen oysters each. Hennessy washed his down with a glass of milk.

After leaving Virget's, the policemen continued south on Rampart, crossing Poydras and Lafayette and finally coming to Girod. Since O'Connor thought that Hennessy was on the Sicilians' hit list, he offered to escort his friend home, but Hennessy wouldn't hear of it. So they said good night right there on the corner of South Rampart and Girod and parted. David Hennessy then turned west and started for number 275, which was between Basin and Franklin. As he approached his home he heard nothing except his own steps on the wet pavement—nothing until the whistle and then, without doubt, the sound made by the fast young feet. The sound bounced off the buildings that lined the seemingly deserted street before being absorbed by the heavy gulf air and low-lying fog. Hennessy's ears must have picked up the signal and relayed it to his brain, but, for reasons we will never know, the brain did not react. So he continued walking until he reached his house. He was just getting his key into the front door when the shooting started.

The buckshot came from almost right across the street—from the corner of Basin and Girod and from a nearby shed. The men who fired at the Superintendent of Police had moved into position from a dark alley, and at such short range they couldn't have missed. To make absolutely sure that they would get him, they had selected four "blunderbusses," or sawed-off folding shotguns, and one double-barreled shotgun, all of which provided a thick cone of fire. The noise was terrible. When Hennessy turned to face the pellets that were coming at him his revolver was already out, and, although he had been hit, he started shooting back. He got off three or four rounds, all wide of the mark, while standing unsteadily in front of his door and bleeding from wounds in the neck and the left side of the chest. One of his attackers came out of the darkness and into the bright street light, knelt to steady his aim, and got off another shot at the swaying policeman before retreating back into the shadows. Now Hennessy was staggering toward the corner. As he tried to make his way toward help, the men with the shotguns came out of the alley and from behind the shed and followed along on their side of the street, keeping up with him and methodically firing, reloading, and firing again as they walked. It was like men-of-war pacing an armed sloop and sending murderous broadsides into their pitifully unequal opponent. David C. Hennessy was getting blown out of the water.

O'Connor and J. C. Roe, another member of the Boylan Police Agency, which was one of the city's private police forces, both heard the shooting. Roe, who was nearest, got there first. In fact, he got there in time to try to shoot back at Hennessy's assailants, but, he was to explain later, his pistol wouldn't work. After getting grazed on an ear, Roe ran away. Then O'Connor, another friend of Hennessy's named Thomas Anderson, and others who had been attracted by the gunfire began arriving. They found the victim sprawled on Mrs. Henry Gillis's porch, a little way down Basin, at number 189.

"Oh, Billy, Billy, they have given it to me and I gave them back as best I could," Hennessy told O'Connor. The Superintendent was lying in blood coming out of six wounds and was unable to hold up his head.

"Who gave it to you, Dave?" asked O'Connor.

"Put your ear down here." Captain O'Connor did as he was asked and was rewarded with an answer.

"The Dagoes did it," said the dying Superintendent of the New Orleans police.[1]

David C. Hennessy died at Charity Hospital at 9:06 the next morning. He had spent most of the night assuring assorted city officials, including Mayor Joseph A. Shakspeare and Police Commissioner W. H. Beanham, that he would be all right. He undoubtedly had also told them, too, that "the Dagoes" got him. After an autopsy, the body was turned over to Francis Johnson and Sons, the undertakers, and prepared for interment. It was taken back to the Hennessy home late that afternoon and stayed there until the following morning, when it was carried by a detail of policemen to City Hall; there it lay in state until 3:00 P.M. Friday. So many people came to see David C. Hennessy's body that some newspapers estimated that the crowds were larger than those that had come to pay respects to Jefferson Davis, who had occupied the same spot ten months earlier. Hennessy was taken off display and brought to Saint Joseph's Church for obsequies that Friday, October 17, and then, at the head of a long procession, to Metairie Cemetery for burial. Within a few months of his murder, David C. Hennessy's body was lying under a handsome monument bought by popular subscription.

Within hours of his death, however, a man hunt was started

for his killers. The New Orleans Police Department had the benefit of a description of the murderers from the victim himself —they were "Dagoes." Sicilians. With that fat bit of information to go on, the entire force was called out and given this simple order: "Arrest every Italian you come across."[2] Naturally, it was impossible to do that, since there weren't more than 200 men in the New Orleans Police Department in 1890 and there were thousands of Sicilians in the city.* So only forty-two suspects were arrested during the twenty-four hours after the murder, and about sixty-five others during the days immediately following. Many were interrogated at police headquarters and released, but dozens of others were held for days in police stations or in the parish prison. Meanwhile, an incensed public began clamoring for justice.

John Journee, a captain who was quickly named acting superintendent by Mayor Shakspeare, and several of his top subordinates thought they knew who had ordered David Hennessy's execution, and why. The perpetrators, they decided, were members of that shadowy collection of thieves and cutthroats known as the Mafia Society. And the reason for the hit had been what the Sicilians themselves called *nu delittu ci grida vindetta*—a "crime" demanding vengeance.

Most journalists and historians interested in the so-called Italo-American incident of 1891 say that the Mafia was introduced into New Orleans in 1878 by a burly Sicilian fugitive named Giuseppe Esposito, alias Randazzo, who was wanted in Italy for kidnaping, extortion, robbery, murder, cutting off an English minister's ear, and other serious crimes. They have credited Esposito with establishing the Mafia in New Orleans the way others have credited Garibaldi with the Italian unification—as a fact beyond serious question.

Although murders and other crimes of violence had been going on in the Italian (or Sicilian) ghetto before Giuseppe Esposito showed up, they were put down as being either outgrowths of family feuds or personal hits by vindictive free-lancers. When Esposito and some of his friends arrived from the old country, however, they formalized their criminal escapades. They are said to have systematically pillaged suburban sections of the city and

---

* Sicilians and Italians were listed separately in the "Nativity" category of the crime section of the *Annual Report of the Superintendent of Police;* see, for example, the report for 1892.

isolated plantations along the Mississippi, set up hide-outs and rendezvous points in the unmapped marshes, swamps, and bayous throughout the area, and shaken down Italian merchants for protection money. The charges are undoubtedly true. But, in doing those things, Giuseppe Esposito wasn't performing any criminal activities that Henry Plummer hadn't also performed, and performed better. Other Italian-American gangsters soon began getting in on the act, and as the 1870s turned into the 1880s loose-knit groups of Italian criminals formed in New Orleans, as well as in other southern and eastern cities. They were collectively called the Mafia by those in the non-Latin establishment who associated them with the *mafiosi* in Sicily and who looked on them and their sordid activities with a mixture of horror, disgust, and contempt. There was a Mafia in Sicily composed of hoodlums, so, the reasoning went, Sicilian hoodlums anywhere must have been in the Mafia. But the reasoning seems to have been incorrect. The Sicilian criminals in New Orleans were, in reality, gangs in the Plummer mold, though, for ethnic reasons having to do with the Italian family structure, they usually contained several relatives. They were in no sense masterminded by "dons" who sliced up territory like so much lasagne and who had fearsome tentacles reaching everywhere. But portraying them as the North American branch of an international crime cartel united by blood and booty satisfied many Americans' taste for violent antiheroes and gave law-enforcement people truly worthy adversaries. This alien-conspiracy syndrome is nicely described by Dwight C. Smith, Jr., the director of institutional research at the State University of New York at Albany, in his *The Mafia Mystique*.[3] In any case, it was the murder of David C. Hennessy and the events following it that actually started the Mafia-conspiracy theory in the United States. Italians from Naples to Ragusa were considered by many Americans of the late nineteenth and early twentieth centuries to be hopelessly crime prone.

In describing events surrounding the New Orleans Mafia incident, and especially the Sicilians involved in it, John S. Kendall, the author of a three-volume history of the city,[4] makes this remarkable observation: "It was a system of terrorism founded on fraternity, which could not exist save for the peculiar character of the Southern Italian mind. Suspicious of the government, the Italian of the Neapolitan provinces, Calabria, and Sicily was, and perhaps still is, instinctively an enemy of the police."[5]

Giuseppe Esposito's undoing had started at the hands of a wife he left behind in the old country. Not long after his arrival in New Orleans, he had fallen in love with and married a young widow with two children. When the first Mrs. Esposito found out about the second, she apparently went into a Latin rage. She then went in to see the *carabinieri* and told them where her husband was living. The *carabinieri* told the people at the Ministry of Justice, who told the people at the Foreign Office, who told the Italian consul in New York, who wrote to the police in New Orleans asking for help in capturing and extraditing the fugitive. And that's how David C. Hennessy, a gambling specialist, got in on the case.

After narrowing the list of suspects, Hennessy thought he had his man, so he got an artist named Hoeppner to make a sketch of him surreptitiously. The drawing was sent to Italy, where, as luck would have it, it was compared with another, made years before by an American artist who had been kidnaped and held for ransom by Esposito's gang. The artist had been the guest of a prince and had been mistaken for his host by the kidnapers. So the only way he had been able to prove that he was who he said he was had been by making a good picture of his captor. Esposito had liked that picture so much that he had allowed vanity to overcome wisdom. He had sent a ransom note for the artist to the prince on the back of it. The prince had paid the ransom, the artist was released, and, of course, the drawing was dropped into Esposito's police dossier. And that was how the *carabinieri,* after seeing Hoeppner's picture, were able to assure the New Orleans police that the man known there as Randazzo was really Giuseppe Esposito, the scourge of Sicily.

Esposito was duly arrested by Hennessy, another New Orleans detective, and two New York policemen, named Mooney and Boland. He was put on a ship for New York and, from there, taken back to Sicily under heavy guard. While he was still in jail in Manhattan, his friends in New Orleans raised $5,000 for use in hiring lawyers and meeting other expenses necessary to fight extradition, but the plan collapsed when the man entrusted to carry the money to New York embezzled it. A legal defense probably wouldn't have mattered, anyway. The Italians wanted Esposito so badly that they had sent a warship to collect him. He was taken back to Palermo under heavy naval guard and, in December 1881, was convicted on six of eighteen counts of murder.

Giuseppe Esposito was then sentenced to death, but King Umberto I commuted the punishment to life imprisonment in deference to the wishes of parliament, which disapproved of the death penalty.[6]

Esposito's friends and accomplices in New Orleans would not believe that he had been betrayed by a mere woman. Instead, they suspected a local Italian named Abruzzi, and his chest was therefore destroyed by shotgun pellets one night as he came out of a meeting in Screwman's Hall, at the corner of Exchange Place and Bienville Street. Another Sicilian, named Arditi, was arrested, charged with the murder, tried, and acquitted. That was followed by mumbling around the city that the jury had been bought. The law-enforcement establishment and many leading citizens also heard that there was bitter resentment among Esposito's friends over David Hennessy's role in his capture and deportation. So the Esposito episode constituted one popular indictment against the New Orleans Italians, and against those from the Mezzogiorno in particular, at least where Hennessy's murder was concerned.

A second, and more credible, indictment had to do with Hennessy's role in the celebrated Provenzano-Matranga feud and court battle. The feud seems to have started when the Matrangas moved in on the Provenzanos' business, which consisted mainly of unloading fruit at the city's docks. When the banana business became important, in about 1887, many Italians went into it, either as importers or as stevedores and other dock and transportation workers. A great deal of money was at stake, especially for immigrants from a chronically poor background, so competition for contracts was fierce. And the most relentless competition developed between Anthony and Charles Matranga and Joseph and Peter Provenzano, with the former having come out on top by the spring of 1890. So, one night in early May of that year, the Matranga brothers and five of their employees were ambushed as they returned home from unloading the steamer *Foxhall*. As their wagon passed a clump of weeds at the corner of Claiborne and Esplanade, a shotgun went off, and Anthony Matranga was hit in the leg. There was no doubt in anyone's mind that the attack had been the work of the Provenzanos, so they were arrested, charged, and put on trial.

And they were convicted. They were convicted in spite of what were unmistakable efforts by the police to establish alibis for them. Police testimony at the trial was so blatantly in favor of the defendants that the newspapers and some prominent citizens of New Orleans charged that the law-enforcement officials were trying to shield the Provenzanos. The police angrily countered by demanding an investigation, and, after examining witnesses at great length, a grand jury exonerated the officers. Although David Hennessy did not testify at the Provenzano trial, it was generally understood that the accusations of friendship for the Provenzanos had been directed at him, too. Understandably, the Provenzano family asked for a new trial, and their appeal was pending in criminal court when Hennessy was murdered.

Whatever David Hennessy's relationship with the Provenzano brothers, word got around after the trial that he had collected a great deal of evidence against the Matrangas—new evidence, which he planned to give under oath at a retrial. Obviously, said the wags, the Matrangas couldn't be expected to let him take the stand with information that would hurt them. The wags even said that the Matrangas had argued with Hennessy over the way the Provenzanos were treated while in jail; that he had been "paying the board of the prisoners" and allowing them certain luxuries not shared by ordinary inmates.[7]

When David Hennessy was murdered, then, just about every non-Italian in New Orleans accepted it as fact that Italians in general, and Sicilians in particular, were the scum of the city, were corrupting society, and had been directly responsible for the killing. They suspected the Matrangas in particular, and they reacted with a fury that had been building for years.

The morning after David Hennessy was shot, notices signed by prominent citizens appeared in the city's newspapers calling on the people of New Orleans to attend mass meetings and form committees "to assist the officers of the law in driving the murderous Mafia from our midst."[8] The notices, in effect, constituted warnings to the city administration that it was expected to endorse the committees. The administration was prepared to do even more than that. After Hennessy's death and the funeral that followed, Mayor Shakspeare, feeling heat from the notables in the city, issued this telling message to the City Council, which was called into special session within hours of the dead Superintendent's burial:

Vigilante!

It is with the profoundest grief and indignation that I make you the official announcement of the death of David C. Hennessy, superintendent of police of this city. Grief at the loss of a true friend and an efficient officer; indignation that he should have died by the hands of despicable assassins. He was waylaid and riddled with bullets almost at his doorstep on last Wednesday night, and he died on Thursday morning at 9:06 o'clock.

The circumstances of the cowardly deed, the arrests made, and the evidence collected by the police department *show beyond doubt that he was the victim of Sicilian vengeance,* wreaked upon him as the chief representative of law and order in this community, because he was seeking the power of *our American law* to break up the fierce vendettas that have so often stained our streets with blood. Heretofore, these scoundrels have confined their murderings among themselves. None of them have ever been convicted because of the secrecy with which the crimes have been committed and the impossibility of getting evidence from *the people of their own race* to convict. Bold, indeed, was the stroke, aimed at *their first American victim.* A shining mark have they selected on which to write with the assassin's hand *their contempt for the civilization of the new world.*

We owe it to ourselves and to everything that we hold sacred in this life to see to it that this blow is the last. *We must teach these people a lesson that they will not forget for all time.*

What the means are to reach this end, I leave to the wisdom of the Council to devise.

It is clear to me that the wretches who committed this foul deed are the mere hirelings and instruments of others higher and more powerful than they. These instigators are the men we must find at any cost.

For years past the existence of stiletto societies among the Sicilians in this city has been asserted.

Appeal was made to me by a prominent Italian during my former administration to protect him from blackmail and murder, but, as he was afraid to give any names, I could no nothing for him.

It is believed that these horrid associations are patronized by some of the wealthy and powerful *members of their own race* in this city, and that they can point out who the leaders of these associations are.

No community can exist with murder societies in its midst. These societies must perish or the community itself must perish.

The Sicilian who comes here must become an American citizen and subject his wrongs to the remedy of the law of the land, or else there must be no place for him on the American continent. This sentiment we must see realized at any cost, at any hazard.

The people look to you to take the initiative in this matter. Act promptly, without fear or favor [my italics].[9]

The Mayor also took the occasion to announce that his life, too, had been threatened by the Sicilians, though he didn't get around to accusing anyone in particular. The council then authorized the creation of a special citizens' committee, "whose duty shall be to thoroughly investigate the matter of the existence of secret societies or bands of oath-bound assassins, which it is openly charged have life in our midst and have culminated in the assassination of the highest executive officer of the police department, and to devise necessary means and the most effective and speedy measures for the uprooting and total annihilation of such hell-born associations; *and also to suggest needful remedies to prevent the introduction here of criminals or paupers from Europe* [my italics]."[10]

That committee, composed of the staunchest and most influential men in the community, was formed within twenty-four hours of its authorization by the city council. Although the mayor appointed eighty-seven leading citizens to the special body, it quickly became known as the Committee of Fifty, since that was the number stipulated by the council. Edgar H. Farrar, a well-known lawyer, was appointed chairman on Saturday, October 18. He was to be largely responsible for the committee's policies and for their effects, none of which could have been foreseen on that busy autumn morning.

The leaders of the committee tackled their assignment with what can only be described as relish. They immediately rented an office on the fourth floor of the Cotton Exchange Building and began collecting evidence against everyone suspected of having been involved in the murder of David Hennessy, that is to say, against the Matranga family, its organization, and anyone connected with it. "Suspected" is not quite accurate. There was no doubt whatever in the minds of everyone on the Committee of Fifty, or in the minds of the general public, that the Matrangas had been responsible for the hit. Accordingly, the committee geared itself to trying to prove it. Police officials and the courts were advised of any evidence that came to light, but the committee's actual deliberations were kept secret. In fact, it very quickly began to take on the aura of a special tribunal or the kind of special police panel that has frequently bobbed up in New Orleans in times of political or social difficulty. The Committee of Fifty was, in fact, to form the spiritual foundation for the vigilante group that, the following March, lynched eleven men trapped in the city prison and created an international sensation involving the President of the United States and causing rumblings of war with Italy.

While the Committee of Fifty was gearing up for the task ahead, the police continued to scour New Orleans for the culprits. Hearing that they were wanted, Charles Matranga and a friend named Rocco Geracci went to police headquarters and turned themselves in. Others were arrested, starting the night of the shooting and continuing through the weekend, until, as has been said, more than a hundred had passed through the city's police stations. Many were released. Many were not.

The grand jury held its first meeting on November 9 and handed up indictments against nineteen of the accused on the twentieth—eleven days later. Indicted for murder and for shooting while lying in wait with intent to murder were Peter Natali, Antonio Scaffidi, Charles Traina, Antonio Bagnetto, Manuel Politz, Antonio Marchesi, Pietro Monastero, Bastiano Incardona, Salvador Sinceri, and Loretto Comitez. Nine others were indicted for being accessories before the fact: Asperi Marchesi, the fourteen-year-old, Joseph P. Macheca, James Caruso, Charles Matranga, Rocco Geracci, Charles Patorno, Frank Romero, John Caruso, and Charles Pietza.

Now the legal maneuvering started. All the accused except Patorno were represented by five lawyers, including a former judge, Thomas J. Semmes, and that created another sensation. Semmes was one of the most famous and therefore most expensive jurists in the South, and was a former attorney general of Louisiana and member of the Confederate Senate. The four other lawyers, plus the two representing Patorno, were also known to be good and were therefore also expensive. The *Times-Democrat* was to report, the following March 17, that between $50,000 and $75,000 had been raised by the Mafia in New Orleans and other cities to pay for the defense of the nineteen, but if the money really was raised by the underworld it's unlikely that the newspaper would have gotten accurate figures. No matter. The point was that the suspects were obviously able to lay their hands on more money than any decent citizen could expect to see in a lifetime. And the lawyers who got that money wasted no time earning it.

On Saturday, November 30—the day the prisoners were arraigned—a motion was made to quash the indictments on the ground that the court stenographer had been in the grand-jury room while the evidence was being collected and the indictments formulated. Judge Joshua G. Baker, of Section B of the Criminal District Court, who was the trial judge, ruled in favor of the defense on December 9. The *Times-Democrat* reprimanded the prosecution for its blunder.

A second grand jury was impaneled almost immediately, and four days later handed up identical indictments. A second arraignment took place on December 16, and this time the defense pointed out that two members of the new grand jury (one of whom was R. M. Walmsley, its foreman) were members of the Committee of Fifty and, in addition to their obvious prejudice, had actually contributed money to the prosecution. Judge Baker said that he couldn't see the relevance of that motion, so he set it aside, and on December 22 all the prisoners entered pleas of not guilty. The case was then shelved so the court could deal with what was left of the Provenzano-Matranga trial, which this time ended in acquittal for the Provenzano brothers. In one of those truly interesting legal quirks, the lawyers who had prosecuted the Provenzanos on behalf of the Matrangas would have to switch to defending their clients against charges of murdering Hennessy, and those who had defended the Provenzanos would end up assisting in the prosecution of the Matranga group. The lawyers no doubt enjoyed the challenge of reversing roles.

Before testimony began, the prosecution asked for an order of severance, meaning that it wanted to prosecute some of those indicted but not all of them. It would not explain why it wanted the severance, but the defense gladly accepted the motion, and so, therefore, did Judge Baker. The defense lawyers claimed that the move was as good as an admission by the state that it had no real evidence against the ten who had been severed. The accused now consisted of both Marchesis (uncle and nephew), Matranga, Scaffidi, Bagnetto, Politz, Incardona, Macheca, and Monastero. These, then, were to stand trial for murder or for being accomplices to a murder.

All were kept in the parish prison, which was about a mile from old Saint Patrick Hall, where the trial took place. And every day, from the start of the trial on February 16 to its conclusion about a month later, the prisoners made the round trip in a large mule-drawn wagon known as the Black Maria. As the wagon creaked over the streets of New Orleans, bringing the prisoners to court in the morning or back to their cells in the late afternoon, urchins would run after it and shout tauntingly to those inside, "Who killa de chief?" But the taunts were the least of their inconveniences.

From the time the Italians were taken into custody in mid-October, there had been an unending barrage of threats against them and, in several instances, actual violence. On the day of Hennessy's funeral, a friend of his named Thomas Duffy had become so enraged that he had rushed to the prison, asked to see Antonio Scaffidi, and then shot the man in the neck. Duffy was sentenced to six months in the same prison, which many in the city thought was a great shame.

Ostensibly because of threats of violence, and on the advice of the Committee of Fifty, the sheriff early issued orders forbidding all contact between the prisoners and anyone on the outside except their lawyers. That included newspaper reporters and one Dominick C. O'Malley, a private detective and a close friend of Matranga's, who was to figure prominently in the coming days. The defense immediately started mandamus proceedings against the sheriff, whose name was Villere, on the ground that visitors were necessary for the preparation of the Sicilians' defense. Mandamus was denied, but with the proviso that the prisoners be allowed to have visitors only during certain hours. Matranga appealed to the state supreme court and lost.

There was also a privilege system within the prison, known as "captains of the yard," in which favored prisoners were used to control the others—in an unofficial capacity, of course. And, as often happened elsewhere when trusty systems were used, the prisoners not in power were brutalized by those who were. Some of the Sicilians in the parish prison were severely beaten and, under threats of more and worse violence, were robbed. The situation became so serious that Pasquale Corte, the Italian consul in New Orleans, wrote to Mayor Shakspeare complaining about it. Shakspeare answered, almost testily, "The rumor of maltreatment of the suspects is, I am satisfied, without foundation. On the contrary, I greatly fear that consideration for their personal comfort and the wishes of their friends has been carried beyond the limit of prudence."[11] Not mollified, the diplomat wrote another letter, this one to the grand jury, and had the satisfaction of seeing that body conduct an investigation, which resulted in two yard captains' being indicted for assaulting and robbing fellow prisoners; both were punished. Corte also started keeping the Italian Embassy in Washington apprised of developments in New Orleans.

The Committee of Fifty was meanwhile doing its best to seal the prisoners' fate by less physical, but certainly more lasting, means. Farrar, its chairman, sent a tart letter to O'Malley, the detective employed by the Sicilians to gather evidence on their behalf, demanding that he drop the case and instantly end all communications with the Italian colony and the trial witnesses in particular. He also was warned to stay away from the parish prison and the criminal court building. The Irish detective answered Farrar's letter in kind, telling him to mind his own business. The committee also sent letters to the city's newspapers asking that reporters not be allowed to interview witnesses and be prohibited from writing accounts of their testimony.

Just about everyone in New Orleans, and certainly among the city's establishment, had taken sides by the time the trial started. Those arrayed against the Sicilians insisted that O'Malley and the lawyers working with him could not have been paid except with huge sums of dirty Mafia money. And, to make matters even worse, two shiploads of new Sicilian immigrants—about 1,800 of them—arrived just before the trial began. Their appearance sent another wave of anger and revulsion through the city's middle and upper strata. Mayor Shakspeare, who coldly observed the new arrivals personally at the docks, stated for publication that they were to be admitted only in strict compliance with the immigration laws. Feelings against Sicilians were running very high in New Orleans when the Hennessy murder trial opened.

During the trial's twenty-six days, a total of 319 witnesses was called to give more than 800 typewritten pages of testimony; sixty-seven of them supplied evidence for the state in four days of continual talking. Soon after testimony started, Manuel Politz apparently became deranged and wildly indicated that he wanted to confess. An interpreter was brought in, took some kind of confession, which was not made public, and gave it to the district attorney, who refused to accept it. In the days that followed, Scaffidi, Antonio Marchesi, young Asperi's uncle, Politz, Bagnetto, and Monastero were positively identified by witnesses as the men who had run from the scene of Hennessy's ambush and thrown away their shotguns (the weapons had been found a few blocks from the policeman's house). Incardona was identified as having been at the scene of the crime earlier in the evening, but the prosecution eventually dropped the case against him for insufficient evidence. Macheca was named by four witnesses as the man who, using the name Peter Johnson, had rented the shack in which the killers hid before the shooting; he allegedly had rented it from none other than Pietro Monastero. Asperi Marchesi turned state's evidence and admitted that he had whistled to signal Hennessy's approach. Because of his testimony, and also because he was considered to be nothing more than a tool of the alleged conspirators, the charges against him were dropped. The evidence against Charles Matranga, who provided an alibi for where he had been at the time of the murder, consisted of the anger he had openly expressed against Hennessy because of the policeman's seemingly one-sided efforts on behalf of the Provenzanos. Since Judge Baker considered that to be insufficient for conviction, he ordered the jury to acquit Matranga when he charged it.

The jury went out at 6:15 on the evening of March 12 and delivered its verdict at 2:53 the following afternoon, a Friday. Jacob M. Seligman, a jeweler and the foreman of the jury, reported to Judge Baker, the lawyers, the defendants, and a room packed with newspaper reporters and other observers that he and his fellow jurors had been unable to reach a verdict for Politz, Scaffidi, and Monastero. The other six, he said, had been found not guilty. There was absolute silence. Then there was pandemonium. Even as reporters raced to their offices, charges of jury tampering were spreading out of the building and onto the streets of New Orleans like a shock wave. Readers who had followed the testimony, and who had long since come to the conclusion that Politz, Scaffidi, and Monastero were without question guilty of having killed David Hennessy, were incredulous. Their disbelief was to be echoed two months later in the report of a grand jury that investigated the circumstances surrounding the verdict: "We cannot be mistaken in the assertion that the verdict was startling, amazing, a bitter disappointment, shocking to public opinion, and provoking the repeated accusation that some of the jury had been unfaithful to their high office."[12] That grand jury's indictment was to charge that three or four members of the Hennessy murder jury had been unlawfully controlled; six men representing the defense, including

Dominick O'Malley and one of the lawyers, were indicted for attempted bribery. The indictment also asserted that terror was used against the jurors; at one point during the trial, the light in the jury room went out, leaving the jurors in total darkness. It was proved that the electrical wires had been cut.

As the immensely relieved Sicilians were taken back to the parish prison in the Black Maria that Friday the thirteenth, another contingent of children fell in behind and again taunted the men inside with their refrain of "Who killa de chief?" This time, however, the words were edged with the same anger and frustration felt by their parents. An editorial writer at the *Picayune*, preparing his copy for the next day's edition, was calling the verdict "a thunderbolt of surprise to the masses of the city."[13] It was more than that. It was generally considered to be nothing less than an absolute outrage—a stiletto thrust at the very heart of American law and order.

Nobody of standing in New Orleans had minded when the Sicilians confined their executions to "Vendetta Alley," as the section of Decatur Street between Dumaine and Saint Philip was popularly called. In fact, every corpse found there represented one less of the vermin. But David C. Hennessy, the Superintendent of Police, was quite another matter. If they could kill him and get away with it, no one would be safe. Even Mayor Shakspeare had said he had been threatened. It was therefore abundantly clear to the notables of New Orleans on that afternoon of Friday, the thirteenth of March, 1891, that an example was going to have to be made of young David Hennessy's murderers, irrespective of the jury's verdict. And, as everyone knew, there was one sure way to accomplish that. It was an American's inalienable right to correct the mistakes made by the institutions that were supposed to be responsible to him. The citizens of a democracy giveth, and the citizens of a democracy taketh away.

The New Orleans Vigilance Committee officially came into being between four and five o'clock that afternoon in the law office of W. S. Parkerson, at 7 Commercial Place. Parkerson was to say later, in the *Illustrated American,* a New York magazine, that he returned to his office that afternoon and found fifteen or twenty prominent citizens waiting for him. He didn't explain why they had decided to meet there, in spite of the fact that he was younger and less prominent than most of them, but the answer—

and one he wouldn't have wanted in print—was probably that he had earlier set up a shadow organization for just the kind of contingency that had developed. One thing is certain, however: the membership rosters of the Committee of Fifty and of the Vigilance Committee show many of the same names.

That afternoon meeting in Parkerson's office seems to have accomplished nothing more than setting up a much larger meeting for nine o'clock that night at a hall near Royal and Bienville streets. A notice was written at the second meeting for distribution to newspapers coming out the following morning. The notice was, by 1891, typical of hundreds of others that had appeared across the country during the preceding century.

MASS MEETING

All good citizens are invited to attend a mass meeting on Saturday, March 14, at 10 o'clock a.m., at Clay Statue, to take steps to remedy the failure of justice in the Hennessy case. Come prepared for action.[14]

The notice was written by none other than Edgar H. Farrar, the first chairman of the Committee of Fifty. Two of Parkerson's lieutenants, John C. Wickliffe and Walter D. Denegre, seem to have had relatives on the Committee of Fifty, since a T. C. Wickliffe and a George Denegre appear on that body's roster. And perhaps, because of a typographical error, J. C. Wickliffe and T. C. Wickliffe were one and the same.

What is especially interesting about the men who formed the New Orleans Vigilantes, though, is not the fact that they were notables; such committees, as has been seen, were almost always led by the elite. Rather, it is their openness that is so startling, considering what they had to lose, at least in theory, by advocating extralegal action against the men in the parish prison. But they did it anyway, and that, more than anything else, testifies to the enormous support they had on virtually every level of New Orleans society. Farrar's notice was signed by fifty-seven very prominent citizens of New Orleans—fifty-seven men who, without any question, knew that they were calling on their fellow citizens to storm the parish prison and kill the Sicilians. Before the night of the thirteenth was over, a cache of guns had been moved from A. Baldwin & Co., a hardware store, to Frank B. Hayne's home, at the corner of Royal and Bienville, not far from the Clay Statue. Hayne was one of the elite who had signed Farrar's notice, one of the subscribers to the death manifesto.

By ten o'clock on the morning of March 14, Canal Street around Clay Statue was jammed with a mostly quiet and orderly crowd waiting to get stirred up. Then Parkerson, who had been elected chairman of the Vigilantes the night before, arrived with J. C. Wickliffe. The two leaders, followed by certain members of the crowd, immediately walked around the statue three times, apparently to show the others that they were to be the ones who would take up arms and spearhead what just about everyone knew was coming. That little rite seems to have been worked out in committee session the night before. Everyone else watched in silence, many holding copies of the *Picayune* containing the death order that had brought them there but also containing an editorial that said, in part, "We trust and believe that the object of the meeting is wholly in the interest of peace as is the interest of justice. The names of the gentlemen who have signed the call would seem a ready guarantee of peaceful intentions, and so we accept them." Others carried copies of the *Times-Democrat*, which agreed on the need for a mass meeting to discuss the "grave and threatening situation," but which also cautioned against turning the assemblage into a mob.[15]

"People of New Orleans . . ." W. S. Parkerson looked around from his perch on the statue of Henry Clay, saw at least a thousand receptive faces and probably twice that number, and began haranguing them as persuasively as he could. He inflected as though he were in court, and, as he must have known, in a sense that's exactly where he was. "Affairs have reached such a crisis that men living in an organized and civilized community, finding their laws fruitless and ineffective, are forced to protect themselves. When courts fail, the people must act. What protection, or assurance of protection, is there left us, when the very head of our police department—our chief of police—is assassinated in our very midst by the Mafia Society, and his assassins again turned loose on the community? The time has come for the people of New Orleans to say whether they are going to stand these outrages by organized bands of assassins, for the people to say whether they shall permit it to continue. I ask you to consider this fairly. Are you going to let it continue?" The young lawyer heard a chorus of "No, no, bring on the Dagoes." He began whittling his words to a finer point.

"Will every man here follow me and see the murder of D. C.

Hennessy vindicated?" The crowd roared approval and started calling for an assault on the parish prison. They called at the top of their lungs for the blood of the prisoners.

"Are there men enough here to set aside the verdict of that infamous jury, every one of whom is a perjurer and a scoundrel?"

"Yes," shouted everyone in the crowd who wanted to be a man. "Yes," they screamed in counterpoint, "on to the prison and hang the murderers."

"There is no more infamous a thing in this city than Dominick C. O'Malley," added Parkerson, trying to make himself heard.

"Hang him. Shoot him."

"I now pronounce him a suborner of witnesses, a briber of juries, and the most infamous thing in this community. I now, right here, publicly, openly, and fearlessly denounce him as a suborner and procurer of witnesses and a briber of juries. Men and citizens of New Orleans, follow me. I will be your leader."

He stepped off the statue's pedestal to thunderous applause and calls for action from the contorted faces. Parkerson was followed by Denegre and Wickliffe, but they had difficulty making themselves heard because of the noise. By the time Wickliffe's turn came, he was almost drowned out in the shouting and screaming, but he managed to issue the final orders for the assault.

"Very well, gentlemen, the committee has selected your officers, who are ready to lead you. Will you go?"

"Yes. Yes." The street reverberated with enthusiasm.

"Then, gentlemen, let's go and do our duty. Mr. Parkerson is your leader. Mr. James D. Houston is your first lieutenant. Your second lieutenant is myself. We are prepared to do our duty. Are you?" They told Wickliffe, with two more tumultuous yeses, that they were, indeed, fully and eagerly prepared to do their duty. They were prepared to tear the Sicilians apart. "Then," said John C. Wickliffe, his voice now almost inaudible in the din, "come on."[16]

The angry and excited people who followed the New Orleans Vigilance Committee that morning were not vigilantes. They were a mob led by Vigilantes—about sixty members of the city's elite—and they constituted the vital mass support the committee needed in order to storm the parish prison. And, because they were a mob, they didn't march in orderly fashion to the prison; they ran to it, the way they would have run if they had been soldiers trying to take an enemy position. The Vigilantes, composed mainly of those who had signed the death notice, led one contingent to Royal and Bienville, where they picked up their guns. Meanwhile, hundreds of others, the rhetoric ringing in their ears, dashed down Royal, Bourbon, Dauphine, and even relatively remote Rampart Street, picking up fresh recruits at every corner. Within ten minutes of Wickliffe's having said "Come on," an estimated 6,000 people had gathered outside the New Orleans parish prison, and almost everyone wanted to see blood.

The building, while it stood, was formidable; a large, gloomy brick structure occupying the entire block bounded by Orleans, Treme, Saint Anne, and Marais streets. The Fourth Police Precinct Station was set into one of its massive corners. The main entrance was on Orleans, in the middle of the block, and was protected by a heavy iron grille. Beyond the grille was a vestibule and, beyond that, a second set of bars, which sealed off the corridor leading to the areas where prisoners were kept. Breaking through both sets of bars was out of the question. No matter. They weren't going to have to do that. There also was a side entrance, which would prove extremely vulnerable.

The men inside the prison who were responsible for guarding it also seem to have been vulnerable that morning, as was the entire city administration. Among those in the crowd around Clay Statue who had scattered after Wickliffe finished his short oration were two city detectives who had jumped into a cab and raced to the prison to warn Captain Lem Davis, who was in charge of it, that the citizens of New Orleans were on their way to storm the place. No one seems to have briefed Captain Davis before then, and if he had read the newspaper that morning he apparently hadn't believed what it said. Governor Francis T. Nicholls was in the city that day, but he made no effort to call out troops or do anything else to head off what he had to have understood was an impending tragedy. Mayor Shakspeare was not even in his office that morning. Corte, the Italian consul, had no doubt whatever about the Vigilantes' intentions. So he tried frantically to locate Shakspeare, but was told repeatedly that His Honor couldn't be found. Sheriff Villere was not to move decisively until it was too late. The Vigilantes, then, had been taken at their word—"Come prepared for action"—by all the people who had showed up at the statue, by the detectives who also had come to watch and listen, by newspaper editors, and by at least one diplomat. Yet those who might have been expected to know the mood of the city and the intentions of its elite better than anyone else—the Mayor, the Governor, the Sheriff, and others in the administration—did nothing. And in doing nothing they did a great deal.

Parkerson and most of the other Vigilantes, followed by their part of the mob, reached the prison at 10:20, jamming Orleans Street and waving their pistols, rifles, shotguns, and knives. The lawyer then stepped up to the iron grille protecting the main entrance and formally demanded that the prisoners be handed over. Davis, who by then had posted his handful of deputies at some, but not all, of the other doors, made an equally formal refusal. If the deputies were armed, they never used their guns; most made quite a show of guarding the main entrance (with its two sets of heavy bars), while leaving a wooden door on Treme Street totally unprotected. That door led to an apartment occupied by Davis and his chief clerk, then into a vaulted passageway, and finally into the prison's main corridor and all other sections of the place. The wooden door on Treme therefore offered the logical point of attack, and that's exactly where Parkerson, Wickliffe, and the others headed after Lem Davis went through the motions of refusing to give up his prisoners. None of the other entrances was tested by the Vigilantes; they knew precisely where to go to get into the parish prison.

An improvised battering ram and a large paving stone wielded by a black man quickly turned the door into splinters, and once it had been smashed the leading element of the mob looked at what had been done. They just stood there for a moment, looking. Wickliffe urged cool action. Someone else shouted, "Now we have the prison; we'll bring those people downstairs and the law will be vindicated in broad daylight. We'll have a public execution."[17] That, at least, was the plan. In typical vigilante fashion, the leaders wanted formal executions for display value. But it wasn't to happen quite like that. Only two were to be dragged into the sunshine and strung up; the others were going to die inside.

The Sicilians had been turned loose, just before the mob arrived, and told to fend for themselves. All the other prisoners had been locked in ground-floor cells around the so-called white yard, one of the large courtyards within the prison. Davis had suggested to the terrified men that they hide in the women's quarters, and some, including Bagnetto, ran there. Sinceri and Politz managed to squeeze into an old packing case that had been turned into a kennel for Lem Davis's bull terrier. The kennel was in a dark corner under a rear staircase, and, under any other circumstances, it wouldn't have been thought to be big enough to hold two men. But Salvador Sinceri and Manuel Politz understood that they were squeezing for their lives, so they squeezed as hard as they possibly could. Peter Natali made a dash for the washhouse and hid under a bench in its far corner. John Caruso ran downstairs and joined the non-Italian prisoners; he was then locked up with them and was therefore going to survive. Bastiano Incardona followed the gallery to the second floor, found a box used for discarded rubbish inside a closet, and crawled into it. He, too, was going to end the day alive. Joseph Macheca, Antonio Scaffidi, and the elder Marchesi ran up to the "condemned" cells on the third floor, hoping to get inside one of them, but they found all of them cleared and locked. Those cells were in plain view of the courtyard below, and within easy shotgun range. When Macheca's body was found a few hours later, fragments from a club he had used to try to break into one of the cells were found in his fist. Charles Matranga and Charles Patorno pried loose some wallboards in a distant room beyond the women's quarters and squeezed into the opening. They, too, would live.

Although about 6,000 were crowding the streets around the prison and surging outside the now open doorway on Treme Street, only twenty-five to thirty men were actually allowed inside by Wickliffe, who guarded the portal. These were the Vigilantes. All of them seem to have been carrying shotguns picked up from the arsenal at Hayne's apartment, and those guns were the passes required to get inside. When everyone who was supposed to be inside had gotten in, they were separated into squads. Each squad began looking for Sicilians.

One group ran up the stairs to the "hotel," or the section where those prisoners who paid a little for better food and quarters were kept. They found it empty. Another group charged into the courtyard beneath the condemned cells and, looking up, were no doubt delighted to see Macheca, Scaffidi, and Marchesi trying desperately to break into one of the cells. Those in the courtyard raised their shotguns and opened fire. The three men above them, trapped like animals, were cut down where they stood.

Their blood spattered against the cell bars they hadn't been able to open. It then ran along the floor and dripped into the courtyard.

Bagnetto, Geracci, Monastero, Traina, Comitez, Romero, and James Caruso were found huddling inside the women's quarters, where Lem Davis had advised them to go. All were dragged out screaming and pleading for their lives and, except for Bagnetto, were shot on the spot. They were shot just outside the door to the women's quarters. They were not merely shot; they were torn apart by the shotgun pellets. The men using the guns riddled them with hundreds of rounds and, in fact, stopped shooting only when the gunsmoke became so dense that they no longer could see clearly. The smoke must have made their eyes smart and the noise probably made their ears ring.

At that moment nine of the Italians had been slaughtered, but someone evidently decided that the mob outside had to be satisfied, too, so Bagnetto and Politz, who had meanwhile been found (though Sinceri was not), were dragged out to the street.

Manuel Politz, now completely helpless and half out of his mind, was roughly hustled onto Saint Anne Street by a powerfully built sugar planter named Ross. Someone produced a rope, tied it around Politz's neck, and pulled him to the corner of Saint Anne and Treme. He was strung up on a lamppost on that corner, and, while he struggled against the rope that was choking him, the crowd immediately around him was cleared so that a group with Winchesters could empty them into him. Manuel Politz was hit a dozen times, so the pain of the rope didn't last very long.

Five minutes later, Bagnetto, a noose already around his neck, was brought out of the building. He had been found lying on the floor in the women's quarters pretending to be dead, and begged for his life as the men with the shotguns slipped on the noose and fastened it securely. A tree on Treme Street was selected for a gallows, so a boy climbed it and tossed the other end of the rope over a branch, and several in the crowd grabbed the rope and started to hoist Bagnetto. Then the branch snapped. So the execution had to start all over again, this time using a sturdier limb. Antonio Bagnetto kicked and struggled until his neck broke, and that made the people watching him cheer wildly. A good lynching could be very festive. It was 10:50. Everyone who was going to die that day had done so.

Three of those lynched had been tried and acquitted, five had not been tried, and three others had been tried but the jury had not delivered a verdict on them. Asperi Marchesi, who was also in the prison, wasn't harmed. The boy and the other seven who remained of the original nineteen were later freed, and further prosecution against them was dropped. But few, if any, in the mob were thinking about that as they milled around, studying what had been done. Many said they still wanted Dominick C. O'Malley. Climbing onto a first-floor window sill, Parkerson addressed that subject.

"I have performed the most painful duty of my life today," he said, after ticking off the names of his victims. "If you have confidence in me and in the gentlemen associated with me, I ask you to disperse and go quietly to your homes." Some yelled that they wanted O'Malley, too. "I pledge you that O'Malley shall be dealt with. Now take my word for it. Mob violence is the most terrible thing on the face of the earth. I called you together for a duty. You have performed that duty. Now go to your homes, and if I need you, I will call you. Now go home," said W. S. Parkerson, "and God bless you." "God bless *you*, Mr. Parkerson," shouted the grateful people in the street, lifting the lawyer onto their shoulders and marching him back to the statue of Henry Clay.[18]

Dominick O'Malley stayed in hiding for several weeks, and by the time he surfaced, the mood of New Orleans had quieted to the point where his life no longer was in danger. Jacob M. Seligman, the jury foreman, also stayed well out of sight until his neighbors had calmed down.

Within hours of the mass lynching, however, it became a national sensation and the subject of heated debate throughout the country and overseas. Even as Parkerson was being carried at the head of a triumphant procession back to the statue, Pasquale Corte was wiring the news of what had happened to the Italian ambassador in Washington.

The Louisiana papers generally approved of the Vigilance Committee's actions, although the conservative *Picayune* rebuked the city government for not having taken measures to protect the prisoners. In an editorial published on April 2, the paper said:

No measures for the protection of the prisoners were undertaken beyond what a handful of wardens and turnkeys were able to accomplish. They deserve the highest praise, but, abandoned by the higher authorities, they were powerless to accomplish anything. . . . The people, or an armed body of the people, had practical possession of the city, with not even an official remonstrance against them, until they had accomplished their purpose.[19]

The *St. Louis Post Dispatch* said acidly that "it is hoped that the leading citizens will get the same punishment they meted out to the Mafia." The March 19 issue of *The Nation* slammed New Orleans as being the worst-governed city in the country.[20] The *New York Tribune* charged that no one was safe in a community like New Orleans, since a personal enemy could create a popular belief that his intended victim was guilty of a crime and then have that person killed by a mob similar to the one that had executed the Sicilians.

The *San Francisco Chronicle,* on the other hand, defended the lynchings this way:

. . . We cannot deny that the safety of society is the thing of paramount importance, and that if it cannot be secured under and by means of the forms of law, it must be secured without them. No one will deny there may be times when it is the duty of good citizens to disregard the letter of the law in order to carry its reason and spirit into execution, and although the remedy is a desperate one, its propriety can no more be questioned than its efficiency.

The existence of a secret organization of murderers and assassins seems to have been conclusively demonstrated. . . . New Orleans had its choice, either to overstep the bounds of the law or to live in constant terror of lawless and conscienceless aliens who regard murder as a duty and assassination as a pastime, and its people took the heroic remedy and exterminated the assassins.[21]

Even more to the point, the *Pittsburgh Post* explained that the incident in New Orleans and others like it were "essentially American in character, and when considered as a whole, are not ebullitions of the anarchial spirit, but of the self-governing capacity, which is the basis of the American character in political and civic needs."[22]

That observation may have been true enough, but it did nothing to placate the Italian government, which reacted quickly and firmly to the New Orleans massacre. Italian diplomats had been watching the situation in New Orleans since the nineteen "*mafiosi*" had been arrested. Corte had sent that note to Mayor Shakspeare protesting the treatment of the prisoners and had gotten no satisfaction from the official. Shakspeare's denial of wrongdoing in the prison and other developments relating to the New Orleans Nineteen had been faithfully reported to Baron Fava, the Italian minister in Washington, and also to the Foreign Office in Rome, which had at one point instructed Fava to file a protest with Secretary of State James G. Blaine. The Italians had gotten particularly annoyed with the part of Shakspeare's council address that said, "The Sicilian who comes here must become an American citizen and subject his wrongs to the remedy of the law of the land, or else there must be no place for him on the American continent."

On October 21, 1890—one week after David Hennessy's murder and five days after the suspects had been rounded up or turned themselves in—Secretary Blaine had sent a cable to Governor Nicholls about the protest from Rome and had been assured by Nicholls that the Governor did "not apprehend any trouble." That assurance, plus the encouraging conclusion of the grand jury regarding maltreatment of the men in jail, had been enough to calm the Secretary of State and, apparently, the Italian government, which had let the matter drop. Then, on March 14, 1891, Baron Fava received this telegram from his government's consul in New Orleans:

MOB LED BY MEMBERS OF COMMITTEE OF FIFTY TOOK POSSESSION OF JAIL; KILLED ELEVEN PRISONERS; THREE ITALIANS, OTHERS NATURALIZED. I HOLD MAYOR RESPONSIBLE. FEAR FURTHER MURDERS. I ALSO AM IN GREAT DANGER. REPORTS FOLLOW.[23]

That telegram, of course, was also immediately relayed to Rome. In a matter of hours, Marquis di Rudini, the Italian Secretary for Foreign Affairs, was wiring Fava in Washington instructing him to denounce the lynchings and urge that steps be taken to protect the Italian community in New Orleans. The protest was duly handed to Blaine, who called the incident a "deplorable massacre" and passed the essence of the Italian protest on to Governor Nicholls. Nicholls answered by assuring the Secretary of State that all was again tranquil in New Orleans and that a grand jury was even then investigating the "whole subject." The *Times-Democrat*, which by that time had turned into the Vigilantes' staunchest supporter (very possibly because its editors felt they had to close ranks with their fellow Louisianians), criticized the Governor for not sending Blaine a "scorcher" in reply.

The *T-D* particularly didn't like Blaine's having called the incident a "deplorable massacre" and hinted nastily that bureaucrats in Washington and Rome ought to mind their own business.

Blaine's assurances to Rome that the killings had not been directed at the Sicilians for racial reasons, that the whole matter would be investigated by a grand jury, and that Italians in New Orleans would continue to be protected according to treaty rights did not satisfy Rudini, who got off another telegram to Baron Fava, this time ordering him to demand punishment of the murderers and get an indemnity for the victims' families. Fava, of course, did as he was told.

Now the American Secretary of State thought he was being pushed too far. He interpreted the demands to mean that Rome wanted a guarantee that the leaders of the New Orleans Vigilantes would be indicted and convicted and that payment definitely would be made to the dead men's families. Since he decided that complying with the demands would amount to federal interference in Louisiana affairs, he refused to act on either of them. His discussion with Fava, in fact, seems to have been an angry one. James G. Blaine apparently thought that the Italians, who didn't seem to know as much about American politics as he did, were trying to push him too hard. Here's how Baron Fava recounted Blaine's words:

"I do not recognize the right of any government to tell the United States what it should do. We have never received orders from any foreign power, and we will not now begin. Please inform Marquis di Rudini that the Federal Government cannot give the assurance which he requires, and that it is a matter of total indifference to me what persons in Italy may think of our institutions. I cannot change them, still less violate them."[24]

On March 31, Baron Fava told Blaine that, on orders from Rome, he was going to leave Washington as quickly as possible and that the secretary of the legation would be in charge of all current business. Stout diplomatic ties had now been frayed to a single precarious thread. Newspapers in Britain, Germany, and France heartily endorsed the Italian position and called it a proper and fitting response to American "dilatory diplomacy."

Then talk started in Boston, New Orleans, and other United States port cities about the likelihood of an attack by the Italian navy, which in 1891 consisted of twenty-two excellent heavy warships, making it the fourth most powerful fleet in the world. The very day Baron Fava told Secretary of State Blaine that he was packing his bags and going home, the *Times-Democrat* pointed out that the United States had only one good battleship and it wasn't even completed. Although no one in Washington above the rank of file clerk took the war scare seriously, all the talk about it was enough to renew interest in the navy, and, as a result, the United States was to have a relatively powerful fleet when it got into the Spanish-American War, seven years later.

On May 5, a New Orleans grand jury handed up indictments against Dominick C. O'Malley and five others who had worked for the Sicilians. The documents charged attempted bribery and placed nearly all the blame for the miscarriage of justice (in court and in the parish prison) on the private detective. It refused, however, to indict any individual for the actual lynchings, since they had "embraced several thousand of the first, best and even most law-abiding citizens of the city." The grand jury went on to explain that no harm had been done to persons or property other than at the prison and that the magnitude of that isolated affair made it "a difficult task to fix guilt upon any number of the participants."[25] Not one of the Vigilantes, in other words, was going to be punished for the lynchings, because so many had been involved that it was considered impossible to pinpoint specific individuals. It doesn't seem to have mattered that fifty-seven men had signed their names to an ad for an execution that ran in the newspapers.

It should be noted that legal recourse against vigilante attacks did not develop seriously until the federal government got involved in the civil-rights upheaval of the mid-1960s. Until then, provided they did not victimize members of their own local elites, vigilantes usually operated with considerable sympathy on the part of local lawyers, judges, and juries. As was the case in New Orleans and elsewhere, in fact, the political and legal illuminati often participated, directly or otherwise, in vigilante operations. This was due in many instances to close local friendships and common economic interests, as well as to a deep-seated belief in local and states' rights. It was also due, though, to the fact that many nineteenth-century American jurists believed that lynching was a reasonable response to an inadequate legal system. In the view of many of those lawyers and judges, due process amounted to an obstacle course, made the more unwieldy by the granting of new trials, the necessity of using undependable juries (meaning bribery or intimidation prone), and excessive use of pardons. For them, the *repression* of crime, for the sake of social order, was more important than due process after the fact, and their characteristic answer to Washington's anger went something like this: We know our problems and their solutions better than you do; we'll handle them in our own way, so just mind *your* business, not ours.

That was precisely the case in Neshoba County, Mississippi, in June 1964, when three civil-rights activists—Michael Schwerner, James Chaney, and Andrew Goodman—were lynched by Ku Klux Klansmen, after being set up by Cecil Price, a Neshoba deputy sheriff. The trial of the accused killers could not be held for three years, partly because Federal District Judge W. Harold Cox, a segregationist, obstructed the proceedings and partly because a local grand jury refused to hand up an indictment. Convinced that Mississippi had no intention of trying the Klansmen under homicide statutes, the federal prosecutors had to dust off a vague law against conspiracy to deprive citizens of their civil rights (passed in 1870). Seven Klansmen were eventually found guilty by a federal jury and were sentenced to a maximum of ten years each in prison.[26] That, then, was the way the federal government managed to get into the antivigilante business.

In his annual message to Congress on December 9, 1891, President Benjamin Harrison called the New Orleans Mafia incident "a most deplorable and discreditable" one and "an offense against law and humanity." He also told Congress that the affair had not been the result of animosity toward the Italian people, that he was sorry about the disruption of relations between Washington and Rome, and that an indemnity would, indeed, be paid. The money, $24,330.90, was taken out of the diplomatic emergency fund and offered by Blaine on April 12, 1892. The Italians accepted it graciously, and, although Harrison was severely criticized by some newspaper editors and congressmen for having weakened American sovereignty, relations with Italy soon normalized and most traces of hard feelings disappeared.

Summing up the results of the lynchings in his *History of Louisiana*, published in 1904, the learned Professor Alcée Fortier explained that they had had a salutary effect on the Italians of the state and that no more acts of violence were committed by the Mafia.[27]

That may well have been true, but if it was, then others picked up the slack. New Orleans police records show that the number of arrests made for all crimes in 1892 totaled 21,812, against 22,449 in 1891—a decrease of slightly less than 3 per cent.[28] If Professor Fortier was correct, the unthinkable had happened in New Orleans in 1892—the Mafia had been replaced by other criminals.

9

The Compleat Vigilante

Judge Waller was one of the magnates of Orodia. There were not many magnates there yet, and it was easy for him to be at the top of the heap; but he was the kind of man who might be expected to stay at the top.

He had been a judge in Virginia City, and the title had stuck to him after he had left the bench and turned his attention to the founding of a new city.

Lots in Orodia were going off like hot cakes, and Judge Waller was busy and prosperous.

But business was over for the day, when he sat in his office one evening, cleaning up his desk preparatory to closing his neat little white-washed office.

Consequently, he was a little surprised when a stranger stepped in.

This stranger was a tall and brawny man, rather roughly dressed, unshaven, considerably travel-worn, and looking as if he had just come from an extensive tramp.

Judge Waller's keen gray eyes "sized him up" at once, and as he resumed his seat at his desk he partly opened a drawer in which lay a cocked revolver.

He invited the stranger to be seated, and inquired his business.

"Is this Judge Waller?" he asked.

"Yes."

"Lived long in these parts, I understand."

"Rather long, considering that this is a new country."

"Lived in Virginia City, and been a judge."

"Yes."

"Reckon you know who's who and what's goin' on about as well as most anybody."

"I am largely acquainted and pretty well posted."

"Well, Judge, what I want to get at is this. I am told that you have Vigilantes in these parts."

"So I have heard," replied Judge Waller.

"Of course you ain't one of them, and you don't know who they are, or anything more about them than anybody else does. But I've a notion that if a stranger should want a sound and square opinion about what he ought to do to keep out of trouble, you would be likely to give it to him."

"I can give my opinion, of course."

"Well, Judge, how would those Vigilantes be apt to treat a rough citizen who should come here and want to settle down and go straight?"

"I don't believe they would trouble any man who is disposed to behave himself. Are you that sort of citizen?"

"I may say that I am. Where I come from I was known as Cheyenne Charley."

"And your real name is Charles Rentz."

"Hullo, Judge! So you know me?"

This is excerpted from "Clip, the Contortionist; or, the Vigilantes of Montana," by Edward Willett, author of "The Typo Detective," "Fearless Phil," "The Roving Sport," etc., etc., and appeared in the January 29, 1884, issue of *Beadle's Half Dime Library*.[1] It is prototype vigilante pulp, of the kind that literally millions of young Americans, for more than seventy years, paid their nickels to read. As such, it is instructive. Willett, if that was his real name, set the scene in a town called Orodia, about a hundred miles from Virginia City and Bannack, where the Plummer gang had been strung up almost exactly twenty years earlier.

Cheyenne Charley, of course, has come to Orodia for evil ends; he has drifted in to hook up with the Cautious Crooks, an outlaw band whose recognition signal consists of one man saying "C-R-O" and another answering "O-K." Cheyenne has taken the precaution of asking Judge Waller, one of the pillars of the community, about the strength of the local vigilantes, and, after doing so, meets Spence Symmes. Both are Cautious Crooks, and after they exchange recognition signals Cheyenne Charley gets drunk. Here's the conversation they have while riding out of Orodia the next morning. They are headed for a secret rendezvous. Spence Symmes is talking.

"You had better leave it alone if you can't manage it better than that. . . . And right here I must give you some solid advice, and I mean to talk to you like a father. We will stand by you; but none of us are bound to stand by a man who won't stand by himself. So, if you expect to stay with the Cautious Crooks, and take their chances, you have got to keep a level head and be careful not to slop over. . . . Just now we are mighty particular about walking straight and keeping out of all sorts of scrapes that don't pay, because the Vigilantes are getting too strong and too sharp for us to fight."

"I have been looking into that business," remarked the man from below. "Just before I met you I saw one of those Vigilantes, and had a talk with him."

"Who was that?"

"Judge Waller. He is one of their head men, if not the boss of the gang."

"How do you know that?"

"I knew it by the way he talked, and he knew all about me."

"Yes, they seem to know everything, curse them! and that's why we have to be so quiet and careful."

The Cautious Crooks don't seem to be quiet and careful enough, though. Before long, Cheyenne and Spence meet Sam Bunker, another member of the gang, who gleefully leads them to his run-down but conveniently secluded ranch. Bunker's evil jubilation quickly turns to frightened rage when he gets close enough to his front door to read the sign nailed to it.

There was good cause for his profanity, which was indulged in mainly to cover a feeling of intense terror.

Tacked to the rude door of the cabin was a piece of white cardboard, on which was figured in black the likeness of a skull and a pair of crossbones, underneath which were the figures 3–7–77.

This was the usual symbol of the Vigilantes, by which notice was given to the occupant of the cabin that he must clear out and be seen no more in that region.

Between rage and fear the man was almost out of his wits, and his comrades waited patiently until lack of breath, rather than lack of language, caused him to subside.

Sam Bunker manages to get over his terror and, with Cheyenne Charley, Spence Symmes, and the other Cautious Crooks, holds up a wagon carrying the payroll for the men working on the railroad. The railroad, it should be noted, is expected to bring civilization and commerce to Orodia. They hold up the wagon in the middle of the night, use weapons of the "best quality" to kill some of the guards, and are only prevented from committing more atrocities by our young hero, Clip Saunders, who happens upon the scene. Clip manages to do a perfect imitation of the sounds of an approaching troop of cavalry, thus scattering the outlaws before they have a chance to carry off most of the money. But, irrespective of the fact that most of the payroll has been recovered, the guards are dead, and that signals a call to action.

Messengers had been sent as far as Virginia City, and there was such a gathering of the clans for immediate vengeance as had not been seen in a long time.

The members of the Vigilance Committee were undoubtedly on hand, though nobody pretended to point them out.

There were no masks among them, nor was there any attempt at disguise or uniform; but everybody knew that they were there, mingling with the other citizens, and that the business of pursuing the outlaws would be under their direction.

Eight harrowing pages later, the relentless Vigilantes catch up with the Cautious Crooks, in part with the help of Clip Saunders.

The Vigilantes were resolute and thorough in their purpose of exterminating the band of robbers that had been the terror of the region about Orodia.

When they had found their hiding place and driven them from it, they lost no time and omitted no effort in the work of clearing them out.

Day after day, and night after night, they searched the hills and forests for stray members of the gang that had claimed Spence Symmes as a leader.

They strictly obeyed their instructions, and shot down without mercy all they found who refused to surrender.

Those who surrendered—and they were very few in number—were hanged, as a farmer nails dead hawks on his barn as a warning to other hawks.

Even the isolated settlers—not always unsuspected of sharing the booty of the plunderers—from whom they had been accustomed to seek shelter and supplies, turned against them, refusing them the slightest favor, and aided in hunting them down.

They could only die or leave the country, and the few who got away considered themselves very fortunate.

Thus the region was finally cleared of its worst characters, and it was no longer necessary to post on houses or cabins or tepees the skull and crossbones and mystic numbers of the Vigilantes.

Cheyenne Charley manages to escape the wrath of his pursuers for a while, but, after turning up broke, hungry, and thirsty (for whiskey) at some ranch, he is handed over to Judge Waller. The Judge is, as Cheyenne has suspected, a ranking Vigilante. In due course, the prisoner is convicted in court for murder and sentenced to be executed, but, Willett tells us, the law's delays prevent the sentence from being carried out, and Cheyenne Charley eventually escapes from prison and disappears.

There are several significant elements in the tale Willett has constructed, elements shared by practically all vigilante fiction and, therefore, ones that have to a considerable extent shaped American thinking on the subject.

Most important, the author treats his vigilantes not as a temporary organization, formed to cope with a specific problem and then disband when the problem has been erased, but as a pervasive and shadowy force that is a permanent part of society—a small standing army, always available in times of emergency. Willett's vigilantes are around all the time, scrutinizing everyone who comes into their region and always ready to deal with those they think are undesirable. This permanence, plus the fact that only the best and bravest citizens belong to the secret organization, lends a definite aura of legality and moral sanction to the brotherhood; it, rather than regular lawmen, is the broadly accepted and rightful guardian of the community. This theme is explicit in "The Ghost," written by Max Brand and published in *Adventure* in 1929, in which the local vigilance committee, not the sheriff, puts a price on a notorious bandit's head and even selects a gunman capable of getting him.

Never in the history of Murrayville had there been so grave and dry-throated an affair. William Collins, the head of the vigilantes, addressed the assembly. He rehearsed the list of the Ghost's outrages, pointed out that what the community needed was an experienced man-hunter to direct their efforts, and ended up by asking Silver Pete to stand up before them. After some urging Pete rose and stood beside Collins, with his hat pushed back from his gray and tousled forelock and both hands tugging at his cartridge-belt.

"Men," went on Collins, placing one hand on the shoulder of the man-killer, "we need a leader who is a born and trained fighter, a man who will attack the Ghost with system and never stop after he takes up the trail. And I say the man we need is Silver Pete!"[2]

Brand, who certainly was one of the best-known and most prolific fashioners of western fiction, invests Collins with the attributes of a combination sheriff, mayor, and all-around wise man, who is looked to for guidance by everyone in Murrayville, vigilantes and nonvigilantes alike. Everyone seems to know that Collins is the leader of the organization, and, judging by the fact that the meeting is held in public, presumably with other vigilantes present, the group evidently is taken for granted as being the region's main law-enforcement organization. Nowhere is a sheriff or a marshal in evidence (although Brand suggests that Murrayville is an old, established community, and even mentions that posses can't find the clever culprit), and the very fact that even the vigilantes themselves are reduced to hiring a nasty gunslinger further makes the point.

For both of these writers, as well as for scores of others, including Owen Wister, vigilantes weren't temporary lethal outgrowths of inadequate law-enforcement systems; they *were* the law-enforcement systems—the ultimate law-enforcement systems. And if that's the case—that they existed permanently, just above or below the more apparent badge wearers and gavel pounders— then they were part of the infrastructure, and therefore quasilegal. And it follows from that premise that their executions, too, were quasilegal. Thus was the American's right to be his own ultimate lawman firmly established in fiction by writers who read newspapers and tried to justify with their pens what they perceived as reality. In this way, vigilantism reinforced itself; the writers embellished and justified real-life vigilante actions, and real-life vigilantes were able to derive at least some moral sanction by reading the literature on the subject. "Clip, the Contortionist," "Redtop Rube, the Vigilante Prince," and many other such pulps were circulating years before the New Orleans Mafia incident. James Weir's *Lonz Powers: or, the Regulators: A Romance of Kentucky*, treated vigilantism favorably, too.[3] And going hand in hand with the fiction, of course, were Dimsdale's classic on the first big Montana action and Bancroft's *Popular Tribunals*.

If the vigilantes were placed solidly within the infrastructure and given the right to take the law into their own hands, it followed that those who wore the badges and used the gavels, who sat on the juries and prepared writs, had to be denigrated. Willett makes a point of comparing vigilante justice, which is sure and swift, with the legally constituted variety, which is fumbling, bogged down in a quagmire of stupid formalities, and unpredictable. He uses Cheyenne Charley as an example of the outlaw who passes through the court system and even into prison only to escape without ever paying for his crimes. It is clear that Cheyenne is a vehicle telling us that courts and jails cannot be depended upon and that the only sure way to settle a badman's hash is to string him up ourselves. Brand, in "The Ghost," doesn't even deign to get the local lawman into the story, but, rather, places the mantle of authority on Collins, the leader of the vigilantes. Wister insists that when the law isn't being enforced by regularly constituted authorities it is the citizen's right to take it into his own hands, since he created the law in the first place and it is therefore his tool. The moral survives as one of the oldest and most deeply held American beliefs: if you want something done right, do it yourself.

The efficiency of vigilante operations and the accuracy with which badmen are fingered are another theme running through the literature, at least until *The Ox-Bow Incident*. Besides being cheaper than housing and feeding the wretches and paying sheriffs and deputies to capture them, judges and juries to try them, and jailers to guard them, vigilante solutions are always quick and highly efficient. Furthermore, vigilantes always get the right men. That watchful eye always knows what's happening, in most cases better than does the sheriff, who only gets paid to catch criminals, but who is rarely victimized by them. Judge Waller startles Cheyenne Charley (and us) by casually dropping the fact that he knows Cheyenne's real name. Obviously, the vigilantes' intelligence system is superb. And there is no escape for those of the Cautious Crooks who fail to get out of the territory in time; if they resist the avengers they're shot down like dogs, and if they surrender they're hanged like hawks on a barn door. No innocent pigeon ever seems to have been hanged on that door before *Ox-Bow*. Americans, after all, have traditionally liked clear-cut winners and losers, heroes and villains, good and evil. Even if it means going into extra innings or into sudden-death overtime after the fourth quarter, there must be a winner and a loser, or we feel unsatisfied.

Another thread running through nineteenth- and early-twentieth-century vigilante mythology has it that only the best people belong to vigilante groups and that their motives are always honorable. They are distinguishable from savage mobs of crazed lynchers because they have patiently put up with their problems longer than any rabble could, have contemplated the alternatives in the coolest and most deliberate way, and have finally taken the trouble to organize. They then do what must be done with deep sorrow, as one morality edges out another. The choice is always painful, but, for the fictional vigilante, ultimately unavoidable. It is a choice made easier by the nature of his enemies, who are always murderers, horse thieves, rustlers, coach or train robbers, crooked gamblers, vicious drunkards and derelicts, or corrupt officials (or all of the above). No one ever joins a vigilante group, or starts one, in order to grab someone else's land or possessions, find refuge from the law or protection from enemies, or liquidate fellow citizens because of their race, religion, or politics.

Finally, the pulp writers and novelists did just enough reporting to lend authenticity to what they were churning out. Wister was sent to Wyoming for health reasons as a young man, and his experiences there, coming relatively soon after the frontier closed, left deep impressions and provided a great deal of firsthand information. He then interpreted what he had learned. Willett, whatever the extent of his travels, managed to inject into his vigilante piece the facts that Orodia was in the vicinity of Virginia City and that the vigilantes used the dreaded 3–7–77 as a signature. Brand, whose real name was Frederick Schiller Faust, graduated from the University of California at Berkeley and was reasonably familiar with western lore. He wanted to be a poet, but turned to the pulps for a living. His formula was simple: "Action, action, action is the thing. So long as you keep your hero jumping through fiery hoops on every page you're all right. . . . There has to be a woman, but not much of one. A good horse is much more important."[4] How close, then, were these writers to the truth? In some cases, they were close enough.

On Friday evening, July 20, 1860, James A. Gordon, a man in his twenties who had an evil reputation, particularly for his disposition when drunk, walked into a saloon in Denver, liquored up, and then took two shots at another "low" character, named "Big Phil." Both rounds missed, and "Big Phil" ran out of the place. That seems to have angered Gordon, who swallowed a few more drinks, picked up two companions, named Fitzpatrick and Rookerbone, and went to the Louisiana Saloon. They drank some more there and at one point smashed their glasses against the front door.

A stranger in town, John Gantz, who was a German from Leavenworth, Kansas, watched as the three carried on. Gantz apparently was popular in Leavenworth, seems to have been offending no one in the saloon, and was only watching the action, when Gordon decided that he didn't like him. Without provocation, Gordon hit Gantz and knocked him down, so the German scrambled to his feet and also ran away. But James A. Gordon was by then in a drunken rage. He chased Gantz onto the street, dragged him back into the drinking dive, and again knocked him down. He then sat on Gantz's chest, held him by his hair, and squeezed the trigger of his pistol, with the muzzle a few inches from the terrified man's face. He squeezed the trigger four times, but the thing wouldn't go off, so Gordon became angrier. It did go off the fifth time, though, blowing the German's brains all over the floor. James A. Gordon sobered very quickly and got out of Denver with a small group of Vigilantes close behind.

The Denver Vigilantes had started as miners' courts in 1859, when the town had only three homicides and one duel. The following year, however, bloodshed ran rampant, as did armed robbery and crooked gambling. In his *History of Denver,* published in 1901, Jerome C. Smiley struck a note close to the hearts of many present-day Americans when he noted that "the desperadoes, influenced by their gregarious instincts, took more naturally to the town where there was at the time less unity of purpose among the people and more individual absorption in personal affairs."[5] In other words, criminals found it easier in those days to operate in a larger, more impersonal, and busier environment than they did in rural areas, where residents were more keenly aware of what was going on. That fact of life was well known to the residents of Denver and other cities a hundred years later. And, besides violent criminals, Denver in 1860 was overrun by claim jumpers and, as Smiley put it, by "a horde of thieves whose operations ranged all the way from robbing clotheslines to stealing a saw-mill."[6] The real absence of law enforcement, due mostly to the region's ambiguous political status in 1860 (it was to become a territory the following year), had given rise to the typical miners' courts and, when crime started going completely out of control, to the almost inevitable vigilance committees.

At any rate, James Gordon fled eastward, narrowly escaped capture at Fort Lupton, and kept going. Ten miles outside the fort, his pursuers shot his horse out from under him, but he continued on foot and finally made his way into Indian Territory. Meanwhile, back in Denver, money was raised for use in chasing and capturing Gordon, no matter where he went, and one W. H. Middaugh volunteered to take up the pursuit. What happened next is important.

Middaugh went to Leavenworth (Denver was just inside the Kansas Territory in 1860), had himself appointed a deputy United States marshal, picked up a court warrant for Gordon's arrest, got a Leavenworth deputy named Armstrong, and began tracking the killer. They caught up with him on the prairie near Humbolt, in the Kansas Territory, and, undoubtedly gratified by their accomplishment, brought him into Leavenworth. And there the United States court set James A. Gordon free on a writ of habeas corpus based on technicalities.

When the large German community in Leavenworth heard about Gordon's having killed Gantz and then been freed by the court, it formed a mob, grabbed Gordon, and managed to get a rope around his neck three times while kicking and punching him and tearing off every stitch of his clothing. Each time the noose was forced over Gordon's head, Middaugh and some military officers managed to get it off again, while Gordon begged them either to surrender him to the mob or to kill him immediately. He was finally rescued from the enraged Germans and ended up being put in a military prison by a detachment of soldiers sent out to rescue him, Middaugh, and the officers. After being told by the authorities in Leavenworth that they would not give up Gordon without the correct papers, Middaugh hopped a coach for Denver, gathered affidavits, other evidence, and some witnesses to the Gantz murder, and returned to Leavenworth. After still more delays, the prisoner was finally handed over and was taken back to Denver in chains.

James A. Gordon went on public trial in a grove of cottonwoods below Wazee Street on Saturday, September 29, and was found guilty the following Tuesday. The trial was presided over by a chief judge and two associate judges, and three men each were appointed counsels for the people and for the defendant. After a jury (whose number and composition haven't survived) voted Gordon guilty, the three judges announced the verdict to a large crowd in front of Nelson Sargent's Tremont House, in nearby Auraria. The crowd was asked to pass on the jury's verdict and, almost unanimously, it seconded the decision. Judge A. C. Hunt then sentenced Gordon, who was present, to be hanged the following Sunday. And he was.[7]

It must be noted that W. H. Middaugh conscientiously had himself appointed a deputy and picked up a warrant before going after Gordon. Furthermore, rather than spiriting his prisoner back to Denver for a popular trial, he took him back to Leavenworth and turned him over to a United States court (the warrant undoubtedly stipulated as much, but Middaugh's compliance showed that he was trying to do the correct thing). He was rewarded by seeing the court free Gordon—an act that would have done nothing to calm the already disgusted citizens of Denver. Middaugh nonetheless rescued his former prisoner from a lynch mob that wanted to do the Vigilantes' work for them, probably risking his own life in doing so. Finally, Gordon was publicly tried by men who made no secret of their identities, and the jury decision was put to a vote by the citizenry at large. In retrospect, it's hard to see how the Denver Vigilantes could have been fairer, given the dire circumstances and the bitter frustration that went with the use of the regular court system.

"We never hanged on circumstantial evidence," said W. N. Byers, looking back on vigilantism in Denver in 1860, and specifically on the execution of another outlaw. "I have known a great many other such executions, but I don't believe one of them was ever unjust. But when they were proved guilty, they were always hanged. There was no getting out of it. No, there were no appeals in those days; no writs of errors; no attorney's fees; no pardon in six months. Punishment was swift, sure and certain. Murderers almost always confessed their crimes."[8]

The James A. Gordon episode and scores like it, then, made excellent grist for the fiction writers who were shortly to fire the imaginations of millions of Americans with the exploits of vigilantes—with tales that Americans wanted to hear about them—

selves. Here's another episode, also typical of scores more, that they didn't want to hear about: the Pierce City Chinese lynchings.

Pierce City, Idaho (now called simply Pierce), sits high in the Bitterroot range, in the Orofino district, between Lewiston and, much farther to the east, Bannack, Virginia City, and the Missouri River and Musselshell sections of Montana. In other words, Pierce City, in 1885, was in the heart of the northern vigilante belt. Between 1862 and 1864 the Lewiston Vigilantes had executed thirty-one men. During about the same period the Bannack and Virginia City organization, as we have seen, had accounted for thirty others, and sporadic outbreaks by smaller groups had continued throughout the 1870s, bringing the grand total to more than a hundred, according to some estimates. "Rangers" in the Sun River region, close to the Canadian border, had operated between 1870 and 1884, and the year they wound down the deadliest of all American vigilance committees—the one led by Granville Stuart—had accounted for thirty-five alleged horse and cattle thieves in the north-central part of the region. Whereas the group that hanged Henry Plummer and his gang had generally been praised by the commentators of the time, Stuart's vigilantes had taken some severe criticism, because they had operated outside a far better law-enforcement system.

By 1885, then, the men of Pierce City, in the Idaho Territory, were very well versed in the theory and practice of vigilantism. They also had an abiding hatred for the Chinese—a hatred that, throughout the decades following the Civil War, was shared by many white westerners, particularly in Idaho, Colorado, and California (fifteen Chinese had been hanged in Los Angeles in 1871, for example, following the murder of a white man).[9]

The trouble in Pierce City started on the morning of September 10, 1885, when D. M. Fraser, one of the two leading merchants in town, was discovered to have been murdered. Not only had the popular and well-established shopkeeper been murdered, the residents of Pierce City saw, but he had also been "terribly chopped to pieces in his own store," with a bloody hatchet and knife that were found lying on his spattered floor. There were even grisly bloody footprints near the body.[10]

Since the other leading merchant in Pierce City happened to be one Lee Kee Nam, it was on him that suspicion immediately fell. It figured, after all. First, there was the mercantile rivalry.

Second, everyone knew that the Chinese liked to do their killing with hatchets and knives, rather than cleanly, with guns, the way whites did.

Word of the murder spread quickly, and as it did men from the area, including a contingent of twenty or twenty-five from Lewiston, began riding into Pierce City to make sure that justice was done. The best thing to do, they decided, was to form a vigilance committee and get at the truth. The deputy sheriff in Pierce City seems to have had a smooth working arrangement with the Vigilantes; they ignored him and he ignored them.

In that there were no legal problems where the Vigilantes were concerned, then, they went right to the heart of the problem. They grabbed Lee Kee Nam, put a noose around his neck, hoisted him, and let him drop. Lee Kee Nam passed out. Then they brought in his partner, made him look at the apparently dead body, and warned him that if he didn't confess to Fraser's murder he, too, would swing. The terrified man began babbling that it had been Lee Kee Nam, acting alone, who had committed the murder. Lee Kee Nam revived at that point and was told that his partner had placed all the blame on him. He reacted by launching into a counterincrimination, after which a bitter argument took place in which each accused the other of having been solely responsible for the crime. Somehow three other Chinese—a barber, a gambler, and a pimp—were also implicated, and they, too, were picked up. In true vigilante style, the suspects had been captured while the trail was still warm and, by intimidation, had been made to 'fess up. Satisfied that they had gotten Fraser's killers, the leaders of the Pierce City Vigilance Committee now made a show of handing them over to the deputy sheriff, who obediently took them into custody. He then swore in a half-dozen other deputies and, on September 18, loaded his prisoners into a wagon and set out for Murray, the Shoshone County seat. The wagon didn't get very far, though.

A few miles out of Pierce City, while passing through dense timber, the lawmen and their wagonload of prisoners were stopped by a large group of heavily armed and masked men. The deputies were relieved of their weapons and told to go back to Pierce City, which, of course, they did.

None of the masked men who took part in the executions of the Chinese that day seems to have described the event, but the *Nez Perce News* later carried an item reporting that the hangmen

236

hadn't made a clean job of it: "When the sheriff's posse returned later in the day, they found the five Chinamen hanging by the necks on a pole lashed to two pine trees. The pole had been broken and lashed to a center post, so that the victims must have been hoisted twice."[11]

If it hadn't been for the widespread anti-Chinese feeling and resulting violence in much of the West at that time, the Pierce City incident might well have been chalked up as just another isolated vigilante action and let go at that. But violence and the threat of it against Asians had reached serious proportions by the late summer of 1885, and not only influential Chinese-Americans, but also the Chinese government, had become openly concerned. Two weeks before the Pierce City lynchings, white miners on strike at the Union Pacific's Rock Springs, Wyoming, coal mines had attacked a camp full of Chinese workers and shot at everyone in sight. The Chinese were "coolie" labor, working for "coolie" wages, and that was no good where white trade unionists were concerned. The editor of the *Idaho World* summed up the situation beautifully: the Chinese must be refused all employment and totally ostracized; otherwise, "the Mongolian will become a fixture on this coast and remain a menace to labor and a nightmare to civilization."[12]

With feelings like that heavy in the air, the Chinese merchant community in Portland sent its own agents into northern Idaho as soon as it heard about the lynchings outside Pierce City. The agents were under orders to investigate the hangings and protect the interests of the Chinese in the area. The results of their investigation convinced the Chinese agents that the five executed men had, indeed, been guilty of murdering D. M. Fraser and had deserved their fate. Quite another report, however, was sent to the Chinese consul in San Francisco. That other document concluded that the killings had been groundless and, more important, had been racially motivated. The consul got off a note to the Chinese minister in Washington, the minister asked Secretary of State Thomas F. Bayard for the customary investigation, and Bayard, in turn, passed the request on to Edward A. Stevenson, who had been appointed territorial governor after the hangings happened. Although Stevenson was a new appointee, he had been in Idaho since leaving the California gold fields in 1863, had built a fortune in mining and farming, and knew Idahoans reasonably well. His reaction to Washington's meddling and to the

request for an investigation of the Chinese lynchings is instructive.

For one thing, although Stevenson first heard about the Chinese government's request for an investigation in April of 1886,
he had known about the hangings right after they happened,
from reading the newspapers. Yet he had done nothing about
them until asked to by the Cleveland administration. Then, after
promising the Secretary of State that he would go to northern
Idaho at the "earliest opportunity" and "try to obtain the facts
connected with that disgraceful outrage," he still did nothing for
the next three months, except to report that road conditions were
making his fact-finding trip impossible.[13] In fairness, Stevenson
did manage to avert violence, after the Boise Anti-Chinese
League set May 1 as the deadline for all Chinese to get out of the
territory, by issuing a proclamation directing the bigots "to use
every precaution to prevent all riotous demonstrations."[14] There
were no riots.

Edward A. Stevenson decided, in midsummer of 1886, that the
snow had finally cleared sufficiently to allow him to travel into
vigilante territory. His first stop was at Lewiston, where he con-
sulted one of that city's most prominent lawyers. They seem to
have talked politics as well as vigilantism, because when Stevenson left Lewiston he carried a remarkable letter of introduction
to the justice of the peace at Pierce City. The letter carefully
explained the circumstances that had brought Stevenson to that
remote place. The territorial Governor, the letter continued, was
poking around only because the State Department, in Washington, wanted him to do so on account of the official Chinese
complaint. The Lewiston lawyer asked his friend the justice of
the peace to show the Governor and his party every courtesy and
extend every facility so they could "arrive at the real causes of
the Execution." The Governor "does not want names as to parties
who took part in the hanging; but the cause which lead to it."
And, being a good lawyer, the Governor's friend left nothing to
the imagination of the leaders of Pierce City. He added that a
full investigation was to take place, and "let it Clearly appear
that the Chinamen who were hung were the real murders [sic]
of Mr. Fraser, and that they were hung for committing the Act,
and for that only." For good measure, the lawyer handed the
Governor a list of all the Chinese in Pierce City who could be

expected to provide information substantiating the dead men's guilt.[15]

So Governor Edward A. Stevenson continued on to Pierce City and conducted what he was later to assure the Secretary of State had been a thorough investigation. The deputy and his posse, Stevenson would inform Bayard, had been so frightened by the masked Vigilantes that they had been unable to recognize any of them. Furthermore, he would explain, while it was regrettable that the people around Pierce City had taken the law into their own hands, he had no doubt "that the Chinese hanged, were the identical parties, who so cruelly, shockingly and brutally murdered, without the least provocation (except jealousy) one of the best citizens of Idaho."[16]

Governor Stevenson ended his investigative report with a lecture to the Secretary of State on the problems westerners were having with the Chinese. There was no point in trying to conceal the fact, he explained, "that many such devilish acts have been perpetrated by Chinese; and their low filthy habits; their highbinder political societies, together with their low dens of infamy, prostitution and opium smoking, have disgusted our people." Finally, Governor Stevenson pledged that all the Chinese in Idaho would receive protection under the law while they remained there, but he expressed the hope, on his own behalf as well as that of his constituents, that "the day is not far distant when Congress will relieve us of their presence."[17] Since the authorities in Washington lacked other channels for investigation, they and the Chinese government had to be content with Governor Stevenson's account of the circumstances surrounding the Pierce City vigilante incident and put it down to the imperatives of local rule. New Orleans, of course, was only five years in the future, and "Clip, the Contortionist" had long since turned yellow in dark attics from Georgia to New Hampshire.

The pulp writers and others who helped forge vigilante mythology in the latter half of the nineteenth and the beginning of the twentieth centuries had a rich field to mine, but they dug selectively. They chose to resurrect and dust off the out-and-out villains and match them, time and again, against the forces of good as represented by what they took to be the popular will. That formula worked essentially for two reasons: it was uncomplicated, and it told Americans that they were as good and strong and free as they wanted to think they were. And, of course, Americans lapped it up. Many, who think of vigilantism only in terms of the smashing of the back-country desperadoes in South Carolina, the liquidation of the Plummer gang, or the come-uppance of the likes of James A. Gordon, still lap it up. They do not relate the vigilante-type groups that formed during the Revolutionary War, to spy on neighbors and intimidate them because of suspected leanings toward the Crown, with the late Senator Joseph McCarthy's purges of the early 1950s or with the Hollywood Blacklist. They do not make the connection because they have not been taught to do so, even though the vigilante reaction in time of "civil emergency" has been more or less continual.

Although the Maryland militia stopped the British from taking Baltimore in mid-September 1812, for example, its success didn't prevent the formation of a Committee of Vigilance and Safety in that city two years later. And one of the first steps taken by the Baltimore Vigilantes was to appoint a subcommittee to investigate anyone who at any time had "expressed sentiments inimical to the American cause or to the defense of Baltimore." Several suspects were actually arrested by their fellow citizens and either jailed or sent out of the city.[18]

"Civil emergency" vigilantism continued up to and throughout the Civil War, and almost always involved abolitionist and pro-slavery activities. New York and Philadelphia had vigilance committees to help runaway slaves as early as 1838, and three years before that Fairfax County, Virginia, had started an antiabolition committee. Such groups multiplied throughout the North and the South during the 1840s and 1850s. The Fugitive Slave Law, which was the only benefit the South got from the Compromise of 1850, was quickly nullified by Northern vigilantes in Buffalo, Poughkeepsie, Syracuse, Springfield, Boston, and elsewhere. The so-called Jerry Rescue, which took place in Syracuse in 1850, was one of the more spectacular instances of prewar slave-related vigilantism. Jerry McHenry, a well-known and well-liked escaped slave, was seized and taken before a federal commissioner for deportation. Before McHenry could be sent south, though, a group that included the Reverend Samuel J. May, a distinguished minister, grabbed the prisoner from the clutches of federal officers and spirited him to Canada. McHenry's pursuers are said to have had great difficulty awakening the sleepy tollgate keepers along the escape route. Eighteen men were indicted for breaking federal law; none was convicted.[19] That is myth material.

This is not. In 1942, shortly after the Japanese attack on Pearl Harbor, thousands of Japanese-Americans were put into detention camps in the West. Officials explained that the Japanese were being locked up for two reasons: first, it was good for the country, and, second, it was for the protection of the Japanese themselves. Generalizations, many of them based on the old anti-Oriental racism going back to the 1850s, were rife: the Japanese, naturalized or not, would forever owe their first allegiance to their mother country; the Japanese were dedicated militarists and could therefore be expected to become spies, saboteurs, and fifth columnists; the Japanese—those diabolical little "monkeys" portrayed in Wallace Beery and Randolph Scott Marine movies— had deliberately clustered around major ports and cities so that they could be of maximum use to their invading brothers (it was even alleged that they had insidiously planted flowers and vegetables in such a way as to point toward major targets for the benefit of "Nip" bombardiers).

The other argument for locking them up concerned their own safety and doesn't seem as farfetched as the first one. In the months immediately following Pearl Harbor, a half-dozen Japanese-Americans were murdered, and at least twenty others were subjected to acts of violence, all politically motivated. "Unless you remove all Japanese, alien and American born, from California, we the people will slaughter them," one patriot is said to have warned President Roosevelt.[20] On January 16, 1942, an official of an agricultural marketing organization wrote to Congressman John Z. Anderson that Filipinos in the Imperial Valley of California were "drawing names of individual Japanese out of a box to be 'taken care of' by those drawing the names."[21] Not long after that, the specter of vigilantism appeared full-blown. The sheriff of one California locality reported that he had heard "rumblings of vigilante activity," and other law-enforcement officials were soon echoing the statement. The mayor of Olympia, Washington, wrote to Attorney General Francis Biddle that unless all Japanese, 'irrespective of citizenship" were removed from the West Coast, "there will be a recurrence of the old time vigilante action that will effect a removal in its own peculiar way."[22] That letter was dated February 17, 1942.

At about the same time, the children of the United States were treated to the first installment of a new comic-strip hero: the Vigilante. Greg Sanders, the crime-fighting troubadour of the plains, rode into the November 1941 issue of *Action Comics* sporting a red bandanna, a white ten-gallon, and a blue shirt. Besides a pair of six-shooters, he carried a rope (referred to as a lariat, never as a noose).

"WHO IS THIS VIGILANTE ――," creator Mort Weisinger and artist Mort Meskin (a Brooklyn-born pulp addict, who had won his spurs on the BMT subway) asked rhetorically. "From across the western plains and into the streamlined East flashes a mystery rider symbolic of frontier America—the Vigilante—heroic champion of law and order, who battles twentieth-century criminals with weapons of the range in a ceaseless one-man stampede against all lawlessness! Follow the victory trail of the Vigilante as he rounds up public enemy number 1 with smoking six-guns and twirling lariat."[23]

Greg Sanders, it turned out, had been born in Wyoming and had inherited "the sterling qualities" of his grandfather, an Indian fighter and "stalwart frontiersman" (who also had worn red, white, and blue clothing while shooting Indians whom he called thieving sidewinders). Greg's father had been a "fearless county sheriff," who had managed to teach his son the law of the range—"to bring to justice those engaged in corrupt practices"—before he was killed by a gang of stagecoach bandits. After Sheriff Sanders was murdered, Greg stood over his grave and solemnly vowed to follow the family tradition and use his heritage to become "The Vigilante, nemesis of all crime from border to border!"[24]

Fortunately, Greg Sanders was blessed with a superb voice, so he went east and worked for law and order under the guise of the Prairie Troubadour, a guitar-strumming milksop in the tried-and-true Clark Kent–Billy Batson tradition.* Before long, Greg

---

* Superman, Batman, Captain Marvel, Green Hornet, the Shadow, Submariner, Red Ryder, Straight Arrow, the Lone Ranger, and other similar comic characters who evolved from the pulps were also true vigilantes who performed mightily to keep the mythology alive. Most, like the Lone Ranger, began their wars on crime only after they had somehow been victimized and

was thrilling radio audiences with his renditions of "Home on the Range" and other cactus classics. Off stage, though, girls tended to treat him as the pansy he seemed to be, and readers could only despise those dumb girls for not being in on the secret. Outside the studio, though, he jumped on a supercharged motorcycle, picked up a faithful young companion named Stuff, the Chinatown Kid, and zoomed off on regular nocturnal prowls in the name of justice and the American way. He sang a far different tune after the sun went down.

> Oh, some play games for
> sky-high stakes,
> and some play penny-ante . . .
> But those who gamble with the law,
> must pay the VIGILANTE![25]

That, in fact, was exactly what had happened to Leo M. Frank, a Jewish factory superintendent in Georgia, who was accused in 1913 of murdering a fourteen-year-old working girl when she tried to collect a balance due on her wages of $1.20. Frank was found guilty of murder by a properly constituted court, but, because several facts in the case were in doubt, the governor commuted the death sentence to life imprisonment. That decision aroused such hostility that mobs threatened the governor's own life, and he had to call out the militia for protection. Anti-Semitism was in the air in Georgia during World War I, and the fact that the governor had formerly been a member of the Jewish law firm that defended Frank only fueled Jewish-conspiracy talk. Leo M. Frank gambled that the law would find him innocent. He lost. He then gambled that the law would keep him safe in prison. He found out that he had lost on that, too, when a fellow prisoner severely wounded him while trying to slit his throat. Finally, he gambled that the law could at least keep him inside the place, but, tragically, he even lost on that. Vigilantes broke into the

---

had not been able to get redress from bumbling authorities; they initially took the law into their own hands out of frustration. Having once been hurt by the forces of evil, they used the single episode as an excuse for unending *Bam-Pow-Crack-Smash-Thud-Clunk*-style retribution, and only turned the evildoers over to the police or sheriff after they had been satisfyingly punched, tossed headfirst into a wall, half-drowned, terrorized, or given a "flesh wound" by an expertly directed bullet. It should be noted here that the Lone Ranger's fabled silver bullets, which he used like calling cards, came straight out of the 3–7–77 tradition, as did Palladin's "Have Gun—Will Travel" cards a generation later.

prison about a month after the attempt on his life, dragged him out, took him in an automobile a hundred miles to a secluded place near the murdered girl's home, and hanged him from a tree.[26] Leo M. Frank, like James P. Casey, Lee Kee Nam, Manuel Politz, and all the others, truly paid the vigilante.

. . . 5000 stalwart youths . . . determined faces shining with eagerness . . . gather in a torchlight, midnight tribunal to ride greed, lust and murder out of town.

Skies Blaze Red . . . 5000 torches light the heavens . . . 10,000 glowing faces flame with eagerness.

SEE—the gigantic mobilization of young courageous manhood.

FEEL—the fury of the mob.[27]

That could have been written by a correspondent covering a youth rally in Hamburg in 1933. And it *was* written in 1933, not by William Shirer, but by a press agent for Paramount studios, who ground it out as part of a press release for Cecil B. De Mille's *This Day and Age*. The picture, like others made during the depths of the Depression (including *Gabriel over the White House* and *The President Vanishes*), was a response to a craving for authority by a shaken and bewildered nation, which read, as it sold apples and stood on bread lines, that Adolf Hitler had solidified Germany and that Benito Mussolini had accomplished what was perhaps the greatest miracle of the century—he had made Italian trains run on time. In America, nothing was running on time, and time seemed to be all Americans had. So many of them went to the movies and saw *This Day and Age*, the story of a town's teen-agers who abandon the hedonistic joys of dating and jalopies to almost lynch a gangster named Garrett (played by Charles Bickford), who has eluded a murder charge by using a "million-dollar mouthpiece."

"Legality was presented as a barrier to the truth," notes film historian Andrew Bergman. "In his courtroom scene De Mille used a montage of law books, objections being raised, and fingers pointed in order to show how due process was in fact a symptom of social illness; it had become a shield for shysters. Rather than observing all the technicalities of the law, the students want direct action, and an eye for an eye. They kidnap Garrett and lead him to a brickyard, where thousands more wait, bearing torches and giving high school cheers. 'We haven't got time for any rules of evidence,' cries their leader, as the gangster is bound and slowly lowered into a pit full of rats, until he confesses. No matter how De Mille tried to finesse his point ('It was not the intention . . . that high school students should tackle their local racketeers in the same way'), the moral was simple: serious ends merited any means necessary. And the Hitlerite rhetoric of the press copy, obviously shaped to somebody's conception of the film's major selling point, only deepens the importance of *This Day and Age*'s playing to the mob." The reviews, Bergman adds, were generally hostile.[28]

The reality of vigilantism as it moved off the physical frontier and into the mid-twentieth century, then, was not so much widespread disdain as acceptance, provided it fitted the conceptions in the mind of the beholder. Put another way, vigilantism is bad when those evil people do it, but acceptable when we good people do it. There are very few in the present liberal establishment, for example, who think that slavery was a good thing. If they felt strongly enough about the matter, they probably would be prepared to say that the abolitionist vigilantes who sent Jerry McHenry safely on his way to Canada did a fine and noble thing. In that instance, vigilance was socially beneficial, whether or not it broke the law. The same people, however, would probably condemn the Fairfax antiabolitionists as being thickheaded beasts for using identical tactics to keep slaves from escaping. Along with most of us, I think slavery is evil, but that's not the point; the point is that the Fairfax vigilantes thought it was a good and useful thing, and they therefore also thought that extralegal methods for keeping it going were thoroughly justified.

Likewise, the Italian-American who is familiar with what happened in New Orleans in 1891, the Irish-American who knows about the consequences of what occurred in San Francisco in 1856, and the Jewish-American who knows about Leo M. Frank and others of his faith find no apparent contradiction in condemning those lynchings, on the one hand, and in mumbling darkly about what "they ought to do" to spic and nigger dope fiends, rapists, and murderers, on the other.

Vigilantes are always frightened and angry people—people guarding their advantages or their right to gain more advantages—who feel compelled to use direct and often violent action to intimidate or crush those threatening them. Tolerance and accommodation have always been expendable commodities, not just in the United States, but everywhere. But the dichotomy between American social ideals and day-to-day practice has become even more glaring against the backdrop of all the civil-rights and brotherhood rhetoric. The liberals of the Kennedy enlightenment managed to paint themselves into the proverbial corner by bombarding their countrymen with the appealing notion that they were, at heart, a just, compassionate, and tolerant people who only needed some guidance, through civil-rights legislation, to find the true track to the heaven they deserved. It was pure fiction, of course, but no politician ever got re-elected by informing his constituents that they were capable of reacting viciously and could be depended upon to do so, regardless of statutes forbidding it, when they were threatened or frustrated. Their socioeconomic expectations were raised, and they were told that if only they obeyed the law everything would be all right. Yet everything is far from all right. Conflict still lies across the land, as it always has, during our seemingly interminable voyage through hard times and rising expectations. And, as usual, vigilantes are close behind.

10

And Now . . .

PUBLIC NOTICE

THE TIME HAS COME

With our Democracy deteriorated into hypocracy . . .

With violent crimes, murder, dope, rape, kidnapping, holdups, robberies, cattle rustling, vandalism, beatings and torturing of people, young and old, and all other acts of crime and violence . . .

With little or no respect for law and order . . .

With little or no law enforcement . . .

With little or no justice in our judiciary courts . . .

THE TIME HAS COME FOR ACTION

By the law-abiding citizens of Montana, and all of the other forty-nine states of our great republic of the United States of America.

If there are one, two, three thousands or more of red-blooded Americans in Montana who are willing and interested in bringing law and order, justice and honesty back to our State, who are willing to fight or die for their homes, safety and loved ones, will they please contact me at once.

There will be posse comatatus committees, organized throughout

247

Vigilante!

Montana and forty-nine other states of our great republic of the United States of America very soon.

All persons interested in organizing posse comatatus committees and all persons belonging to this organization must be twenty-five years of age or older, married and own property.

They must be law-abiding citizens with a clean record.

There will be no shootings or hangings except for murder, kidnapping, rape and cattle rustling.

Lesser crimes will be handled according to the seriousness of crimes committed.

Please remember that it was the <u>Vigilantes,</u> organized over one hundred years ago when Montana was only a Territory, organized by our forefathers, that brought law and order to Montana.

What our forefathers did over one hundred years ago we can and must do today to restore law, order, and freedom to the people of the United States of America.

All citizens interested in posse comatatus committees please contact me as soon as possible in person or by mail at Stevensville, Montana, 59870.

SIGNED AND DATED this 24th day of April, 1974 by

Captain Loren J. B. Nedley

This is a vigilante broadside tacked up in Montana during the spring of 1974.

"After being mugged, beaten, robbed, and my house broken into and vandalized I decided to organize a Vigilante organization here in Montana," says Captain Loren J. B. Nedley, the eighty-one-year-old gentleman who penned that document. "Before too long all members will wear a badge and gun. We work in cooperation with all law enforcement members. We do not go out looking for criminals unless asked to by the sheriff or F.B.I. However if we catch anyone in the act of Rape, Kidnapping or Murder they will be shot *dead*. There are three new faces in Hell for breakfast in Montana," he adds.

Nedley has claimed 2,000 vigilantes in his state, nearly 20,000 in Idaho, and more than 2 million nationwide. The first annual convention of the Posse Comitatus of Montana and the United States of America was held, appropriately enough, in Virginia City, where the Plummer gang got its comeuppance, on June 21 and 22, 1975. The fact that only nine vigilantes showed up, however, suggests that Nedley's group was somewhat thinner, or perhaps less motivated, than he cared to admit. And not only were Nedley's vigilantes disarmed when they got to Virginia City, but they were relieved of their hardware by Kemp Coit, the town marshal, who hailed from Martha's Vineyard and who saw his first action during the 1968 student demonstrations in Chicago. It was ignominious for the vigilantes, but, as any of them would have been quick to point out, it figured; America is going to the dogs.

Talk during the convention had to do mostly with the destruction of the Constitution by "Communist Trotskyite Jews" and other enemies, ranging from the United States Forestry Service to rock-music fans. The Reverend Richard G. Butler, head of the Fundamentalist church of Hayden Lake, Idaho, complained that the Constitution was no longer being taught in the nation's schools. Arwood Stickney, a Missoula sanitation man, vented his frustration by charging that the criminal in America today is "out on the streets before the victim is in the hospital." Slim Deardorff, a Montana horseshoer, checked his twin .357 Magnums. Captain Nedley told of his vision: "I wouldn't be surprised to see all these mountains full of guerrilla warriors" one day.

To organize a *posse comitatus* ("power of the county"), says Nedley, "get eight trusted men. Go to the county court house and register as a Sheriffs Posse Comatatus Committee. Then pass the information to the next county and the next. Accept only honest married men over 25 years old. The main thing is to get involved and organized before we have a communistic take over of our Country."

Many of Nedley's neighbors have apparently dismissed his call for vigilance as so much harmless nonsense. His claim that the reference to the "three new faces in Hell for breakfast" meant that three evildoers had been "shot *dead*" was shrugged off by local lawmen, who said that everyone in their area was present and accounted for. And M. E. Carver, another Montanan, added that "we have come too far to return to vigilantism. Let us all carry a gun and do not kill, only in self-defense." So speaks the voice of moderation.

If Nedley's description of his organization's size and intentions was overblown (a common denominator of activist groups across the political spectrum), it was nonetheless interesting that a sheriff's *posse comitatus* should crop up in Wisconsin at the same time. That group described itself as a front-line defender of con-

249

stitutional government against an international conspiracy to control the world, according to the *Minneapolis Tribune* of December 15, 1974. Law-enforcement officers and state officials have called the group "a dangerous bunch of vigilantes who don't want to pay their taxes or abide by land-use laws."

The Wisconsin vigilantes admitted that they were dangerous, but only to the real enemies of the United States: Nelson Rockefeller, Pope Paul VI, Jews, blacks, and anyone favoring regional government, the United Nations, the graduated income tax, or fluoridation. Eugene Lind, a county posse chairman, has predicted that those in the international conspiracy are getting ready to erase state lines.

"They've already got plans for 22 super-states planned around the major river basins," explained the vigilante leader. "Then they're going to start more chaos. Can you imagine what a complete truckers' strike, like we almost had last year, would do to our cities? People would be killing each other for food. That's when they'd bring in the United Nations troops to restore order. Only they'd never leave. And the only members of the U.N. big enough to take over the U.S.? Russia and China. You can read it in the Bible."

Posse leaders go on to explain that county sheriffs are the only legal law-enforcement officers in the country and that when a sheriff refuses to stop unconstitutional activities (such as governmental interference in what someone does with his own land) the posse is obliged to do so. That authority, they insist, comes from common law. So far, this *posse comitatus* has carried writs, not ropes; the state organization has filed suits in federal district court against about 200 state officials, including Governor Patrick J. Lucey, who is being sued for treason because of a letter he wrote indicating support of the United Nations. Wives of state officials are being sued for condoning their husbands' political actions.

But the new vigilantes are not so naïve as to think that they will get anywhere in courts already rotten with corruption and filled with communistic dupes or plain dopes. Thomas Stockheimer, the state chairman of the Wisconsin posse, has been quoted as saying that his vigilantes were prepared to die defending their God-given constitutional and natural liberties. "Others talk," he said. "We're storing up beans and bullets and preparing for the fight." Stockheimer went on to denounce the John Birch

Society as being a "tool of the establishment. You can't trust the John Birch leaders. They aren't patriots. Those guys are bought and paid for."

Stockheimer, Lind, and other vigilante leaders have refused to say how many members they have, because they're afraid that the FBI would then be able to identify them. They have registered in eight Wisconsin counties, though, and claim to have unregistered posses in thirty-six others. *Posse comitatus* groups also have registered in Washington, Oregon, Michigan, California, Idaho, and, of course, Montana.

"So far, basically, they're just talking," said Robert Repaske, a Wisconsin assistant state attorney general, and one of those being sued. "But it's only a matter of time before they step across the line. Something's going to happen."[1]

Over in Idaho, meanwhile, it was more of the same: the grandsons of American frontiersmen brooding over crime and what they saw as an insidious bureaucratic conspiracy to sap their freedom the way blood could be taken from an eagle—one unnoticed drop at a time, until it was too late. The enemy was seen in Idaho, as in many areas west of the Mississippi and south of the Potomac, as being the federal government—an amorphous horde of lazy or dangerous or stupid or conspiratorial (or all of the above) liberal-radicals, who were out to bleed the American way of life to death.

"It has been said of you and others of your ilk, that you now have the bureaucratic tit so far down your throats that you can no longer even taste the milk. Please be assured that an ever increasing number of good, genuine and solid citizens of this state, more and more, are convinced that the general welfare would be far better served if you and many others of your fellow travelers would just 'knock it off' and go on direct relief," wrote Asael Lyman, "A Cooperating Member of the [Idaho] Vigilant Committee of 10,000," to Keith Higginson, director of the Idaho Department of Water Administration. The letter, written on November 12, 1973, castigated Higginson because two state Fish and Game Department agents allegedly had entered the property of two brothers named Calvin and Cecil Green and arrested their employees for moving gravel on the property and thereby altering the shape of the Snake River. Lyman also complained bitterly in the letter that rules drafted by the Department of Water Administration allegedly to prohibit livestock from grazing along streams in order to protect fish were another case in point. Higginson denied that the fencing off of streams was part of his department's program, but Lyman insisted that he and others in Idaho would not be fooled. The same Committee of 10,000 made network television during the late winter of 1973–74 when it announced that it would take reprisals against rustlers who were trying to steal large quantities of cattle because meat was bringing high prices.

"Cattle and horses must not be left any longer to stray about in any such loose way," Lyman wrote at the bottom of a copy of his letter to Higginson that he sent to this writer. He was quoting a letter, dated May 2, 1866, written by one Daniel H. Wells to settlers of the southern Utah Territory. They *"must be strongly guarded by a force sufficiently strong to protect them from falling into the hands of an enemy, who if he sees there is no chance of getting a single hoof without first getting a bullet, will then, and not til then, most likely desist."*

Others in Montana and Idaho were at the same time explaining that their vigilantes were full of so much hot air. But the phraseology of at least one of those moderates was, in itself, very interesting.

"I'll place this request for new recruits into the Montana Vigilante Party on the city hall bulletin board," wrote M. E. Carver, after reading Nedley's broadside in *Harper's Weekly*.

"I doubt if you get much response, as ideas change fast here in South Central Montana. Just a year ago the people in this section of Montana were unhappy about cattle rustling. At that time hunters and others came onto the farmers property and helped themselves to his beef cattle. They butchered and branded cattle and hauled the calves away." But, he went on to say, "it is dumb to hang a man for stealing an animal, anytime. One hundred years ago many a man was hanged by the neck until dead, who hadn't been involved in the theft of an animal.

"True, many murders and rapers go unpunished in Montana, because we take into consideration what caused the man to commit these offenses.

"Most of our troubles come from outside the Nation and the State.

"We have had three outside influences during the past 15 years which hasn't helped us much. First the drugs and Vietnam; second the employing of out of State educators; and third bribery on the part of the Federal government. They tax our income and then use it to bribe us into spending it the way they feel fit. Who is calling the shots around here, anyway?"[2]

In California's lush San Joaquin Valley, still another *posse comitatus* was, at least in part, calling the shots in early September 1975, during the United Farm Workers' attempt to unionize fruit and vegetable pickers and other laborers. At Stockton, a posse claiming a hundred members, including three women, kept organizers off tomato farms with the threat of violence. About forty of the vigilantes were armed; many had handcuffs dangling from their jeans and wore sheriff-style badges; a pickup truck with a bumper sticker reading "God, Guns & Guts Made U.S. Free" held a stack of "citizen's arrest forms" and a citizen's-band radio for use in co-ordinating the defense of the vast farmlands in the area. The vigilantes held the union organizers at bay for three days before deciding to abandon their skirmish lines and allow lawmen to take over (a fight between posse members and sheriff's deputies at one point led to some arrests on charges of assault with a deadly weapon on a police officer). The California vigilante operation was important for two reasons. First, it spread quickly; the San Joaquin group was organized that February, but by September there were twenty-two similar *posses comitatus* in California. Second, the Californians didn't confine their activity to nailing up harmless broadsides that merely bemoaned the state of the nation; they actually turned out, with their guns, radios, and arrest forms, to establish a physical presence, and not only held off the union organizers but also grappled with law-enforcement officers. In other words, the California vigilantes proved that they would, indeed, use force when they thought it was needed. Clearly, then, the concept of the *posse comitatus* was spreading and taking on a serious dimension by the autumn of 1975.

On July 31, 1974, while Captain Nedley was tacking up his broadsides, the Wisconsin *posse comitatus* was stashing beans and bullets, and the San Joaquin group was still only a tempting dream, Edward A. Foster was being locked up in the Maine Medical Center's P6 psychiatric ward. Foster, a two-year veteran of the Portland Police Department, was being held under close observation after he suggested to three other policemen that they form a "death squad" to take care of repeated criminal offenders who were not being punished sufficiently by the regular legal process.

Witnesses at a series of hearings in district court and at the state Civil Service Commission told of discussions between the twenty-six-year-old patrolman and other members of the department in which he complained about the shortcomings of the judicial and correctional systems. The talk, held during off-duty hours, over beer, allegedly ended with Foster's proposing to his three comrades that they take the crime situation into their own hands. According to at least one of the three other policemen, Foster's plan called for one of them—a former sniper in Vietnam—to execute three hardened criminals and bury their bodies at a local highway-construction site. Foster also allegedly "offered to buy a 12-gauge shotgun" and pay for it himself. The accused said that he could not remember mentioning the purchase of such a weapon, but he did recall proposing the use of a specific kind of gun for the assassinations and also having come to the meeting with a list of three possible victims and their police records.

After first denying that he had suggested the formation of the death squad, Foster admitted to having talked about it, but insisted repeatedly that it had only been a "practical joke." At least one of the officers to whom he made the suggestion had taken it seriously enough, however, to report it to their superior. Three psychiatrists examined Foster and came to a split decision on the state of his sanity, ranging from characterizing him as not paranoid to calling him "a moderate to extreme paranoid personality" and "unfit to be a policeman." Although no criminal charges were placed against the exuberant young policeman, he was fired from the force. "Every good policeman is frustrated with the criminal justice system and talks of a death squad at one time or another," Edward A. Foster was quoted as having explained in his own defense.[3]

But it went beyond talk in New York. On October 10, 1974, Julio Torres, a forty-year-old suspected drug addict, died at Jacobi Hospital two days after he was brought in suffering from the effects of a beating with a wrench, a broken bottle, metal pipes, and sticks. A month later, two Hispanic brothers and a man named John P. Corcoran, who was on the list for appointment to the police department, were indicted for manslaughter in the case by a Bronx grand jury. According to the police, the defendants had decided to move against addicts in their Bronx neighborhood who were using a vacant apartment as a "shooting gallery" and had started on Torres. The police added that all three of the suspects had called themselves "vigilantes."[4]

The Julio Torres incident was unique in only two regards: suspects had been caught, and they had called themselves vigilantes. Otherwise, what happened to Torres seems to have been happening sporadically around the city for years, and particularly in such addict-infested high-crime areas as the Lower East Side, the South Bronx, and the Crown Heights section of Brooklyn. The problem, of course, is proof; no one who participates in a vigilante-type execution (as opposed to settling a grudge) is likely to come to the police and admit it. Furthermore, one of the most popular ways of executing junkies and pushers is to toss them off roofs, a simple expedient that has the advantages of being cheap and highly efficient and not involving a murder weapon.

"When an addict goes off a roof, we can't make a diagnosis on whether he was pushed or whether he fell," says Dr. Michael Baden, Deputy Chief Medical Examiner for the city of New York, and a man who quite routinely performs autopsies on drug addicts. "If somebody is shot or stabbed, we *can* make a diagnosis of homicide, but otherwise, there's nothing in the autopsy finding to tell you it was a homicide. . . . Some junkies may have been thrown off buildings; invariably, there aren't effective witnesses to tell the police what happened. It could exist, though. We had a couple of cases where guys were thrown off roofs in '72 and '73. There has been a big increase in junkie homicides, though. In 1970, 50 addicts were killed; last year, it was 300-something." Dr. Baden was referring to 1973.

Santos Santos, a.k.a. Santos Laguana, is, or was, a case in point. According to a homicide report filed by detectives of the Forty-second Precinct, in the Bronx, the twenty-seven-year-old drug addict was thrown from the roof of 522 East 159th Street at 7:10 on the evening of Saturday, July 14, 1973. Thirty minutes later, the victim was brought into Lincoln Hospital, dead on arrival, and the autopsy listed the cause of death as a fractured skull and lacerations of the brain, liver, spleen, and aorta, plus internal hemorrhaging. Those who had witnessed the plunge explained to the detectives that they had seen Santos jump, or at least fall, from the roof. None would venture a guess, though, as to how he might have accomplished that with his hands and feet tied.

The important point here is that in New York, as in virtually every other part of the country, vigilantism remains a clear outgrowth of class warfare, but not necessarily one involving cattle barons and WASP Minutemen against rustlers and Communists. The impoverished but law-abiding residents of a ghetto neighborhood, who own small shops and are working hard for a better life for themselves and their children, are, relatively speaking, the economic elite of the area. As such, they see the drug addict, holdup man, and mugger in exactly the same way as the wealthy cattlemen who joined the Leavenworth, Kansas, Committee of Vigilance in 1856 saw the low-class bandits who threatened their way of life and economic goals. Wealth and position are relative, and, no matter how little people have or how tenuous their social position, they tend to protect what they have from those one notch lower who are threatening to take it all away from them. The knowledge of what had happened to the eleven Sicilians lynched in New Orleans in 1891, for example, did nothing to keep the middle-class Italians in Newark's North Ward from threatening similar action against rioting blacks in 1967. By 1967, the Italians in Newark had turned into the haves, and many of them were damned if they were going to let a bunch of black have-nots destroy what they had worked so hard to build. Similarly, there are people in Wisconsin today who are convinced that Jews have horns and that the very religious Hasidic Jews, in particular, are loathsome demons incarnate, who are out to do all the things Adolf Hitler had warned about: seduce innocent Christian girls, poison forever the pure Anglo-Saxon bloodline, and steal everyone's money (while at the same time somehow being Communists). It therefore seems ironic that a band of bearded Hasidic Jews in New York's Crown Heights section started modern passive (nonaggressive) vigilance, in May 1964.

They called themselves Maccabees, after a Jewish family that led a fierce fight for freedom against the King of Syria in the second century B.C. And what they did seems ironic, but isn't, because Hasidic Jews were very much a part of the establishment in Crown Heights in 1964, and they had every intention of remaining so. In addition, they were well aware that their beards, side curls, and traditional Old World wide-brimmed black hats and long coats made them objects of ridicule among many non-Jews, and especially among the blacks in the neighboring Bedford-Stuyvesant ghetto. Although the leaders of the Hasidic community in Crown Heights were reluctant to single out blacks as their chief tormentors during that difficult spring of 1964, they made no secret of the fact that the vast majority of muggings, beatings, and robberies were being done by blacks who prowled through their neighborhoods looking for easy victims. The Jews in Crown Heights, many of them refugees who had barely escaped the holocaust, were also well aware of the fact that Jews, and particularly ultra-Orthodox Jews, were classified by their predators as pale and pudgy pacifists, who would not fight back. They were being attacked, they felt, because they were allowing themselves to be attacked. And the police were spread too thin to be of much help in protecting their homes and shops and the pay envelopes they brought back from jobs elsewhere in the city. So they decided, early in 1964, after a rabbi's wife was dragged out of her apartment and slashed while fighting off a rapist, and after a group of Jewish children was attacked and beaten by young blacks, to protect themselves. There were some large, muscular Jews in Crown Heights in the spring of 1964, but it was difficult to tell that because of their long black coats.

The "protective patrol force," as it was called, went into operation with about 120 volunteers, four radio-equipped patrol cars, and a command post in a drab storefront at 459 Albany Avenue. The command post contained only a desk, some chairs, a large map of Crown Heights, a telephone, and donated radio equipment with which to keep in contact with the cars, each of which held six reasonably burly men. None of the men were armed, but all patrolled with orders to overwhelm the enemy when possible, and only if impossible to call headquarters for help. Headquarters was then supposed to call the police—the last resort.

"We don't believe in the vigilante system in any society," grumbled Deputy Police Commissioner Walter Arm. "That's what we have police for. We're aware of the situation and we're trying to do the best we can." But the best did not seem to the Hasidic Jews to be good enough.

"The police know what we are doing," said Rabbi Samuel Schrage, the man who organized the Maccabees. "We didn't ask them if we could do it because we didn't expect them to sanction it." Yet there was nothing illegal about the patrol force, so there was nothing the police could do to stop it. When two police-men—a captain and a sergeant—came to the storefront two weeks after the Maccabees began their nightly patrols and asked if they could be of assistance, they were politely but firmly put off. They were told that they would be called if needed.

The cars prowled from about eight in the evening to five in the morning, constantly scanning for any signs of trouble and staying in almost continuous radio contact with the command post. Among the volunteers during those first months were twenty non-Jews—twelve whites and eight blacks—who worked on Friday nights, when the Jews were having their Sabbath. During their first ten days, the Maccabees were instrumental in three arrests: two suspicious men were observed breaking into a catering estab-lishment and were held for the police, and a purse snatcher was caught in the act, wrestled down, and also held until the police arrived. The number of such instances would increase into the dozens as the year progressed. Many of the area's 500,000 resi-dents would then begin coming out on the streets again, because of the roaming patrol cars.

Did the Maccabees lessen crime in Crown Heights? Yes, said the *New York Times,* which reported in March 1966 that crime in the area had fallen off to the point where the patrols could be reduced and finally eliminated. Yes, said Rabbi Schrage a decade later. "When I started the Maccabees, the blockbusters were all over the place. People were panicking. Now the blockbusters are no longer here. The homeowners are too solid. The streets are safe. Economically, the middle-class blacks and Jews have great rapport, and politically there's tremendous rapport between the Jews and officials like Shirley Chisholm and Vander Beatty."[5] Police unhappiness over the Maccabees notwithstanding, it should be noted here that Rabbi Schrage's accomplishment was officially acknowledged by the city of New York when he was appointed assistant executive director of the Youth Board in June 1966. True to tradition, vigilantism had served as a means of political recognition for one of its leaders.

The concept of car patrols began spreading as crime soared in the mid-1960s. In December 1964, twenty-four residents of Port Chester, New York, formed a "vigilante group" to cope with rowdy youngsters from nearby Connecticut who were taking advantage of New York State's law allowing eighteen-year-olds to drink. After a series of brawls, beatings, and acts of vandalism in Port Chester, the group decided that police protection was insufficient, and loosely organized patrols were started. In March 1966, after several women in the Midland Beach section of Staten Island, New York, had been attacked, the Midland Beach Progressive Association organized nightly unarmed radio-car patrols in co-operation with the police. In March 1966, while the Maccabees were winding down, a radio-car citizens' patrol patterned after them was started in Brooklyn's Bushwick section. The organization had been in the planning stage for several months when, that March, a robbery-killing and a rape became the catalysts for action. This time the patrol force, consisting of fifteen volunteers, was headed by a Lutheran minister, the Reverend Samuel L. Hoard. It was supported by a dozen Protestant and Catholic churches in the area. The East New York, Brownsville, and Flatbush sections of Brooklyn began radio-equipped vigilante patrols the following January, with 350 members using five cars. Their task, they said, was to spot and "discourage" criminal activity and to co-operate with the police. In June 1967, a force of about fifty private guards armed with shotguns started patrolling in Houston, Texas, after several businesses almost went under because of robberies and burglaries. And by 1975 the radio-car vigilance patrol was an established concept in scores of cities throughout the country, including Camden, New Jersey, where "Towne Watch" patrols started, not only because of a worsening crime wave but also because of "widespread abuse of police power," and Duluth, Minnesota, where gas-station owners began nightly patrols to thwart the stick-up men who were victimizing them. What the gas-station operators did, other Duluth businessmen could do, too. So, in February 1975, the owner of a second-hand-goods shop in Duluth said that he and other businessmen were thinking of either hiring a private patrol agency or "forming our own vigilante committee," in an effort to stop burglaries. Arthur Davis, the owner of that store, said that he was not satisfied with the quality of police protection; he claimed to have had ninety-six break-ins in five years, "and they [the police] haven't recovered 15 cents worth of merchandise."

And there were foot patrols, block associations, and tenant groups, sometimes hiring guards but usually doing it themselves, with walkie-talkies and clubs. They sprang up in New York's Delano Village housing complex, in North Harlem, in December

1964, and, that same month, along Manhattan's West Side, and specifically on Riverside Drive, West End Avenue, and 103rd Street, where heroin addicts suddenly began responding to a price rise for the drug by increasing their robbery and burglary activities. On March 3, 1967, thirty-five tenants, most of them women, in New York's large Peter Cooper Village housing project formed a "temporary vigilante committee" to patrol the buildings and grounds in the wake of a series of rapes and muggings. The apartment dwellers accused both the police and the Metropolitan Life Insurance Company, the owner of the buildings, of not supplying adequate protection and then insisted that they would therefore have to protect themselves.

Seeing that citizens seemed determined to organize, with or without official co-operation, municipal governments began deciding, by the end of the 1960s, that they would be better off getting in on the act, rather than see the crisis of confidence continue to worsen. In 1973, New York's Mayor John Lindsay began providing matching funds to block associations for the installation of back-yard lighting, television monitoring units, and automatic-eye house alarms. The people in such block associations started carrying police whistles, were called "block watchers," and were officially granted responsibility for looking out for their neighbors' safety. A year later, in April 1974, the Fort Worth Police Department set up a twenty-eight-man anticrime force composed of uniformed lawmen and city-paid civilians; one captain, three sergeants, twelve uniformed officers, and twelve civilians were sent on crime-prevention patrols in a desperate effort to ease a crime rate that had jumped 20 per cent the previous year (and that was causing increasing numbers of businessmen and other citizens to grumble about police incompetence).

One of the aspects of the rising crime rate of the 1960s that had largely been overlooked by criminologists and the more affluent whites in America was the fact that blacks, Hispanics, and other racial minorities were getting hit worse by criminals from their own communities than were whites elsewhere. Before the middle of that decade, it hadn't really occurred to the well-to-do white whistle blowers that black families in Harlem, Bedford-Stuyvesant, and similar communities were also being terrorized by hoodlums, thieves, burglars, purse snatchers, muggers, and armed robbers.

In October 1967, the Reverend Oberia D. Dempsey, pastor of the Upper Park Avenue Baptist Church, and the "unofficial mayor of Harlem," organized Operation Interruption, an "armed police militia" designed specifically to counterattack drug addicts in that community. The Reverend Mr. Dempsey set up a core of 200 active members, who were officially armed with clubs (and unofficially armed with more lethal weapons), and about 2,400 others who concentrated on patrol work, citizen escort, and informing the New York Police Department, the FBI, and the Federal Narcotics Bureau of drug activity in the Harlem community. The armed members were clearly mandated to stop crime when they found it, with or without help from the police. (Captain William J. O'Rourke, of the Twenty-fifth Precinct, was quoted by the *New York Times* as having admitted that the police in the neighborhood were proving unequal to the task of stopping drug-related crimes and as saying that he wanted to work closely with the vigilance organization.)[6] In October 1968, blacks in Pittsburgh started nightly unarmed "vigilante" patrols to reduce crime and also because of racial tensions with white groups in the city. In January 1969, a Community Patrol Corps emerged in the black ghetto of Detroit, with about twenty young blacks in paramilitary uniforms trying to ward off not only criminals but also allegedly brutal white policemen. That group was given a $50,000 grant from the New Detroit Committee, a local Urban Coalition group.

Racial vigilantism in the mid-1960s developed parallel to, and in some cases as part of, the anticrime side of the reaction. Richard Maxwell Brown reports that, from May 1965 at least through 1966, a black organization called Deacons for Defense and Justice operated in Jonesboro and Bogalusa, Louisiana, to protect civil-rights workers (many of them white) and black area residents against the Ku Klux Klan, red-necks, and the police. The black self-protection group used an armed-patrol-car system and by May of 1966 claimed 7,000 members in Louisiana and sixty loosely federated chapters in Mississippi, Alabama, Florida, and the Carolinas.[7]

White vigilantes were said to have been active in Cleveland, Ohio, during the summer of 1968, when racial violence flared there, and may have been responsible for the unsolved deaths of two blacks. Even as that summer of '68 wore to a close, militants on both sides were mumbling about vigilance.

"Several observers here worry that the continual friction in Cleveland will lead to more militancy on the part of Negroes and to a growth of fascism among whites," reported the *New York Times* on September 3, 1968. "A black nationalist suggested that if things got worse he hoped to see black city officials 'lead us in the streets with guns' and more than one white policeman was overheard advocating 'a take-over by the military' because, he said, civilian rule had failed.

"Many Negroes here, very few of whom say they would have joined with the militants involved in the shooting, do feel a need to protect themselves against the police and in some instances against white citizens. Two of the Negroes killed during the tension were miles away from where the gun battles occurred and in areas where white vigilantes are active. National Guardsmen who sealed off the Negro slums during the disorders also turned back several carloads of white men attempting to enter the area." That same summer, "nightriders" in Irasburg, Vermont, harassed the Reverend David L. Johnson, a black accused of adultery with a white woman; an antiblack group calling itself Fight Back formed in Warren, Michigan; and the Home Defense Association of Oakland, California, was started to protect the white community against black marauders. The two latter organizations seem to have been patterned after the best-known white vigilance group to come out of the racially turbulent 1960s—Anthony Imperiale's renowned North Ward Citizens' Committee of Newark, New Jersey.

Although few of them may have thought so, the Italian-Americans in Newark's North Ward had a great deal in common with the Hasidic Jews in Crown Heights, the Reverend Mr. Dempsey's black armed patrols in Harlem, and other embattled groups that saw themselves threatened from below. A considerable majority of the North Ward's 43,000 residents were lower-middle-class Italian-Americans during the hot summer of 1967, and many of them were at the same time aspiring to more while feeling that they were being dragged down to less. They were service-station operators, luncheonette owners, bakery employees, bartenders, cocktail waitresses, bus and taxi drivers, and others with either blue collars or off-white ones. During the years between World War II and the mid-'60s, those people, many of them the children

And Now . . .

of immigrants, watched with growing apprehension as Protestants—white Protestants—deserted the community for the
greener pastures of suburbia and were replaced by blacks from
the city's Central Ward ghetto. They watched as their formerly
middle-middle-class neighborhood began to deteriorate into a
shabby, ticky-tack patchwork of graying multiple-occupancy
dwellings and corner bars with phony brick façades, faded pic-
tures of Miss Rheingold, and the odor of quiet resignation mixed
with boilermakers. The men who passed their time in those bars
during the first week of July 1967 were acutely aware of what
was happening to them and their community; they talked about
it a lot—about the decay and "the niggers." They talked about
the blacks pretty much the way the people in New Orleans had
talked about the Sicilians seventy-six years before. The country
and their city were overrun with "niggers and Communists and
Communist niggers," they told one another, and the crime and
radicalism were destroying everything. The North Ward
bounded the Central Ward, and the Central Ward, as they all
knew, was packed full of lazy, mean-minded niggers, who were
buying dope and knives with welfare money—*their* Goddamned
tax money.

The Central Ward was, indeed, on welfare in July of 1967.
More than half of Newark's 400,000 population that year was
black, and most of the blacks lived in the Central Ward, which
was a festering ghetto. One-third of Newark's housing was substandard in 1967, and the worst houses were in the Central
Ward. Unemployment in black sections like the Central Ward
was officially set at 12 per cent, but unofficially went as high as 20
per cent, and an estimated 17,000 households were existing on
incomes of less than $3,000 a year. By July 1967, the city of
Newark led the nation in relative crime rate, incidence of vene-
real disease, and maternal mortality. All that Goddamned federal
and state tax money was being shoveled into the Central Ward,
the people in the North Ward explained to one another over and
over again in July 1967, and it wasn't doing any good. The federal and state bureaucracies were seen by many in the North
Ward, as elsewhere in the United States, to be composed in the
main of either liberal-criminal-lunatics or agents on the payroll of
world communism, who were instructing the niggers on how to
destroy America and actually paying them to do so. Anthony

Imperiale was to put it this way to a Nutley, New Jersey, audience the following May, after the riots that were to make him a vigilante leader and eventually a politician:

"You've been fortunate not to have been hit by a riot yet, because you know that the enforcement of law is what the taxpayer depends upon. This is how we feel safe. This is that one thin line between us—law and order, the boys in blue. . . . If Chief Justice Earl Warren, if the Supreme Court is gonna continue to pass laws to benefit the Commies, to benefit the radicals who are bent on the destruction of the United States, then it is up to you, the decent citizens, to stand up and be counted. Because when you're not watching, they're sneaking the Commies and the radicals right in under you. And it's happening in your town as well as mine."[8] He was telling them to be vigilant, as his people in the North Ward were being vigilant. They cheered and applauded.

The Newark riots that began late on the night of July 12, 1967, were part of a wave of civil disorder that swept across America all that summer and well into the next and that was the result of long-festering grievances deep within the neglected and abused slums of the nation. The riots in Newark started the night the police arrested and apparently brutalized a forty-year-old black cab driver named John Smith, a chess-playing musician with one year of college and an honorable discharge from the army, but who was working without a license because of eight or nine accidents. Shortly after nine-thirty that night, residents of a housing project across from the Fourth Police Precinct Station saw Smith being dragged inside by the arresting officers. Within minutes, at least two civil-rights workers had gotten calls from a hysterical woman who told them that Smith was being beaten by the police, and when Smith's employer, the Safety Cab Company, got word of his arrest, it was relayed to the fleet's other drivers. Several black community leaders had to push past an angry mob, less than an hour after the arrest, in order to get into the precinct house to see Smith. A quick examination of the driver convinced both the black community leaders and a senior police inspector on the night watch that Smith needed medical treatment. Within minutes, Molotov cocktails had exploded against the side of the orange-red brick building, police in riot gear were rushing out the front door, a rock barrage was coming down from the roofs across the street, and events were in motion that would leave the city in partial shambles less than a week later, with $10.2 million in property damage, 1,029 business establishments looted or otherwise damaged, National Guardsmen patrolling the streets, and twenty-three persons dead: a white detective, a white fireman, and twenty-one blacks, including a seventy-three-year-old man, six women, and two children.[9]

The North Ward Citizens' Committee was started by Anthony Imperiale a few months after the last of the fires in the Central Ward had been put out and the last of the victims had been buried. It was started, in the autumn of 1967, by Imperiale and others who wanted to save what was left of their community and to show the blacks that what had happened in the Central Ward was not going to happen in the North Ward—or, if it did happen, it was going to cost them plenty of blood.

The leader of the group that then Governor Richard J. Hughes called "vigilantes" was a thirty-nine-year-old ex-Marine: Anthony Imperiale, as he was known to the outside, or "Tony," as he was called by his many friends and followers. He was then, and still is, a slightly over five-and-a-half-foot ball of gristle, with a thick neck, powerful hands, and a hairy bull chest. He joined the National Guard at sixteen and the Marine Corps at eighteen, and it was in the Marines that he had two tattoos put on his arms: lovebirds with an inscription reading "Louise and Tony" and a heart pierced by a dagger, with the widely used "Death Before Dishonor motto." By the winter of 1967–68, Tony Imperiale had done four years in the Marines and some private detective work, operated the Imperiale Association of Judo and Karate (he owns a black belt) and the Tomar Construction Corporation, which did patio work. He at one time wanted to be a policeman, but has said that he was rejected because he was a fraction of an inch too short. No matter. When he headed the North Ward Citizens' Committee, he had a black 1959 Cadillac with a two-way radio, a dining room lined with empty antique guns and loaded new ones, and a headquarters with a police radio, telephones, street maps, judo posters, a bulletin board with press clippings about the committee (pro and con), and other signs of vigilance. It was in that one-story building that Imperiale taught many of the committee's 200 dues-paying members some of the finer points of judo and karate and other things they needed to know for community- and self-defense. There were, in those exciting times after the rioting, a North Ward Women's Auxiliary and a North

Ward Junior Auxiliary, giving every concerned white in the community a chance to pitch in for neighborhood defense. The wives in the auxiliary usually manned the phones, while their husbands, wearing black construction hard hats with "N.W.C.C." painted on them in white, scouted along carefully chosen routes. Paul Goldberger, who was a Yale undergraduate journalist at the time, described such a patrol on a warm evening in May 1968.

Most of the members of the patrol are young, and the cars they drive tend to be old. As dusk falls, the street in front of the headquarters comes alive with the roar of faulty mufflers and the impatient engine revving of youth craving excitement. . . . They talk together with a kind of false bravado.

Imperiale gives the word, and the four-man patrols move out. They follow carefully planned routes, studying the scene, looking for signs of trouble. At first, the police used to stop the cars to search them for weapons, and some such searches still occur. "They never find any guns," says Imperiale, "because we never carry any. It would be stupid." The patrol is intended to prevent conflict, he says, not start it.

For Imperiale, a patrol consists of driving from one corner gathering of white youths to another. Invariably he is recognized, and he knows most of the boys by their first names. "Hi ya, Angelo." "Waddya doin', Stevie?" He urges them to stay cool, stay out of trouble. Older residents often spot his elderly black Cadillac. "Go get 'em, Tony," they shout. "They're out to get you." [That referred to a bomb that had exploded in front of the committee's headquarters a short time before.]

Police calls, monitored at headquarters, are relayed to Imperiale over his car radio. If the call is for a location on his patrol route, he drives over; otherwise, he instructs the headquarters operator to dispatch a nearer car (the patrol assignments are charted on a large map of the city at headquarters).

The crackling of the radio provides a steady punctuation for conversation in the Imperiale Cadillac. He and his followers have absorbed the jargon of radio communications; it pervades their speech. And thus far everything has been 10–4 (O.K.) for the organization—since the patrols began, they have never been involved in a blameworthy incident. Actually, though the potential for excitement is most obviously there, the patrols tend to be boring.

The car draws up to the rear of a pizza palace on Bloomfield Avenue; this is where the white youths of the ward hang out, a good spot to keep track of action. Everybody knows Imperiale (they call him "Big T"), and he seems to know everybody. He favors one boy with a characteristic playful cuff on the cheek (sometimes the cuffs are pretty hard, but no one seems to mind). . . . They crowd around him in obvious awe and affection, and when Imperiale singles out a boy for attention, the youth revels in the sensation.[10]

And, so far as the patrols went, that was pretty much it, night after night: cruising around block after dreary block, checking out the occasional strange black face, and listening to the real police chatter back at headquarters. Officials agreed after the riots that there never was a serious danger of their spreading into the North Ward, but committee members have added that it was their presence that kept the blacks out, not the fact that the mob violence in the Central Ward had spent itself long before the North Ward Citizens' Committee had even gotten started.

In going over the rise and eventual disbanding of the North Ward Citizens' Committee (it had mostly petered out by 1970), a few observations should be made, which, for the most part, are applicable to similar organizations.

The committee was fun. It filled many otherwise dull days and nights in a community that, in a way, was probably almost as bored as its predecessors in earlier times. The after-work world of communities like Newark's North Ward throughout this country consists in very large measure of watching canned comedy on television and more of the same in drive-in movies, bowling, cards, idle gossip, and just plain hanging around. Actually getting to play police, however, is another and far more exciting proposition. Membership in the committee allowed some of the people in the North Ward to act out parts of the police role, using many police toys: patrol cars, two-way radios, street maps on walls (undoubtedly stuck with colored pins), helmets, and so forth. It was not merely passive but fully active entertainment, requiring participation. It permitted women who would otherwise have been left at home to come down and back up those of their men who were out patrolling, and, similarly, it got youngsters onto judo and karate mats and gave them a purpose—to get good enough at self- and community defense so that they could support their fathers when the black catastrophe finally came. Everyone wants to feel important, and riding patrol against a savage horde and in defense of home and loved ones in far more fulfilling and exciting than watching quiz shows or Johnny Carson. Vigilance in any form is interesting because it joins people with a common (and, they think, vital) purpose and gets them out of their homes and onto the streets, where they can interact with friends and perhaps even with enemies and can thereby assure themselves and one another that they are alive.

The committee served as an ideological lightning rod. Although Anthony Imperiale said in 1968 that he was not a member of the John Birch Society, he added that he would not have been "ashamed to be one" and that his choice for the presidency that year was George Wallace (Barry Goldwater being "too wishy-washy"). Members of the committee and its supporters were able to vent their spleen on a series of political issues and feel that they were being heard, particularly at a time when most of the nation seemed to be listening only to those who threatened to riot or who actually did so. "Are there no poor whites?" Imperiale asked in 1968. "But the Negroes get all the anti-poverty money. When pools are being built in the Central Ward, don't they think the white kids have got frustration? The whites are the majority. You know how many of them come to me, night after night, because they can't get a job? They've been told, we have to hire Negroes first." In Anthony Imperiale, then, the disgruntled citizens of the North Ward had someone to whom they could voice their anger and frustration. That facet of the committee was not wasted on Donald A. Malafronte, an administrative assistant to Mayor Hugh Addonizio and a Model Cities Program administrator at the time of the trouble in Newark. "In some ways he relieves tension among his own people because he tells whites what they want to hear," said Malafronte. "We don't believe Imperiale ever laid a hand on anybody. Like LeRoi Jones (the black poet and militant with whom Imperiale was linked by a famous 'hot line'), he belongs in Newark, but on the fringes. We want to forge them both together, with Imperiale on one wing and Jones on the other, but none in center stage, because Newark isn't *all* Anthony Imperiale or LeRoi Jones." Malafronte added, though, that the city was concerned enough about white militancy to keep the North Ward Citizens' Committee under constant police surveillance.[11]

The committee was a stepping stone to politics. As we have seen at other times and in other places, vigilante leaders, from Colonel William Lynch to Rabbi Samuel Schrage, have used the thrust of their power bases to propel them into the regular body politic. Imperiale, an immigrants' son who never went to college, was no exception. While the committee was still at its zenith, the "Big T" was making conscious efforts to polish his rough rhetoric and delivery, to maintain a dialogue with community leaders (like Jones and Mayor Addonizio), and to broaden his political base by insisting that he was against all radicals, black and white, thereby promoting the idea that he had a fair and consistent philosophy applicable to everyone and was not simply a rabid racial bigot. Sure enough, Imperiale entered the race for mayor in Newark in 1970, but was eclipsed when Kenneth A. Gibson, a black, beat Addonizio, who was by then under federal indictment on corruption charges. That campaign in 1970 was bitterly fought along racial lines, but the next one, four years later, was a different story. Imperiale, who had in the meantime gotten elected to the New Jersey Senate, conducted a relatively mild campaign, in which he actually succeeded in getting support from some black ministers. In trying to combat the image of being a white militant, Imperiale was simply facing the facts of political life, since Newark's South and Central wards were heavily black. He lost that election by 42,313 to 33,652, a creditable showing, and had clearly learned a lesson along the way: democratic politics on any meaningful scale is far more complicated and difficult than vigilantism played in a small dark pocket.

Over all, the North Ward Citizens' Committee didn't do much good, but it didn't do much harm, either.

Enough Rope...

VIGILANTISM is an evil. War, too, is an evil. Both observations are a little less than remarkable. The evidence suggests that the majority of men who have laid down their plows and ledgers to pick up guns and ropes have known full well that what they were doing was a kind of evil—evil, but also necessary. Similarly, the pages of history are full of stories of soldiers who committed unspeakable atrocities and who then went home and quite honestly denounced the horrors of war. Both groups have justified their actions on the ground that not to have acted as they did would have meant that they ended up as victims, rather than victors. The argument is, in essence, that it's better to be alive than dead. And, if those are the only alternatives, it's a hard argument with which to quibble. But are they?

In the case of vigilantism, the argument holds up in some cases, but not in most. Furthermore—and this is what makes blanket judgment impossible—there are infinite ways in which people can be victimized and equally infinite ways in which they can perceive their victimization. Consider two oversimplified ex-

270

tremes: the cases of the knife-wielding mugger and the candy-bar thief. If the mugger comes at you with knife flashing and you think that he clearly intends to use it, you can decide that you are in great immediate danger, and you can act accordingly. If someone comes into your candy store and steals a candy bar under your very eyes but you think that the loss of the candy bar is inconsequential, you may decide that you are not in any kind of danger and let the matter pass. Conversely, if you have reason to think that the person coming at you with the knife doesn't mean to use it, regardless of what he says, you may not feel threatened and might therefore do nothing to protect yourself. If the person stealing the candy bar is the hundredth to do so that week and you have been pushed to the point of bankruptcy because of it, you might well become fit to kill at the sight of yet another otherwise petty theft. Jostling during the rush hour on commuter buses and trains has resulted in innumerable embarrassed apologies and ready acceptances, but also in hair pulling, fist fights, and murder. It all depends on the perceptions and dispositions of those involved.

So it is with the vigilante reaction. Every vigilante mentioned on these pages perceived some kind of danger—some kind of threat to his well-being—and every one was disposed to react to that threat with violence. The South Carolina Regulators and the first Montana Committee of Vigilance saw the threat as direct, immediate, and deadly, and both organizations acted (or reacted) in kind. The East Texas Regulators began by perceiving a threat from criminals and ended by transferring the source of that threat, in true feud fashion, to even their most unoffending neighbors; neighbors under the wrong flag were *ipso facto* perceived as enemies. The great San Francisco Committee of Vigilance assigned enemy status to its political and economic rivals and made them the source of all the danger that allegedly plagued the city. The Bald Knobbers perceived the threat to them as coming from the godless and morally vacant within their own mountain society. The threat for the New Orleans Vigilantes came from the mysterious and sinister-looking invaders from an island in the Mediterranean, who conveniently fleshed out the delicious specter of criminal conspiracy.

Each of these representative vigilante organizations, plus all the hundreds of others, did what was evil, and most did what was unnecessary. But I think that others, with members driven to true desperation, did what literally had to be done. For me, making such judgments involves two inseparable criteria: was there a real and immediate danger to life and property, and, short of evacuation, was there a reasonable alternative to vigilante action?

There are some who would argue that evacuation—picking up and moving away, rather than fight—was and is the ultimate reasonable alternative. Turn the other cheek. I think that turning the other cheek on a street corner or in a subway is probably a very rational and mature course of action; turn the other cheek, avoid a nasty fight, go home and cool off, and begin the next day contented and satisfied that you acted in a civilized and sensible way. The same attitude practiced on the American frontier, however, would have spelled disaster. The purely pacifistic family would have had to move on so often that it would most likely have eventually ceased to exist as a functional unit and would therefore have disintegrated. The financial and emotional strains on a farm family forced repeatedly to move away just after a barn had been put up or just before crops were to be harvested would have led to its ruin. On a mass scale, it would have resulted in a highly unstable population of transient and alienated individuals, who themselves would very likely have turned into criminals. It would have led, in short, to precisely the kind of unstable conditions that the honest settlers most feared when they turned to vigilance as a stabilizer. Today's urban pacifist can best understand this by thinking of turning the other cheek, not on a street corner on the way to work, but after repeatedly being kicked out of his or her apartment or office, or having seen both repeatedly robbed and vandalized.

The vigilante actions in this book should speak for themselves. If they do not, though, I would add that I think that what happened in Missouri and New Orleans was utterly senseless, what happened in East Texas and San Francisco was unnecessary, and what happened in South Carolina and Montana was thoroughly justified.

The real and immediate danger to life and property in both Missouri and New Orleans, particularly where vigilante interests were concerned, was negligible, and law enforcement was more than adequate in both instances to cope with what real crime existed. The Bald Knobbers seem to have been very bored people. If the jury in New Orleans was tampered with, it was not the first or the last time such a thing happened, and if none of the other vigilantes understood that a travesty in the jury room did not call for lynchings, the lawyer who led them certainly should have. The crime situation in East Texas in 1840 was serious, but it consisted for the most part of swindling and stealing, not of wholesale murder, so popular justice proved to be a worse cure than the disease. The same applies to San Francisco, especially because that city, too, had a reasonably effective police force and judicial system. Corruption on both sides was rampant, but, again, it hardly justified use of the rope. South Carolina, on the other hand, had neither effective lawmen nor judges in 1767 and was plagued not with urbanized sharpies and petty scoundrels, but with a horde of professional killers, kidnapers, rapists, and plunderers, who would have destroyed society had they not been stopped. And the Alder Gulch region of Montana in 1863 and 1864 amounted to a casebook study of a neurotic community in which residents were being robbed and slaughtered by their elected protector. The choice for them was clear: flee or pick up their ropes.

Having said that the vigilantes of South Carolina and Montana were perfectly justified in taking the law into their own hands, I must now add that they, too, were afflicted with a fundamental problem common to most vigilante organizations and one that makes them particularly frightening to their neighbors: they didn't know when to stop.

Even the best-intentioned groups, seeing the positive effects of their actions and experiencing the exhilaration of wielding power where none had existed before, tended to overdo it. When that happened, just as when sadists moved in and gained control, the organizations were said to have "gone bad." As we have seen, the response usually came from moderators who formed to stop them. Vigilante groups sometimes went bad because their leaders became addicted to power and authority, as happened with Watt Moorman, but more often it was a combination of that and a zeal that put ever-increasing numbers of citizens on the hit list. Once vigilantes had knocked out the killers and bandits, they could lower their sights only a little and take care of rustlers and horse thieves, too. Then gamblers and brothel owners. Then, with a smoothly functioning group still tightly organized and not wanting to be wasted, it was a short step to going after common thieves and anyone who moved his fences in the wrong direction,

273

allowed his livestock to wander, beat his wife, drank too much, didn't go to church, or perhaps even slept too late. Anyone could be singled out for regulating, and since even the best groups were hardly perfect, the new names often owed the vigilante leadership money or had voted the wrong way or had done something else within the bounds of the law to anger the men with the ropes.

Vigilantes do not have to be members of large groups, but they almost always have been, and with good reason: the group provides a measure of anonymity, bolsters courage, and tends to be self-reinforcing. It is conceivable that a loner like Paul Kersey (played by Charles Bronson in *Death Wish*) could roam the streets shooting muggers at will, until he was either killed or locked up, but it's highly unlikely that any rational individual would do so for long. The reason, very simply, is that being a one-man vigilante operation is extremely dangerous and would appeal only to a schizophrenic with a Batman fixation. Group action, however, is almost always far more potent than the sum of its parts acting individually. And the reason goes well beyond the old safety-in-numbers theory.

"The *responsibility* one feels for the consequences of having engaged in antisocial behavior (here broadly defined) may be made insignificant by situations in which it is shared by others, by conditions which obscure the relationship between an action and its effects, or by a leader's willingness to assume all of it. The presence of others facilitates the first of these techniques," says Professor Philip G. Zimbardo, a social psychologist at Stanford University. "After the 1964 slaying of the civil rights workers (Schwerner, Chaney, and Goodman) in Mississippi, it is reported by Huie (1965) that the Klansmen passed the murder weapon from hand to hand, so that all shared equally the responsibility, or so that no one was individually responsible. Similarly, in modern electrocution chambers in American prisons there are often three executioners, each of whom pulls a switch simultaneously—only one of which is operative. In firing squads, one gun is loaded with blanks so that each man may believe he personally was not responsible. Compliance with the demands of a role limits perceived responsibility, as argued by Adolf Eichmann at his war crimes trial."[1]

That is why Samuel Brannan told "every lover of liberty and good order" to "take hold" of the rope that killed John Simpton, the Australian, in San Francisco. We recall that about twenty-five in the crowd did as he had told them to do, so that the responsibility for the lynching was nicely spread out among everyone who took hold and pulled. It is hard to conceive of Brannan's having hanged Simpton by himself. The heavy firing that went on inside the New Orleans parish prison is another example, with everyone shooting, reloading, and shooting again, until they no longer could see through the smoke. Responsibility was therefore shared.

"The loss of identifiability can be conferred by being 'submerged in a crowd,' disguised, masked, or dressed in a uniform like everyone else, or by darkness," adds Professor Zimbardo. "The most prevalent fantasy of children which illustrates the appeal of anonymity is wanting to be 'the invisible man.' "[2] Here, of course, we are reminded of the Bald Knobbers (and, of course, the Ku Klux Klan), who rode at night, under hoods. But we are also reminded of the splendid anonymity that came with being part of 6,000 marchers in San Francisco. It should be noted here that anonymity was a relatively late development among vigilantes. The South Carolina Regulators and the Shelby County Guards made no secret of their identities; later groups began to do so only when society had stabilized to the point where they could possibly be held accountable for their actions to law-enforcement officials. When there were few or no lawmen within hundreds of miles, few vigilantes cared who knew their names or about their escapades. This further underscores the point made earlier that, contrary to what the vigilantes said about their seeking anonymity to avoid reprisals by outlaws, they really did so to avoid incrimination and possible prosecution by the authorities. It still happens, under many guises.

Judith Rodin, an assistant professor of psychology at Yale University, was present at Columbia University during the tumultuous student riots in 1968. She has recalled that when the police first charged into the students, their clubs swinging at any youngster in their path, some of those being attacked began writing down badge numbers. "The cops then began to stop beating them up. They went away. The next time they came back without badges," she says.

The most interesting of Professor Zimbardo's observations on group aggression is the one having to do with its self-reinforcement role. He explains that aggression in a situation in which the individual has become completely submerged in the group may screen out restraint. The aggression therefore becomes more intense and starts to feed and then grow on itself. He gives three examples, but there are many more.

"One of the most terrifying of all sights, according to [Jacques] Cousteau, is the 'dance of death' by sharks when they surround a passive victim. After a dozen or so killer sharks circled an injured baby whale for several hours with no sign of attack, suddenly one bit into its flesh. Within moments pandemonium broke loose; the sharks tore and ripped flesh, leaped over each other, attacked again and again until soon only blood and bones remained." A Johns Hopkins University psychologist reported the same thing, according to Zimbardo, after watching hungry snakes in a cage with live mice. Regardless of how hungry the snakes were, they did not attack for a long time. As soon as the first mouse had been struck, however, more strikes followed in rapid succession, until five or six mice had been killed. "The attack itself appears to provide a self-excitation feedback which stimulates more attack." Finally, Zimbardo cites an art critic's review of an act by Yoko Ono called "Cut Piece" (*Look*, March 18, 1969). "She sat in her best dress and invited the audience to cut it up with a pair of scissors. At first, there was an awful silence. Then—well—it was terrible. Once they started, they couldn't stop. They went wild. She was left naked, of course."[3] Precisely the same thing has happened at sporting events when two or three angry spectators have turned an entire stadium into a scene of frenzy (as happened when more than 300 people were killed and about 500 others were injured in a riot at a soccer match between Argentina and Peru in May 1964).

What does all this mean? It means, basically, that twenty-five people working together against a target are more dangerous than twenty-five of them acting individually: first, because they are more likely to express their aggression freely when they are anonymous and share responsibility for the outcome, and, second, because the actions of each individual have a stimulating effect on the others—each feels freer and is, indeed, motivated to exceed the actions of the others. That hackneyed scene in which the mob remains docile until one member throws a rock, and then everyone is throwing rocks, is an obvious example. Zimbardo has split students into two groups, one taking the part of themselves—students—and the other of the police on a bust. He observed that those acting out the police role got so carried away that they actually roughed up and brutalized the student group; they fell into their roles and acted with the kind of fervor they expected of the police.

It is difficult to tell whether Americans are more violent and insensitive to violence now than they were a century ago. It is tempting to say that they are, but that may be due in part to the fact that we live today, not yesterday, and therefore have no perfect means of comparison. The media explosion puts Charles Whitman, who killed fourteen people and injured thirty-three from his sniping position in the University of Texas tower, right in our living rooms and in full color. Similarly, we have seen the atrocities in Vietnam and Cambodia performed as nightly rituals and therefore assume that we are more violent and insensitive than ever. Yet General Winfield Scott had this to say about the Texas volunteers who invaded Mexico in 1846 and '47: they "committed atrocities to make Heaven weep and every American of Christian morals blush for his country. Murder, robbery and rape of mothers and daughters in the presence of tied-up males of the families have been common all along the Rio Grande." Mexican newspaper editors called them "vandals and monsters," who had been vomited from hell and were "thirsty with desire to appropriate our riches and our beautiful damsels."[4] There may in fact, then, have been as many sadistic lunatics running around in the eighteenth and nineteenth centuries as there are today, if not more, but many of their escapades simply either went unreported or didn't circulate widely.

Now, however, I can sit in a theater and listen to an ethnically mixed audience applaud while Paul Kersey calmly shoots muggers and watches their blood spill out. I can watch Clint Eastwood and his likes "drop" six men in almost as many seconds, some falling into horse troughs with a satisfying splash, others rolling delightfully off roofs, and note that the people around me are giggling. I hear audiences snicker and laugh during scenes of rape, murder, and torture, and it makes me wonder whether the threshold isn't actually rising steadily.

On September 23, 1967, then, 200 students at the University of Oklahoma chanted "Jump, jump" to a mentally disturbed fellow student perched on a tower there. He did. On April 13, 1964, in Albany, New York, many in a crowd estimated at about 4,000 also shouted "Jump! Jump! Jump!" to a man contemplating a similar suicide leap. His seven-year-old nephew was trying to talk him out of it, while adults screamed, "C'mon, you're chicken" and "You're yellow." Some were placing bets that he would leap to his death (they lost), and one well-dressed man was quoted by the *New York Times* as having said, "I hope he jumps on this side. We couldn't see him if he jumped over there."

Zimbardo quotes a letter written to the *San Francisco Chronicle* of February 29, 1969, by some University of California Admissions Office clerks, who accused the police of the bloody beating of students, staff, and reporters without provocation. The letter said that one of the students, being beaten as he was dragged down the stairs, screamed, "Please don't hit me anymore! Won't someone help me?" *The more he begged, the more they hit.* And an American sergeant who took part in the interrogation and torturing of Vietcong prisoners recalled that "first you strike to get mad, then you strike because you are mad, and in the end you strike because of the sheer pleasure of it."[5]

We have seen that the vigilante reaction is very much with us, though sometimes in altered form, and that the potential for violence and brutality still exists, perhaps more so on today's frontier than yesterday's. It remains to speculate, then, on whether vigilantism has a future, and, if so, why.

We have learned several hard lessons about vigilantism while examining its course during the past 200 or so years. It is useful to recapitulate five of the most salient characteristics of vigilantism right here and then apply them to a little projection.

1. The *right* of Americans to become vigilantes stems directly from three postulates that existed in 1776 and that exist, undiminished, today: the sovereignty of the people, the right to rebel, and the law of survival. Americans, in other words, assume that they have the inalienable ultimate right and duty to do whatever they feel is necessary to safeguard what they perceive as their interests, and that includes taking the law into their own hands.

2. Under the right combination of circumstances, Americans are prone to use violence in order to safeguard their perceived interests. They see violence as a legitimate means of protection and will not hesitate to use it when they think that there is little or no alternative. In addition, their

threshold for violence and brutality, if it has not increased, certainly is extremely high and is likely to remain so.

3. Americans understand now, as they have always understood, that concerted group action is likely to accomplish what individual action often cannot, particularly in confrontation situations (as between gangs of thugs and groups of armed citizens). They are, in other words, fully prepared at any given time to form into groups for collective defense—some passive, like the Maccabees, others active, as the current Montana group says it is. For all of their pronouncements about rugged individualism, Americans are addicted to joining garden clubs, parent-teacher associations, Masonic lodges, veterans' organizations, antidefamation leagues, street gangs and clubs, tenant groups, and vigilance committees.

4. By the very nature of the diversity of people in America, coupled with its riches and free-enterprise system, confrontation situations have been and continue to be incessant. The ultimate arbiter of these confrontations, or so it is believed, is the law-enforcement system. It follows, then, that a lack of confidence in that system—in its presence when needed and in its impartiality—is very likely to result in panic and then in thoughts about citizen self-defense.

5. Vigilance committees form only when the upper segment of society feels threatened by the lower segment, when those with something become afraid that those without want to steal it from them. This polarization, actual or imagined, comes only during hard times—such as existed throughout the American frontier experience and during the Great Depression of the 1930s—or during times of racial and religious strife, when the dominant groups think they are socially or economically threatened by their inferiors.

In order to be able to make an educated guess on the prospects for continued or increased vigilantism in the United States, it is necessary to find out, I think, whether the elements just listed are likely to become confluent (if, indeed, they can be said to exist). Going to the police or to the Justice Department is next to useless, and so is poll taking; officials often don't know a vigilante reaction when they see one, and citizens under extreme pressure can be expected to see things quite differently than they do while answering theoretical questions at their front doors. The homicide and robbery rates could jump 100 per cent with no citizen backlash, for example, or they could stay the same and finally provoke a violent reaction. The nucleus of the problem is that there is absolutely no way to tell the precise point at which a given community will have had it and will decide to strike back with a vengeance. Who can ascertain the emotional point at which the fans in a soccer stadium will run riot or predict the moment at which one of the circling sharks will make that first attack? No one knows how far people have to be pushed before they become fit to kill, because people and circumstances vary so much.

The first four elements necessary for vigilante activity—acceptance of the right to engage in it, belief in the alternative of violence, propensity to organize for the common good, and lack of confidence in the system's ability to protect the individual—all exist right now. The first three of these have, I think, been well established. The fourth, too, is very much in evidence: lack of confidence in the system's ability to protect the individual from predators.

There is a definite trend in this country, in rural as well as urban and suburban regions, to view law-enforcement officials and the judiciary as being increasingly incapable of coping with criminals. Stories told by those in the cities who have come home to burglarized apartments only to hear policemen all but dismiss the crimes as inconsequential, compared with what might have happened, are becoming folklore. The burglary victims are being told that they were actually lucky—that it could have been worse. They are being told by the policemen who routinely arrive to make reports that the theft of jewelry, works of art collected over the years, hard-earned television sets, tape recorders, and radios is relatively unimportant. "If you'd been home," the police often assure the stunned victims, "you'd probably be dead right now. Those dope fiends are killers." Having been cleaned out of perhaps $10,000 worth of possessions, the burglary victim is supposed to feel relief; so, too, should the mugging victim who escapes with only bruises; so, too, should the residents of an apartment house in which someone else was robbed and murdered. The relief, if there is any, is very short-lived and is closely followed by an abiding frustration, fear, and bitterness. Those

Enough Rope . . .

emotions are being followed, in turn, by the purchase of large
dogs and guns and, in every city in the country, by the formation
of block watchers and street patrols or by the hiring of guards to
perform the same functions for which an increasing amount of
tax money is being collected.

President Ford, like his predecessor, has assured the "decent,
law-abiding" citizens that life is going to be made tougher for
criminals, that the victim is more important than the criminal—
that, in some unspecified way, America is going to get tough on
crime. Meanwhile, the Mayor of New York, who promised during
his election campaign to put more police on the streets, actually
laid off hundreds in order to alleviate the city's budget crisis.
Some Americans have snickered at New York's problem and have
even shown unconcealed gratification that the big-spending smart
alecks in the Big Apple were finally seeing the years of welfare
socialism and other massive waste catch up with them. But the
Mayor of San Francisco was not among them. At a mayors' con-
ference during the summer of 1975, he warned that nose-thumb-
ing at New York was ill-advised, because New York's problem
today would be shared by other cities tomorrow. Money and time
seem to be running out everywhere, while the nation's haves look
on with growing restiveness.

At the other end of the social spectrum are those who see the
police as instruments of brutality and repression. I am referring
not to amorphous far-left street-corner rhetoric, but to specific
instances of abuse of police power.

On September 15, 1974, police officer Frank Bosco, a white,
shot and killed fourteen-year-old Claude Reese, Jr., a black,
while responding in Brooklyn "to a mistaken radio call about a
burglary." Within a week of that incident, a twenty-two-year-old
black named William Blake was shot in the eye while sitting with
friends in a car outside an all-night restaurant in the Washington
Heights section of Manhattan. The police were, again, responding to a tip that four armed black men were sitting in a car in the
vicinity. When the blacks refused a police demand that they get
out of the car, thirteen shots were fired, one of which hit Blake.
As it turned out, the blacks were armed with hamburgers and
coffee. The massive stop-and-search operation connected with
San Francisco's so-called Zebra killings early in 1974, in which
more than 500 black men were questioned, frisked, and occasionally brought into police stations, aroused a great deal of anger

281

among minorities throughout the country. Following a murder spree in Detroit at about the same time, law-enforcement officials complained that the homicide-clearance rate (solved cases) had dropped from 90 per cent in 1967 to 62 per cent in 1973, because "a considerable confidence gap has developed between police and the community," leading to a "marked decrease in the willingness of citizens, particularly black citizens, to cooperate with the police." It would seem that if those at either end of society's spectrum have one thing in common, then, it is a growing disrespect for those who are supposed to protect them.

Finally, it must be added that during 1974 and 1975 American citizens of every stripe were being deluged by tales of corruption. They were reading about the chief of police and other policemen in a Detroit suburb who were arrested on charges of protecting a $5 million-a-year gambling operation. They were reading that the Pennsylvania Crime Commission had issued a 1,400-page report alleging widespread corruption in the Philadelphia Police Department and that New York City Police Commissioner Michael J. Codd had dismissed nineteen former plain-clothes officers for allegedly sharing in annual pay-offs of $240,000 from Brooklyn gamblers. Of course, as the police pointed out, they were cleaning their own house—but they had cleaned their house in the wake of the Knapp Commission report on police corruption, and yet things had somehow again gone wrong. Maybe the police would always be corrupt. Maybe it's in people's nature to take care of themselves as best they can and not depend on anyone else.

The police usually point out that they are so swamped with crime and so undermanned that they can't hope to cope adequately with all the demands made on them; they physically cannot track down all the burglars and muggers, while killers roam the streets, in many cases trying to kill policemen (and often succeeding). That, they add, is why white policemen sometimes get jumpy and start shooting at suspicious-looking blacks in the night. And the police, in turn, vehemently denounce the court system. I have heard the police in both Washington and New York complain bitterly that the court system in much of America is little more than a turnstile operation in which criminals are set free almost as soon as they're caught. "We bring in a mugger, the judge sets him free on bail because his lawyer got a postponement, and he's out on the street the next day, mugging to pay for his lawyer," a Washington detective once complained. The judges, of course, say that their courts are severely overloaded and that's why there are plea bargaining and endless postponements. True. It's all true. But it nonetheless leaves the proverbial man in the street caught somewhere in the middle of an unresponsive morass that he sees increasingly as swallowing him alive. And there doesn't seem to be anything he can do about it. Well, there may be something.

Now for that fifth element: the confrontation situation between the haves and the have-nots. It has existed since the founding of the Republic, of course, but I mean here a confrontation so severe that, coupled with the other ingredients, vigilantism results. Is it likely to happen?

Sociologists, historians, social psychologists, criminologists, and others interested exclusively in human behavior are not really the ones to ask; while their record for explaining what has happened is fair, they aren't crystal-ball gazers, nor do the best of them pretend to be. It is better to go to Lester R. Brown, Paul R. Ehrlich, and others in their profession. For, although neither of these men has likely given much, if any, thought to vigilantism, they can very likely tell us more about the possibility of severe confrontation situations than all the other social scientists put together. Brown and Ehrlich are environmentalists who are specifically concerned with resource scarcity. And resource scarcity is what class confrontation is all about.

Brown heads Worldwatch, a global-resource monitoring operation intended to pinpoint areas ripe for famine and to suggest means of prevention, and is the author of *By Bread Alone,* a minor classic about food scarcity.[6] Ehrlich, a generalist, laid his claim to fame with the publication of *The Population Bomb,* which is considered to have been a prime mover of Americans toward zero population growth; his latest work is *The End of Affluence,* which deals with the coming restructuring of resource use and how that is likely to affect society.[7]

It is not possible to do justice here to what both these men predict is in store for the inhabitants of this shrinking planet where food and energy supplies are concerned. Suffice it to say that both make compelling arguments that our food and energy resources are rapidly nearing depletion; given even slight continued population growth, the planet soon will very likely no longer be able to feed and warm those on it. The meat scarcity of 1973, the gasoline lines of 1974, and the soaring prices that persisted through 1975 are nothing, they warn, compared with what we are likely to experience in the coming years, unless radical measures are adopted to prevent it. Weak nations (even great big ones, like India) are in imminent danger of collapse, because they lack anything like adequate food and energy, and relatively strong nations (like the United States) are about to undergo monumental restructuring, as their inhabitants are forced to come to grips with shortages that simply will not disappear. Both predict that the coming scarcities will cause a wrenching effect, and both hint darkly that society all over the world will probably go through convulsions while making the adjustment. Americans, according to the prophecy, are now poised on the brink of making the switch from sirloin to soybeans, like it or not. The scarcities, again, are already upon us and, as of early 1976, have in large part contributed to the worst inflation-recession cycle since the Great Depression. So what?

So this: on March 4, 1975, the *New York Times* carried a front-page story that reported that the unemployment rate in New York City had been 10.6 per cent during the previous January, the highest in the nation except for Detroit, and that it had reached 9.3 per cent state-wide—the highest unemployment rate in New York State since the Depression. That in itself was newsworthy, but what made the story particularly interesting was the fact that it also quoted a police spokesman as saying that the rate of reported crimes had turned upward in 1974, after the unemployment rate started moving steeply upward. New York's crime rate was climbing. The unemployment rate was climbing. The clear inference was that some people who were out of work, and who therefore could no longer afford to buy things, were stealing them in increasing quantities. The have-nots, in other words, were robbing the haves with increasing frequency. And, given the reality of that situation as we know it, they were probably robbing the haves not only because they were out of work and didn't have much money, but also because whatever money they did have was insufficient to purchase what they needed. And here is where scarcity enters the picture, too.

Scarcity causes inflation, and inflation widens the gap between the haves and the have-nots. The haves can be depended upon to wail loudly when the day comes that they have to pay a dollar for a quart of milk. They will wail, but if they have children, they also will pay that dollar. The have-nots will not be able to buy the quart of milk because they simply will not have its asking price. So, rather than see their children go without the milk, they can be depended upon to steal it (or, of course, its asking price) from those who have it. If the Brown-Ehrlich crunch comes, and there is every indication that it has already started, then the haves and the have-nots across the planet, including those within "the richest nation on earth," are going to begin confronting one another on a scale and with an intensity rarely seen before. Ehrlich, who is not given to wild sensationalism, has gone so far as to suggest that everyone able to do so begin laying away quantities of canned tuna and other storable food items. He is not the first to recommend a little prudent hoarding, either. If that kind of thing is around the corner, then the have-nots can reasonably be expected to begin making increasingly serious attempts to get hold of the milk and tuna, and, true to form, the haves will then begin thinking about more certain methods to use for holding on to what they own. The struggle may already have begun.

In 1974, the *New York Times* undertook a detailed statistical study of major crime trends in the city from 1968 to 1973. Using police department statistics, and with help from the New York City-Rand Institute, the newspaper charted the courses of four major felony categories: murder, rape, robbery, and burglary. Results showed that, while those crimes had stabilized or decreased in many of the city's most dangerous and poor neighborhoods, they had jumped markedly in outlying middle-class areas. Assistant Police Chief Simon Eisdorfer, commanding officer of all Queens precincts, ventured the guess that crime had jumped in his relatively affluent jurisdiction because of a ten-year apartment-building boom there. "Burglars find it easier to break into apartments than private homes," he was quoted as saying.[8] It was a bad guess. Harlem, the South Bronx, and other ghetto areas where burglaries had either stabilized or gone down are also loaded with apartment houses, and, in most cases, they have far poorer security than those in Queens. The burglars went to Queens because the people there had the milk and tuna fish. It's as simple as that.

What was happening in Queens, New York, was happening nationwide. According to the FBI, murders jumped 116 per cent between 1960 and 1973. During that same period, forcible rape went up 199 per cent, robbery 256 per cent, and auto theft climbed by 183 per cent. Crimes of violence—the kind that most terrify people and provoke reaction—shot up by 204 per cent. As a result, private spending on self-protection—everything from whistles to guard dogs to shotguns—has been growing. As crime rates began making the inner cities increasingly dangerous during the 1960s, people fled to the safety of the suburbs, but they are now finding that they are not safe there, either. Crime has been growing faster in the suburbs than in the cities, and, as we have seen, for a very good reason.

Sociologists, penologists, psychologists, and batteries of other social scientists are now locked in debate over the reasons why increasing numbers of youngsters—in many cases preteens—are committing crimes, why so many assaults against persons are becoming increasingly brutal and senseless, and what, if anything, can be done about it. They tell one another that crime is going up because of the deterioration of home life, because the prison system hardens inmates rather than helping them, because the police are in many cases repressive, and so on.

The answer may be, however, that criminality within the nation's very infrastructure—on the highest political and financial levels—is simply filtering down to those on the street. Corruption on all levels of government is certainly not new, but the media explosion and coverage of the corruption are new, and its tincture spreads to the lowliest segment of society. Every street kid in every city in this country knows about the cops who show up on Thursday afternoons to get their envelopes from neighborhood bookmakers, night-club owners, pimps, and even drug pushers. They have seen that, along with the uniformed officers collecting free drinks and sandwiches, for years. They know firsthand, whether they can express it or not, that there is a real dichotomy between the moralistic propaganda their society dumps on them and the daily events that take place on the street —in the real world. It is old stuff; rotten, but old.

What is new, however, is the realization that even the highest administrators in the Republic have defied and corrupted the system. Seven or eight children packed into a roach-filled cubicle in any city in this country can watch a never-ending procession of really important men breaking the law and not only getting away with it but also actually receiving degrees of admiration from the public. Frank Costello, a thief and a butcher, was mobbed by autograph hounds as he came out of criminal court; it was on television. The Godfather (*all* the Godfathers) is deliberately tinged with Robin Hood–like qualities, such as family loyalty, aid to the neediest in his community, and astounding bravery and dedication. And, of course, he is smart. So are the kids who watch those movies and, even worse, who watch the news. They are in most cases ignorant and impressionable, but they are not stupid. They understand that Robert Vesco's reward for massive theft is the life of a prince in exile in some seemingly exotic land. They have seen a procession of elected officials, including Otto Kerner, Hugh J. Addonizio, Thomas Dodd, and others, spotlighted for using their offices in order to make money illegally. And, of course, they have seen the President of the United States and his closest lieutenants use precisely the same kinds of dirty tricks that their little civics and social-studies textbooks tell them are wrong and against the law. And those people have, by and large, gotten away with it. Those who have gone to jail for political espionage and for what amounted to massive industrial extortion have gotten lighter sentences than a ghetto youngster might expect for shoplifting or hitting a service station. The pardoning of Richard Nixon in the throes of the Watergate scandal, and everything that went with it, offers an immutable lesson, and a very simple one: the biggest shot in America broke the law and got away clean. You've just got to be smart, and you can get away with anything.

Something heavy is in the air in America, sending out signals that are unmistakable to anyone who is sensitive to them. There is increasing impatience with "do-gooder" social workers and anyone who talks about "coddling" criminals. There is now new and increasingly vigorous discussion about reinstituting the death penalty. "We've gone overboard," says Frank Carrington, the executive director of Americans for Effective Law Enforcement. "The criminal-justice system just totally ignores the victims of crime. We are confounded with a bunch of rules, court decisions, a total preoccupation with the rights of the suspected criminal and the convicted criminal. I don't say concern about such rights is wrong. But I think there should be a balance."[9]

Balance is, indeed, the elusive goal—balance, meaning true justice for everyone. When the system's inability to provide equal justice for all people, to safeguard their lives and property, and to promote their happiness reaches the crisis level—and, again, no one knows where that level is—then citizens will assuredly break the law and take its pieces into their own angry hands. At

this rate, such occurrences are not only possible, but highly probable. Should that day come, democratic society will be left in
shambles, with all citizens suffering the consequences equally.
And the direst of the consequences will in all likelihood be the
appearance of a man on horseback who will be carrying some
kind of rope. That man will be the last vigilante.

Notes

1. The Vigilante Reaction

1. Bo Burlingham, "The Unquiet Grave of Fred Hampton," *New Times*, May 31, 1974, pp. 22–27.
2. "Playboy Interview," *Playboy*, April 1974, p. 70.
3. Meir Kahane, *Never Again!* (Los Angeles: Nash Publishing Corp., 1971), p. 278.
4. Richard Maxwell Brown, "The American Vigilante Tradition," in *The History of Violence in America*, Report to the National Commission on the Causes and Prevention of Violence (New York: Bantam Books, 1969), p. 158.
5. Owen Wister, *The Virginian* (New York: The Macmillan Co., 1902), pp. 433–36.
6. Walter van Tilburg Clark, *The Ox-Bow Incident* (New York: New American Library, 1960), p. 47.
7. Wister, *The Virginian*, pp. 391–92.
8. Ibid., pp. 392–93.
9. Brown, "American Vigilante Tradition," p. 183.
10. Thomas J. Dimsdale, *The Vigilantes of Montana* (Helena: State Publishing Co., 1915), pp. 31–32.
11. Richard Maxwell Brown, "Legal and Behavioral Perspectives on American Vigilantism," in *Perspectives in American History*, vol. 5, ed. Donald Fleming and Bernard Bailyn (Cambridge: Charles Warren Center for Studies in American History, Harvard University, 1971), p. 138 n.
12. Brown, "American Vigilante Tradition," p. 196.
13. Ibid., p. 163.
14. Ibid., p. 176.

2. The Honorable Judge Lynch

1. Charles Francis Adams, *Three Episodes of Massachusetts History*, vol. 1 (Boston: Houghton, Mifflin and Co., 1892), p. 179.
2. Adams, *Three Episodes*, vol. 1, p. 198.
3. Ibid., pp. 204–05.
4. Ibid., p. 208.
5. Ibid., p. 249.
6. Richard Slotkin, *Regeneration Through Violence* (Middletown, Conn.: Wesleyan University Press, 1974), passim.
7. James Elbert Cutler, *Lynch-Law* (New York: Longmans, Green and Co., 1905), pp. 3–8.
8. Robert McCluer Calhoon, *The Loyalists in Revolutionary America: 1760–1781* (New York: Harcourt Brace Jovanovich, 1973), p. 295.
9. Calhoon, *Loyalists*, pp. 299–300.
10. Cutler, *Lynch-Law*, pp. 61–62.
11. Ibid., p. 67.
12. Robert B. David, *Malcolm Campbell, Sheriff* (Casper, Wyo.: Wyomingana, 1932), pp. 18–21.
13. Cutler, *Lynch-Law*, pp. 46–47.
14. Ibid., pp. 47–48.
15. Albert Matthews, "Origin of the Term Lynch Law," *Publications of the Colonial Society of Massachusetts* 27 (1932): 260.
16. Matthews, "Origin of the Term Lynch Law," 260–61; see also Cutler, *Lynch-Law*, pp. 73–75.
17. Matthews, "Origin of the Term Lynch Law," 262–63.
18. Ibid., 267–68.

3. South Carolina

1. Richard Maxwell Brown, *The South Carolina Regulators* (Cambridge: The Belknap Press, 1963), pp. 4–6.
2. Brown, *South Carolina Regulators*, p. 7.
3. Ibid., p. 11.
4. Ibid., p. 29.
5. Ibid., p. 31.
6. Charles Woodmason, *The Carolina Backcountry on the Eve of the Revolution*, ed. Richard J. Hooker (Chapel Hill: University of North Carolina Press, 1953), p. 214.
7. Brown, *South Carolina Regulators*, p. 36.
8. Ibid., p. 39.
9. Woodmason, *Carolina Backcountry*, p. 215.
10. Ibid., p. 232.

11. Ibid., p. 233.
12. Brown, *South Carolina Regulators,* pp. 50–51.
13. Ibid., p. 90.

4. Texas

1. Joe B. Frantz, "The Frontier Tradition: An Invitation to Violence," in *The History of Violence in America,* Report to the National Commission on the Causes and Prevention of Violence (New York: Bantam Books, 1970), p. 137.
2. C. L. Sonnichsen, *Ten Texas Feuds* (Albuquerque: University of New Mexico Press, 1957), p. 16.
3. Sonnichsen, *Ten Texas Feuds,* p. 20.
4. Ibid., pp. 11–12.
5. For an account of the Illinois organization of 1841, which claimed two victims, see Alice Louise Brumbaugh, "The Regulator Movement in Illinois" (Master's thesis, University of Illinois, 1926).
6. Sonnichsen, *Ten Texas Feuds,* p. 29.
7. Ibid., p. 32.
8. Ibid., p. 33.
9. Ibid., pp. 33–34.
10. Ibid., p. 39.
11. Ibid., pp. 49–50.
12. Ibid., pp. 53–54.

5. California

1. James O'Meara, *The Vigilance Committee of 1856* (San Francisco: James H. Barry, 1887), p. 12.
2. O'Meara, *Vigilance Committee of 1856,* pp. 13–14.
3. W. Eugene Hollon, *Frontier Violence: Another Look* (New York: Oxford University Press, 1974), pp. 72–73.
4. Hubert Howe Bancroft, *Popular Tribunals,* vol. 1 (San Francisco: The History Co., 1887), p. 181.
5. Bancroft, *Popular Tribunals,* vol. 1, p. 185.
6. Ibid.
7. Ibid., pp. 185–86.
8. Ibid., p. 219.
9. Ibid., pp. 224–25.
10. Ibid., p. 230.
11. Ibid., p. 231.
12. Ibid.

13. Oscar Handlin, ed., *Readings in American History* (New York: Alfred A. Knopf, 1957), p. 293.
14. John W. Caughey, *Their Majesties The Mob* (Chicago: University of Chicago Press, 1960), p. 52.
15. Hubert Howe Bancroft, *Popular Tribunals,* vol. 2 (San Francisco: The History Co., 1887), p. 4.
16. O'Meara, *Vigilance Committee of 1856,* p. 9.
17. Ibid., p. 10.
18. John Myers Myers, *San Francisco's Reign of Terror* (New York: Doubleday, 1966), p. 101.
19. Bancroft, *Popular Tribunals,* vol. 2, p. 36.
20. Ibid., p. 39.
21. Ibid., p. 28.
22. Myers, *San Francisco's Reign of Terror,* p. 108.
23. Ibid., p. 110.
24. Bancroft, *Popular Tribunals,* vol. 2, p. 60.
25. Ibid., p. 72.
26. Ibid., p. 112.
27. Myers, *San Francisco's Reign of Terror,* p. 115.
28. Ibid., p. 120.
29. Bancroft, *Popular Tribunals,* vol. 2, p. 235.
30. Ibid., p. 236.
31. Ibid., pp. 551–55, for all editorial comment.

6. Montana

1. Thomas J. Dimsdale, *The Vigilantes of Montana* (Helena: State Publishing Co., 1915), p. 12.
2. Nathaniel Pitt Langford, *Vigilante Days and Ways* (Missoula: Montana State University Press, 1957) from the introduction by Dorothy M. Johnson.
3. Dimsdale, *Vigilantes of Montana,* p. 15.
4. Hoffman Birney, *Vigilantes* (Philadelphia: The Penn Publishing Co., 1929), p. 62.
5. Langford, *Vigilante Days and Ways,* p. 7.
6. Ibid., pp. 76–78.
7. Dimsdale, *Vigilantes of Montana,* p. 30.
8. Langford, *Vigilante Days and Ways,* pp. 109–10.
9. Dimsdale, *Vigilantes of Montana,* pp. 10–17.
10. Langford, *Vigilante Days and Ways,* pp. 140–42.
11. Ibid., p. 235.
12. Birney, *Vigilantes,* pp. 211–12.
13. Langford, *Vigilante Days and Ways,* p. 249.

14. Ibid., p. 294.
15. Birney, *Vigilantes,* p. 221.
16. Michael A. Leeson, *History of Montana* (Chicago: Warner, Beers & Co., 1885), pp. 289–301.
17. Mark Twain, *Roughing It* (New York: New American Library, Signet, 1962), p. 73.
18. John Wellington Smurr, "Afterthoughts on the Vigilantes," *Montana: The Magazine of Western History* 8 (April 1958): 8–20.
19. Leeson, *History of Montana,* p. 304.
20. R. L. Housman, "The Vigilante Movement and Its Press In Montana," *Americana Illustrated* 35 (January 1941): 40–42.

7. Missouri

1. W. Eugene Hollon, *Frontier Violence: Another Look* (New York: Oxford University Press, 1974), p. 196.
2. *Springfield Republican,* May 11, 1889.
3. Lucile Morris, *Bald Knobbers* (Caldwell, Idaho: The Caxton Printers, Ltd., 1939), p. 51.
4. *Springfield Republican,* December 29, 1888.
5. Morris, *Bald Knobbers,* pp. 55–56.
6. Ibid., pp. 87–88.
7. Ibid., p. 94.
8. A. M. Haswell, "The Story of the Bald Knobbers," *Missouri Historical Review* 18 (October 1923): 30–31.
9. Morris, *Bald Knobbers,* p. 72.
10. Ibid., pp. 110–11.
11. Ibid., p. 126.
12. Ibid., p. 132.
13. Ibid., p. 146.
14. *Springfield Daily Leader,* April 19, 1887.
15. Morris, *Bald Knobbers,* pp. 171–72.
16. Ibid., pp. 237–40.

8. Louisiana

1. John E. Coxe, "The New Orleans Mafia Incident," *Louisiana Historical Quarterly* 20 (1937): 1068.
2. Coxe, "New Orleans Mafia Incident," 1070.
3. Dwight C. Smith, Jr., *The Mafia Mystique* (New York: Basic Books, 1974).

4. John Smith Kendall, *History of New Orleans* (Chicago: The Lewis Publishing Co., 1922).
5. John S. Kendall, "Who Killa de Chief?," *Louisiana Historical Quarterly* 22 (1939): 505.
6. Kendall, "Who Killa de Chief?," 497–501.
7. Ibid., 511.
8. Coxe, "New Orleans Mafia Incident," 1074.
9. Ibid., 1074–75.
10. Ibid., 1075.
11. Ibid., 1078.
12. Kendall, "Who Killa de Chief?," 515–16.
13. Coxe, "New Orleans Mafia Incident," 1085.
14. Ibid.
15. Ibid., 1085–86.
16. Ibid., 1086–87.
17. Kendall, "Who Killa de Chief?," 521–22.
18. Coxe, "New Orleans Mafia Incident," 1088–89.
19. Ibid., 1090.
20. Ibid., 1090–91.
21. J. Alexander Karlin, "The New Orleans Lynchings of 1891 and the American Press," *Louisiana Historical Quarterly* 24 (1941): 191.
22. Karlin, "New Orleans Lynchings," 193.
23. Coxe, "New Orleans Mafia Incident," 1093.
24. Ibid., 1094–95.
25. Ibid., 1092.
26. David M. Chalmers, *Hooded Americanism* (Chicago: Quadrangle Books, 1968), pp. 392–93.
27. Coxe, "New Orleans Mafia Incident," 1097.
28. *Annual Report of the Superintendent of Police for the Year 1892, City of New Orleans* (New Orleans: V. Mauberrett, 1893).

9. The Compleat Vigilante

1. Edward Willett, "Clip, the Contortionist; or, the Vigilantes of Montana," *Beadle's Half Dime Library,* vol. 14, no. 340 (January 29, 1884), in Western Americana Collection, Beinecke Rare Book and Manuscript Library, Yale University.
2. Tony Goodstone, ed., *The Pulps: Fifty Years of American Pop Culture* (New York: Chelsea House, 1970), p. 58.
3. James Weir, *Lonz Powers; or, the Regulators: A Romance of Kentucky* (Philadelphia: Lippincott, Grambo & Co., 1850).
4. Ron Goulart, *An Informal History of the Pulp Magazine* (New York: Ace Books, 1972), p. 134.

5. Jerome C. Smiley, *History of Denver* (Denver: The Times-Sun Publishing Co., 1901), p. 338.
6. Smiley, *History of Denver*, p. 341.
7. Ibid., pp. 343–44.
8. Ibid., p. 349.
9. Robert V. Hine, *The American West: An Interpretive History* (Boston: Little, Brown and Co., 1973), pp. 233–34.
10. Kenneth Owens, "Pierce City Incident," *Idaho Yesterdays*, fall 1959, p. 9.
11. Owens, "Pierce City Incident," p. 10.
12. Ibid., p. 11.
13. Ibid., p. 12.
14. Ibid.
15. Ibid.
16. Ibid., p. 13.
17. Ibid.
18. "Civil Defense in Baltimore, 1814–15: Minutes of the Committee of Vigilance and Safety," *Maryland Historical Magazine*, September 1944, pp. 199–224.
19. *History of the State of New York* (New York: Columbia University Press, 1935), vol. 7, p. 70.
20. John W. Caughey, *Their Majesties The Mob* (Chicago: University of Chicago Press, 1960), pp. 136–37.
21. Caughey, *Their Majesties The Mob*, pp. 136–37.
22. Morton Grodzins, *Americans Betrayed* (Chicago: University of Chicago Press, 1949), pp. 404–05.
23. *Secret Origins* (National Periodical Publications, Inc.), September–October 1973, p. 1.
24. *Secret Origins*, September–October 1973, p. 4.
25. James Steranko, *History of Comics* (Reading, Pa.: Supergraphics, 1970), vol. 1, p. 76.
26. Gay Talese, *The Kingdom and the Power* (New York: World Publishing Co., 1969), p. 169.
27. Andrew Bergman, *We're in the Money: Depression America and Its Films* (New York: Harper Colophon Books, 1971), p. 112.
28. Bergman, *We're in the Money*, pp. 113–14.

10. And Now . . .

1. *Minneapolis Tribune*, December 15, 1974.
2. *Harper's Weekly*, March 14, 1975.
3. *Portland Sunday Telegram*, November 17, 1974.
4. *New York Times*, November 9, 1974.

5. *New York Times,* August 1, 1974.
6. *New York Times,* October 27, 1967.
7. Richard Maxwell Brown, "The American Vigilante Tradition," in *The History of Violence in America,* Report to the National Commission on the Causes and Prevention of Violence (New York: Bantam Books, 1969), p. 203.
8. Paul Goldberger, "Tony Imperiale Stands Vigilant for Lawand-order," *New York Times Magazine,* September 29, 1968, pp. 120–21.
9. *Report of the National Advisory Commission on Civil Disorders* (New York: Bantam Books, 1968), pp. 61–69.
10. Goldberger, "Tony Imperiale," pp. 119–20.
11. Ibid., p. 125.

Enough Rope . . .

1. Philip G. Zimbardo, "The Human Choice: Individuation, Reason, and Order versus Deindividuation, Impulse, and Chaos," *Nebraska Symposium on Motivation,* 1969, p. 256.
2. Zimbardo, "The Human Choice," p. 255.
3. Ibid., p. 260.
4. W. Eugene Hollon, *Frontier Violence: Another Look* (New York: Oxford University Press, 1974), p. 41.
5. Zimbardo, "The Human Choice," p. 244.
6. Lester R. Brown with Eric P. Eckholm, *By Bread Alone* (New York: Praeger, 1974) passim.
7. Paul R. Ehrlich, *The Population Bomb* (New York: Ballantine Books, 1971), and *The End of Affluence* (New York: Ballantine Books, 1974).
8. *New York Times,* December 2, 1974.
9. "The Losing Battle Against Crime in America," *U. S. News & World Report,* December 16, 1974, p. 31.

Bibliography

BOOKS

Adams, Charles Francis. *Three Episodes of Massachusetts History,* vol. 1. Boston: Houghton, Mifflin and Co., 1892.

Bancroft, Hubert Howe. *Popular Tribunals,* vols. 1–2. San Francisco: The History Co., 1887.

Bergman, Andrew. *We're in the Money: Depression America and Its Films.* New York: Harper Colophon Books, 1971.

Birney, Hoffman. *Vigilantes.* Philadelphia: The Penn Publishing Co., 1929.

Boorstin, Daniel J. *The Americans.* New York: Random House, 1965.

Brown, Lester R., with Eric P. Eckholm. *By Bread Alone.* New York: Praeger, 1974.

Brown, Richard Maxwell. *The South Carolina Regulators.* Cambridge: The Belknap Press, 1963.

Calhoon, Robert McCluer. *The Loyalists in Revolutionary America: 1760–1781.* New York: Harcourt Brace Jovanovich, 1973.

Caughey, John W. *Their Majesties The Mob.* Chicago: University of Chicago Press, 1960.

Chadbourn, James Harmon. *Lynching and the Law.* Chapel Hill: University of North Carolina Press, 1933.

Chalmers, David M. *Hooded Americanism.* Chicago: Quadrangle Books, 1968.

Clark, Walter van Tilburg. *The Ox-Bow Incident.* New York: New American Library, 1960.

Collins, Winfield H. *The Truth About Lynching and the Negro in the South (A Plea for White Safety).* New York: Neale Publishing Co., 1918.

Cutler, James Elbert. *Lynch-Law.* New York: Longmans, Green and Co., 1905.

David, Robert B. *Malcolm Campbell, Sheriff.* Casper, Wyo.: Wyomingana, 1932.

Dimsdale, Thomas J. *The Vigilantes of Montana.* Helena: State Publishing Co., 1915.

Ehrlich, Paul R. *The End of Affluence.* New York: Ballantine Books, 1974.

————. *The Population Bomb.* New York: Ballantine Books, 1971.

Goodstone, Tony, ed. *The Pulps: Fifty Years of American Pop Culture.* New York: Chelsea House, 1970.

Goulart, Ron. *An Informal History of the Pulp Magazine.* New York: Ace Books, 1972.

Grodzins, Morton. *Americans Betrayed.* Chicago: University of Chicago Press, 1949.

Handlin, Oscar, ed. *Readings in American History.* New York: Alfred A. Knopf, 1957.

Hayden, Tom. *Rebellion in Newark.* New York: Random House, 1967.

Hine, Robert V. *The American West: An Interpretive History.* Boston: Little, Brown and Co., 1973.

Hollon, W. Eugene. *Frontier Violence: Another Look.* New York: Oxford University Press, 1974.

Horn, Stanley F. *Invisible Empire.* Cos Cob, Conn.: John E. Edwards, 1969.

Kahane, Meir. *Never Again!* Los Angeles: Nash Publishing Corp., 1971.

Kendall, John Smith. *History of New Orleans.* Chicago: The Lewis Publishing Co., 1922.

Langford, Nathaniel Pitt. *Vigilante Days and Ways.* Missoula: Montana State University Press, 1957.

Leeson, Michael A. *History of Montana.* Chicago: Warner, Beers & Co., 1885.

McConnell, William J. *Frontier Law: A Story of Vigilante Days.* New York: World Book Co., 1924.

Morris, Lucile. *Bald Knobbers.* Caldwell, Idaho: The Caxton Printers, Ltd., 1939.

Myers, John Myers. *San Francisco's Reign of Terror.* New York: Doubleday, 1966.

O'Meara, James. *The Vigilance Committee of 1856.* San Francisco: James H. Barry, 1887.

Phillips, C. Coffin. *Portsmouth Plaza.* San Francisco: Nash, 1932.

Rosenbaum, H. Jon, and Peter C. Sederberg, ed. *Vigilante Politics.* Philadelphia: University of Pennsylvania Press, 1976.

Royce, Josiah. *California.* New York: Houghton Mifflin, 1886.

Bibliography

Slotkin, Richard. *Regeneration Through Violence*. Middletown, Conn.: Wesleyan University Press, 1974.

Smiley, Jerome C. *History of Denver*. Denver: The Times-Sun Publishing Co., 1901.

Smith, Dwight C., Jr. *The Mafia Mystique*. New York: Basic Books, 1974.

Sonnichsen, C. L. *Ten Texas Feuds*. Albuquerque: University of New Mexico Press, 1957.

Steranko, James. *History of Comics*. Reading, Pa.: Supergraphics, 1970.

Talese, Gay. *The Kingdom and the Power*. New York: World Publishing Co., 1969.

Twain, Mark. *Roughing It*. New York: New American Library, Signet, 1962.

Weir, James. *Lonz Powers; or, the Regulators: A Romance of Kentucky*. Philadelphia: Lippincott, Grambo & Co., 1850.

Williams, Mary Floyd. *History of the San Francisco Committee of Vigilance of 1851*. Berkeley: University of California Press, 1921.

Wister, Owen. *The Virginian*. New York: The Macmillan Co., 1902.

Woodmason, Charles. *The Carolina Backcountry on the Eve of the Revolution*. Edited by Richard J. Hooker. Chapel Hill: University of North Carolina Press, 1953.

REPORTS

Annual Report of the Superintendent of Police for the Year 1892, City of New Orleans. New Orleans: V. Mauberrett, 1893.

Assassination and Political Violence. Report to the National Commission on the Causes and Prevention of Violence. New York: Bantam Books, 1970.

The History of Violence in America. Report to the National Commission on the Causes and Prevention of Violence. New York: Bantam Books, 1969.

Law and Order Reconsidered. Report to the National Commission on the Causes and Prevention of Violence. New York: Bantam Books, 1970.

The Politics of Protest. Report to the National Commission on the Causes and Prevention of Violence. New York: Ballantine Books, 1969.

Report of the National Advisory Commission on Civil Disorders. New York: Bantam Books, 1968.

ARTICLES

Adams, James Truslow. "Our Lawless Heritage." *The Atlantic Monthly,* December 1928.

Brown, Richard Maxwell. "Legal and Behavioral Perspectives on American Vigilantism." In *Perspectives in American History,* vol. 5, edited by Donald Fleming and Bernard Bailyn. Charles Warren Center for Studies in American History, Harvard University, 1971: pp. 95–144.

Burlingham, Bo. "The Unquiet Grave of Fred Hampton." *New Times,* May 31, 1974.

Burrows, William E. "The Vigilante Rides Again." *Harvard Magazine* 78 (December 1975) pp. 36–41.

"Civil Defense in Baltimore, 1814–15: Minutes of the Committee of Vigilance and Safety." *Maryland Historical Magazine,* September 1944, pp. 199–224.

Claiborne, William L. "New Yorkers Fight Back: The Tilt Toward Vigilantism." *New York,* October 15, 1973.

Coxe, John E. "The New Orleans Mafia Incident." *Louisiana Historical Quarterly* 20 (1937): pp. 1067–1109.

Goldberger, Paul. "Tony Imperiale Stands Vigilant for Lawandorder." *New York Times Magazine,* September 29, 1968.

Haswell, A. M. "The Story of the Bald Knobbers." *Missouri Historical Review* 18 (October 1923): pp. 27–35.

Housman, R. L. "The Vigilante Movement and Its Press In Montana." *Americana Illustrated* 35 (January 1941): pp. 35–50.

Karlin, J. Alexander. "The New Orleans Lynchings of 1891 and the American Press." *Louisiana Historical Quarterly* 24 (1941): pp. 187–204.

Kendall, John S. "Who Killa de Chief?" *Louisiana Historical Quarterly* 22 (1939): pp. 492–530.

Matthews, Albert. "Origin of the Term Lynch Law." *Publications of the Colonial Society of Massachusetts* 27 (1932): pp. 256–271.

Moyer, K. E. "The Physiology of Violence." *Psychology Today,* July 1973.

Mueller, Oscar O. "The Central Montana Vigilante Raids of 1884." *Montana Magazine of History* 1 (January 1951): pp. 23–35.

Owens, Kenneth. "Pierce City Incident." *Idaho Yesterdays,* fall 1959: pp. 8–13.

Smurr, John Wellington. "Afterthoughts on the Vigilantes." *Montana: The Magazine of Western History* 8 (April 1958): pp. 8–20.

Bibliography

Willett, Edward. "Clip, the Contortionist; or, the Vigilantes of Montana." *Beadle's Half Dime Library,* vol. 14, no. 340 (January 29, 1884). Western Americana Collection, Beinecke Rare Book and Manuscript Library, Yale University.

Zimbardo, Philip G. "The Human Choice: Individuation, Reason, and Order versus Deindividuation, Impulse, and Chaos." *Nebraska Symposium on Motivation.* (1969).

THESIS

Brumbaugh, Alice Louise. "The Regulator Movement in Illinois." Master's thesis, University of Illinois, 1926.

Index

Index

305

Index

Hennessy, David C., 193–203, 205–212, 219; and his murder trial, 204–09, 221, and newspaper coverage of, 204–05, 207–09. *See also* Louisiana vigilance, New Orleans
Hetherington, Joseph, 123–24
Hickok, Wild Bill, 130
Higginson, Keith, 251–52
Hoard, Samuel L., 259
Hollon, W. Eugene, 164
Hollywood Blacklist, xiii, 240
Homestead Act, 189–90, 189n
Horton, "Sandy," 91
House Un-American Activities Committee, x
Houston, James D., 212
Houston, Sam, 82–83, 91
Howard, William A., 107
Hughes, Richard J., 265
Humphreys, Squire, and family, 75–77, 79–81
Hunt, A. C., 234
Hunter, Bill, 135, 156
Huston, Tom Charles, 3–5

Idaho vigilance
Lewiston, 1862–64, 22, 145, 152, 235
Pierce City, 1885, and Chinese lynchings, 234–39; Pierce City Vigilante Committee, 236–37, 239
Pseudovigilance, 251–52
Illinois vigilance, 22, 74
Imperiale, Anthony, 5, 262–69
Incardona, Bastiano, 204–05, 208, 215, 217
Indiana vigilance, 74
Ingram, John, 85–86
Iowa vigilance, 74
Italian–Americans, *see* Louisiana vigilance, New Orleans; New Jersey pseudovigilance, Newark
Italy, Government of, 200, 206–07, 213, 217–20, 222
Ives, George, 135–36, 147

Jackson, Andrew, 20
Jackson, Charles W., 68–79, 81, 86
James brothers, 130
Jamison, Gen. J. C., 176–77
Japanese-American racism, 241–42
Jefferson City, Missouri, 189
Jewish Defense League, x, 5, 14
John Birch Society, 268
Johnson, David L., 262
Johnson, James Neely, 119–20, 122
Johnson, Zack A., 185–88, 191–92
Jones, LeRoi, 268–69
Journee, John, 197

Kahane, Rabbi Meir, 5
Kansas vigilance, 256
Kellogg, William Pitt, 21
Kendall, John S., 198
Kentucky vigilance, 74
Kerner, Otto, 287
King of William, James, 99–100, 113–17, 119–21, 124
King, Thomas, 114, 117
Kinney, Nat N., 165–77
Kirkland, Moses, 56, 58, 61, 64
Knapp Commission, 282
Know–Nothing party, 111–12
Ku Klux Klan, x, 6, 14, 161, 222, 261, 274–75

Lane, "Clubfoot George," 155
Langford, Nathaniel Pitt, 21, 134, 139–40, 146–47, 149–51, 153, 157–58
Law and Order moderators, San Francisco, 116–17, 120–23
Layton, Al, 167–68
Leavenworth (Kansas) Committee of Vigilance, 1856, 256
Lee, J. L., 179
Lee Kee Nam, 235–37, 244
Lind, Eugene, 250–51
Lister, of Shelbyville, Texas, 85–86
Little Big Horn, battle of, 128n
Llewellyn, A., 83, 85–86, 88
Lott, John S., 149, 154

306